Religious Schooling in America

Religious Schooling in America

Private Education and Public Life

Steven L. Jones

Westport, Connecticut
London

Library of Congress Cataloging-in-Publication Data

Jones, Steven L., 1971–
    Religious schooling in America : private education and public life / Steven L. Jones.
      p. cm.
    Includes bibliographical references and index.
    ISBN 978–0–313–35189–1 (alk. paper)
    1. Church schools—United States.   2. Religious education—United States.   3. Private
schools—United States.   I. Title.
    LC427.J66   2008
    371.070973—dc22   2008009007

British Library Cataloguing in Publication Data is available.

Library of Congress Catalog Card Number: 2008009007
ISBN: 978–0–313–35189–1

First published in 2008

Praeger Publishers, 88 Post Road West, Westport, CT 06881
An imprint of Greenwood Publishing Group, Inc.
www.praeger.com

Printed in the United States of America

The paper used in this book complies with the
Permanent Paper Standard issued by the National
Information Standards Organization (Z39.48–1984).

10 9 8 7 6 5 4 3 2 1

Contents

Acknowledgments

I must first thank the Institute for Advanced Studies in Culture and its director James Hunter at the University of Virginia. Their material support made this project possible while their camaraderie made it enjoyable. I am grateful as well to the Center for Children, Families, and the Law, and the Center on Religion and Democracy for providing additional support for various stages of this project. Over the last several years numerous teachers and colleagues have prodded my thinking, sometimes quite forcefully, in helpful and productive ways. Krishan Kumar, Sarah Corse, and Jennings Wagoner commented extensively on earlier stages of this work. Mark Graham and Jason Edwards of the Grove City College Department of History deserve particular thanks. James Carper and Karen Keyworth also provided helpful suggestions as the project was nearing completion. Whatever weaknesses remain in this work are surely the result of my failure to heed their advice more fully and are therefore solely my responsibility.

The librarians at the University of Virginia, Catholic University, and Grove City College have tracked down several sources with unfailing perseverance. Without them, I would still be lost in the stacks of their respective libraries. The administration at Grove City College was supportive in many ways as well. I also benefited from the help of several undergraduate research assistants, including Josh Caler, Heidi Haas, James Powell, Andrew Welton, and Rachel Lloyd.

While working on another project with Praeger, Suzanne Staszak-Silva expressed an interest in this manuscript. Her reward for that inquiry was having to put up with my inability to meet deadlines. I am grateful to Praeger for their support.

I owe my greatest debts to my wife, Beth, whose presence in my life is evidence of grace. It is to her and to our children that I dedicate this book.

Introduction

F ew topics galvanize Americans more quickly than their schools. Divisive issues range from vouchers to bilingual education, from the need for national standards to the superiority of local control. Americans are always ready to debate education because they expect so much from their schools, especially from their tax-supported, open-to-all public institutions. Indeed, their expectations go well beyond training in reading, writing, and arithmetic. Schools are one of the principal mechanisms through which Americans address various social challenges, perhaps the most pressing of which ever has been the need to forge a common identity out of America's diverse social origins. In America, schools are the primary institutional means for realizing the national motto *E Pluribus Unum*—out of many, one. Since the rise to dominance of public education in the latter half of the nineteenth century, critics have accused religious schools of undermining that effort. How, their critics ask, can any school that segregates students, both institutionally and ideologically, from the mainstream public schools simultaneously promote national unity and a commitment to the common good? Will not graduates of religious, or faith-based, schools act first on behalf of their religious group, and only secondarily in the interest of the larger community? *Religious Schooling in America: Private Education and Public Life* examines the debate over the place of faith-based schooling in American social and political life.

Suspicion of religious schools and the commitments they reinforce are a long-held feature of American political and educational thought. Though the Supreme Court's 1925 decision in *Pierce v. Society of Sisters* recognized religious schooling as a Constitutional right, it did little to make it more socially acceptable. The "additional obligations" for which parents must be allowed to prepare their children, held inviolable by the Court, were seen as a threat to national unity. Both before and after *Pierce*, educational theorists, political philosophers, and populist political movements such as the Know Nothings criticized faith-based schooling in America. Polls show that even today a majority of Americans believe that the country would be better off if all children attended the public schools. Americans expect their fellow citizens to identify with, and express a sense of attachment to, their nation, its central ideas, and its institutions.

It was their ability to shape public life that ensured the public school's triumph over religious and other private institutions in American educational history. Horace Mann, for instance, praised the potential of the Common Schools to overcome the divisions in American society, particularly those divisions that religious and denominational schools reinforced. Near the end of the nineteenth century, publicly financed, publicly administered schooling emerged as the default educational arrangement for American children. But this supremacy has not gone unchallenged. The religious institutions that in fact predate public education in America have survived, even thrived, over the past century. Multiple religious communities, including those that opposed faith-based schooling in earlier generations, have now embraced it for their children. It is the gradual embrace of faith-based schooling by different religious communities in America, including Catholics, Jews, conservative Protestants (both in Christian day schools and homeschooling), and, perhaps next, Muslims, which accounts for the longevity and continued vitality of religious schooling in America.

Particular systems of religious schooling receive frequent attention in the histories of America's religious communities. While the present work has benefited from several such studies, the approach taken here stresses religious schooling as a more cohesive phenomenon. Advocates of faith-based schooling across religious communities articulate similar reasons for why they take on the added pressure and expense of maintaining their own schools when free, public institutions are readily available. These institutions make possible the discharging of epistemological, communal, and familial obligations held sacred by religious believers across traditions.

Additionally, on the political level these institutions invite the same basic criticisms regardless of their particular religious outlook. Most movements in favor of religious schooling have been accused of undermining national unity. Religious schools, the critics argue, isolate children in overly homogenous social worlds, possibly rendering them incapable of interacting with mainstream America. Of course, the identity and social location of those critics have changed over time. In the nineteenth and early twentieth century they were Protestants arguing against Catholics. By the end of the twentieth century the critics were secular pluralists and in an historical irony it was conservative Protestants that were fleeing public schools, an exodus made possible in part by the social and legal victories won by Catholics a few generations before. Though the contemporary debate takes place mostly among political philosophers and educational theorists, its origins, and its greater significance, are found in the lived experiences of America's religious communities. It is there that parents, pastors, teachers, and children have struggled to build and maintain their own schools, negotiating the terrain of pluralism, religious conviction, dissent, and public responsibility as they went.

Before proceeding, a number of observations are in order. First, I use the terms "religious schools" and "faith-based schools" (or schooling) interchangeably to refer to those educational institutions whose orientation and identity are located primarily in religious communities. Some of these are under the direct control of a particular religious body, for instance a church or denominational hierarchy. Others are largely independent from such bodies, administered by local boards and parents. The National Center for Education Statistics, a division of the U.S. Department of Education, has developed an elaborate classification system for religious schools based on self-identification and associational membership. Catholic schools alone can be congregational, independent, or diocesan. "Christian" schools follow a similar three-fold organizational schema. This organizational diversity renders terms like "church schools" overly narrow. Additionally, the present work focuses not on individual schools, but on the national voices and organizations within each religious community that advocated on their behalf. These voices often spoke in more general terms about the need for schools shaped by their religious commitments and, in some cases at least, with less concern about the particular organizational patterns these schools employed.

Second, I have approached the debate over the place of religious schooling in America thematically rather than chronologically. Thus, when detailing the arguments both for and against religious schooling in the various eruptions of this debate I have focused on voices that were current at the time each religious community embraced this strategy. For instance, though there are several active Catholic organizations that currently lobby on behalf of Catholic schools, it is the early twentieth century National Catholic Welfare Council and their Department of Education that receive attention here. Their defense of Catholic schools is likened to the pro day school voices from the Jewish community in the mid-twentieth century or the advocates of conservative Protestant schooling in the 1980s and 1990s. This is not to imply that contemporary organizations are less important, but the debate is most intense—the schools most under fire—during periods of emergence and dramatic growth. Accordingly, in Chapters 3 and 4 the narrative moves back and forth between criticisms (and defenses) of Catholic, Jewish, and conservative Protestant schooling precisely so that the similarities between the charges are more evident.

Third, there is very little in what follows regarding the academic performance of various school systems. The crisis of confidence Americans articulated in the latter half of the twentieth century regarding public education is surely a part of the growth of Protestant schooling in particular, but it was much less pronounced in earlier debates about religious schooling. Accordingly, I have not delved into the growing mountain of data on school performance except where it intersects with issues of parental choice and the advantages or disadvantages of government oversight. Nor have I included material on how private and religious schools are regulated by the state. Questions of access, teacher certification, and academic accountability are not treated here except as they relate to issues of citizenship and educational freedom.

Finally and perhaps most importantly, while I'm sure my perspective will be evident to the reader, my goal is not to offer definitive answers to the various questions that have been posed regarding religious schooling. Rather, I am interested in the debate itself. How has it changed? How has it remained the same? What does it tell us about the larger issues that surround it, not the least of which is the relationship between religious convictions and the needs of the social order? Although the debate has become, to some extent, the purview of specialists, it is the convictions and actions of ordinary Americans that are at stake here. In keeping with my effort to locate this debate in the lives of those most impacted by it, religious schoolers themselves, I am hopeful that this book will find a readership beyond specialists. To that end, I have tried to present the material and argument in an accessible manner. Education is a contentious topic, and democracies thrive when contentious topics are debated not just in the halls of the academy, but by citizens on the front lines of cultural and political battles. If this book contributes to the public understanding of an important aspect of education and citizenship in America it will have been time well spent.

CHAPTER OUTLINE

Chapter 1 traces the evolution of religious schooling from the last half of the nineteenth century up through today. To be sure, the roots of this approach to education go deeper than the mid-nineteenth century, but the question this book is focused on, namely their place in American political life, took on new dimensions after the rise of public schooling (tax supported and officially nonsectarian). Today, some 90 percent of school-aged children in America attend the public school. Private schools, overwhelmingly religious in character and administration, serve the remaining tenth of the school-aged population. That percentage is largely unchanged since the beginning of the twentieth century. What has changed, however, is the number and character of those religious communities that practice faith-based schooling.

Chapter 2 takes up the reasons why religious communities have embraced this strategy with all its controversy, bureaucratic headaches, and expense when tax-supported public schools are available in virtually every neighborhood? This is not the same as asking why individual parents choose the educational setting they do for their children. This is an important question in its own right, but it assumes the existence of alternative arrangements. This book focuses on the development of just these arrangements. Although the specific motivations for each group differ with historical and social circumstances, at least two broad themes surface again and again, epistemology and piety. On the epistemological level, advocates of religious schooling have stressed the divine underpinnings of all knowledge. Religious traditions, as inheritors and guardians of this knowledge, often construct their own educational institutions to safeguard this knowledge and to guarantee its transmission to the next generation of the faithful. Any school that does not embrace the truths of the religious community runs the risk of stunting the religious development of their children, either by presenting an alternative worldview that undercuts the religious tradition or by more direct proselytization on behalf of a different worldview. Additionally, there are the demands of parental piety. Sending one's children to a religious school (or taking those responsibilities on yourself in the case of homeschooling) is often understood as an act of faith. In many religious traditions, parents are charged by the deity with the responsibility for raising their children up in the way that they should go. Faith-based schooling, then, is promoted as an act of religious devotion on the part of parents.

Chapters 3 and 4 present the two sides in an ongoing debate about the place of religious schooling in American life. Chapter 3 examines the democratic case against religious schooling. The general connections between education and political life have been made plain by generations of philosophers and theorists, including John Dewey, Emile Durkheim, and Edward Shils. This ground has been well covered and my treatment of it is accordingly brief. The real point of this chapter is to show how the links between education and political life have been central to the development of American public education, and have therefore posed two problems for religious schooling in America. First, alternatives to public education have been seen not just as competition for, but as a threat to, public institutions. They leave less capital, economic and social, for public schools. The second, and larger criticism, is that faith-based education undermines national unity by reinforcing sub-communal ties. This is why religious schooling, as opposed to other private arrangements, has been the most controversial. In the eighteenth, nineteenth, and early twentieth centuries, this criticism was wrapped up in the language of patriotism and loyalty. By the middle of the twentieth century it was transformed by the rise of multiculturalism into a concern about the willingness and ability of religious schools to promote pluralism and a willingness to work with others. The basic point of the criticism, however, remains the same. Religious schools shield students from the broader currents of American political and cultural identity (malleable though that is), and in doing so they promote division and discord rather than harmony.

Chapter 4 shows how advocates for faith schools have responded to the criticisms detailed in Chapter 3. They have denied the legitimacy of their critics' charges on almost a point-by-point basis, and have reacted strongly against the idea that they are somehow subverting American unity. It is in their arguments about national unity that advocates of religious schooling have advanced a democratic case for their schools. They see themselves as acting in the best traditions of American independence and freedom. In their eyes, rather than fleeing the "other," they *are* the other, and their existence is a manifestation of precisely the kind of freedoms that are characteristic of American life.

Chapter 5 takes up the teaching of American history in religious schools. History, of course, is one of the primary means of civic education. It is where we learn who we are. It is also where we learn that we belong to something larger than ourselves. In many religious schools, the major figures and events of America's past are examined through the lens of the particular community sponsoring the school. So, for instance, Christopher Columbus was not just the discoverer of the New World but a Roman Catholic, possibly Jewish, a "Bible-believing" Christian, and indebted to Muslims depending upon who is telling his story. George Washington, too, was a special friend to Catholics, Jews, and conservative Protestants depending upon which books one examines. The point of this chapter is not to critique the evidence or arguments made in these various histories, but to show how religious communities have sought to inject their own tradition into crucial moments of American history. It becomes "their" story just as much as "our" story.

Chapter 6 is a brief look at what is currently a very small slice of religious schooling in America, but one that may prove the most controversial–
Muslim schools. Because they are so small a group (currently less than 1
percent of the total private school universe), and because their real emergence even within the Islamic community is just beginning, I have opted
to treat them separately even though many of the same patterns are beginning to surface. My primary goal in this chapter is to provide an overview
of Muslim schooling in America. The amount of suspicion and criticism
they face belies their small numbers. I suspect that many people who drive
by Catholic, Jewish, and Protestant schools every day might find the opening of an Islamic school in their neighborhood somehow more troubling.
Since the rise of militant Islam and especially since the terrorist attacks of
September 11, 2001, the place of Muslims and their various institutions
in America have generated considerable concern. What is being taught in
Muslim schools? Where is their funding coming from? Are they really just a
breeding ground for future radicals? Questions of citizenship and pluralism
will be thrown into particularly sharp relief by Muslim schools, though up
to this point they have not received the attention one might anticipate.

Chapter 7 offers an analytical summary of the debate over religious schooling in America. While I do advance a few ideas on how to move the debate
forward, I do not claim to provide the final answer that will satisfy all sides.
To the contrary, I think the debate is worth having and sustaining as a
means of working out the implications of the institutional and confessional
pluralism so characteristic of contemporary America.

1 Public and Private Schooling in America

For the overwhelming majority of American youth, education and public schooling are synonymous. Although criticizing public schools is nearly a national pasttime, there is an aura of inevitability, even rightness, about their institutional supremacy in the American educational landscape. This was not always so. Private schools, both religious and independent, also enjoy a long history in American society, and in earlier generations their legitimacy was taken for granted just as the public school's is today. How and why the public schools achieved dominance is part and parcel of every history of education course offered in colleges and universities all over America. Explanations range from a focus on superior resources and pedagogy to federalism and secularization. This familiar ground will not be too heavily retrod here. This book focuses on the fortunes not of public schools, but of private religious institutions that in fact predate, and continue to exist alongside of, America's public schools. The modifiers "private" and "religious" might seem redundant, but the history of these institutions shows otherwise. Aside from the obvious fact that not all private schools are religious, the distinction between public and private has not always been clear. For instance, before the rise of what we think of as public schooling, religious groups were intimately involved in the education of children, and many of their institutions received both private and public money. By the early twentieth century, however, public schools were the dominant educational institutions in America, and religious schools were seen competing with, even threatening, public institutions. Private and especially religious schools had to make sense of their place in America's educational landscape under new conditions demarcated by the supremacy of nonsectarian, open-to-all, tax-supported public schools.

Before proceeding with the story of America's religious schools, it is necessary to briefly consider the hegemony of these public institutions, particularly since the very indicators of that hegemony are part of the struggle faced by every system of religious schooling over the last century and a half. The public schools' advantages can be grouped into three categories: legislative, financial, and political. Legislatively, the power of the state upholds public education, the provision for which emerged as an expected part of nineteenth century state government. For instance, in the post-Civil War years the federal government made the availability of public education in the South an issue in the debate over readmission for Confederate states. Most of the southern states were required to present new state constitutions, the provisions of which had to meet with approval from the federal, largely northern, Congress. One of the articles that Congress required was the provision of public schooling for each state's citizenry. Free, public education was quite literally a prerequisite for readmittance to the Union. Both federal attention and resources for public schooling were increasing in the years after the Civil War. The original federal Department of Education (later the Office of Education), for instance, was founded in 1867 to help states establish effective school systems.

Another index of this growing use of legislation to support public education may be found in the development of compulsory attendance laws. The willingness to codify faith in education by enacting it into legislation can be seen as far back as 1642. In that year, the Massachusetts Bay Colony established a body of supervisors, charging them with the evaluation of parental efforts to provide for the education of their children. Over the next several years these laws were revised and amended several times until it was established that all towns of more than fifty households had to provide for instruction in reading and writing for local children. Similarly, all towns of more than 100 households had to establish a grammar school. Of course, enforcement of these laws was difficult, but they do establish the state's prerogative in education in two important ways. First, the state set minimum standards of evaluation for education. The state, then, as opposed to the church or family, was to serve as the guardian of what it meant to educate, and in turn, to be educated. Second, these laws established the state's right to mandate public support for educational provisions. They could require, for instance, adequate funding for facilities and salaries. Thus, while the moral obligation of educating children remained primarily a parental duty until well into the nineteenth century, the seeds for state involvement in this arena were sewn much earlier.

Though the precedents went back for some two centuries, the social chaos of the nineteenth century brought on by industrialization, urbanization, and immigration prompted new efforts to establish free, nonsectarian schools throughout the land. In 1852 Massachusetts passed laws requiring a prescribed amount of formal schooling for free children. This law, which, like its predecessors, was largely ineffective, required six weeks of continuous schooling and six more weeks of noncontinuous schooling each year. By 1870 Massachusetts was still nearly alone in terms of legal support for compulsory attendance, having been joined only by the District of Columbia in 1864 and Vermont in 1867. The legal situation changed drastically during the next two decades, however, with some two dozen states passing attendance legislation between 1870 and 1890.

This is not to say that the compulsory attendance laws were always observed. Inadequate classroom accommodations and indifference on the part of parents mitigated the effectiveness of state measures. The combination of obvious concern for education mixed with rather ineffective laws prompted one historian to call this era the "symbolic phase" of compulsory education to be followed some years later by the bureaucratic stage beginning in the last decade of the nineteenth century. New laws were passed that mandated attendance, but more importantly a network of organizations emerged capable of enforcing these laws. Offices to monitor and record attendance were established, increasing the effectiveness and professionalization of truant officers. And, of course, state funds were distributed on the basis of attendance, a not-so-subtle encouragement for more aggressive enforcement of laws long unobserved. Compulsory attendance was a major part of what Charles Burgess has called the "era of compulsion," in which several behavioral standards upheld by the majority of Americans were reinforced by the coercive power of the state.[1]

Public schools also had a financial advantage over their private counterparts. Public resources for education, even in the early twentieth century, were considerable. In 1900, the total expenditures by public elementary and secondary schools reached $215,000,000 in current dollars. By 1920 it exceeded one billion dollars, a threshold private school expenditures did not cross until 1960.[2] By 1949–1950, the first year that figures for both public and private schools are available from the National Center for Education Statistics, public expenditures reached $5.8 billion, approximately 93 percent of the total spent on elementary and secondary schooling in America. Of course, public schools also enrolled far more students than private institutions did, so it is not surprising that they would have greater costs. Nevertheless, the states, by their power to levy taxes on all citizens, had access to resources that all but the wealthiest private academies could only envy. Since the state's resources are based on compulsion while private institutions must rely on voluntary support in the form of tuition or endowment, it is reasonable to give the financial advantage to the state, at least in terms of access to revenue and planning for contingency. As we will see, competition over finances was part of the struggle between public and religious schools over the entire twentieth century, and continues to be part of the story albeit in a modified form.

Politically and culturally, public schools became the taken-for-granted educative institution for most Americans for a variety of reasons. They were "free," bore the stamp of government approval, and had added social benefits as well. America has long had a peculiar faith in education as a means of overcoming social ills of various kinds, not least among them a growing concern for national unity in the face of immigration and pluralism. The public schools were able to sidestep the disruptive theological and denominational issues that could have derailed their ascendancy precisely because they reflected and reinforced the pan-Protestantism that was widely shared among the American middle-class.[3] No doubt, widespread support for public education was injurious to the Protestant denominational schools as well, but the ability of public schools to serve the cause of national unity was particularly evident when compared to the growing Catholic education system in America. Protestants of all denominations could rally behind the banner of public education not just because it avoided denominational hot buttons, but also because it united them against a common enemy, Rome. Enrollment data supports the notion that by the turn of the twentieth century the public schools were well established as the default educational arrangement for most American children. In 1900 there were approximately 15.5 million students in public schools, the vast majority of which were in grades K through eight. This compares with 1.35 million in private schools, the majority of which were in Catholic institutions.[4]

Given the advantages public schools had over private institutions, one might expect, and indeed some hoped, that faith-based schooling would recede into the background of American education. But the story of religious schooling over the course of the twentieth century is not one of inevitable decline. In fact, just the opposite is true. Religious schooling has shown remarkable staying power. At the turn of the twentieth century public school enrollment accounted for approximately 92 percent of elementary- and secondary-school enrollment in the United States. By 1999, that figure had shrunk slightly to just under 89 percent. Of the 52.8 million students enrolled in elementary and secondary education, 46.8 million were in public schools. Private-school enrollment has grown from 1.35 million in 1900 to 5.9 million in 2000, not counting homeschooled children. In 1999 the National Household Education Survey estimated the number of homeschooled children at 850,000, a number contested by some researchers as too low, meaning that the total number of privately schooled children was at least approaching 7 million by the end of the twentieth century.[5] The National Center of Education Statistics reports that some 85 percent of institutional private schooling is religious in character, and homeschooling too is dominated by religious voices. Religious schools have held their market share not under the conditions of free-market competition, but against public schools that have most every advantage, not least of all the fact that they are free.

Although religious schools have always been an important feature of American education, their place in modern American life can only be understood if we think about their existence since the advent and rise of the public schools. Many religious schools were readily accepted until the cultural superiority of the public schools was articulated over the course of the nineteenth century by figures like the Public School Society in New York City and Horace Mann in Massachusetts. Thus, the history constructed here begins with late nineteenth- century developments in Catholic education. There were, of course, crucial events and personalities before then, but I am primarily interested in the ways advocates of religious schooling have negotiated their place in American life once the shadow of American public education had already been cast. To that end, what follows is not an exhaustive history of faith-based schooling or any one particular religious community in America. Rather, it is an episodic history of when various religious communities embraced the strategy of faith-based schooling over and against public education. As we will see, the religious heirs of the very Protestants that persecuted Catholic schools in the 19th and early twentieth centuries have themselves exited the public schools in increasing numbers over the last three decades. And they were not alone. The key to the longevity of religious schooling in America has been its gradual acceptance by multiple religious communities rather than growth in any one particular religious community. In fact, even as Catholic school enrollment has gone down (though it is still the largest portion of the entire religious school enterprise), the percentage of students in religious schools more broadly has been fairly stable precisely because Jews and Protestants, among others, eventually opted for faith-based schools. But their exit was made possible only because of a century of struggle on the part of American Catholics to build and maintain their own schools, a struggle that culminated in the 1925 *Pierce* decision by the Supreme Court, establishing the right for religious schools to exist.[6]

THE PRECEDENT ESTABLISHED: CATHOLIC SCHOOLING IN AMERICA[7]

"It is of primary importance for our people to realize that human freedom derives from the spiritual nature of man and can flourish only when the things of the spirit are held in reverence.... We need, therefore, to examine carefully what spiritual direction we are giving to our children to prepare them to fulfill their future moral responsibilities to God and to their fellow man."[8] So said the Roman Catholic hierarchy in their pastoral letter of 1950. They went on to argue that "[l]ittle point would be served in intensifying the child's awareness of God during his preschool years, if later

Table 1.1. Parochial School Growth, 1880—1920[9]

Year	Catholic population	Parochial schools	Pupil enrollment
1880	6,143,222	2,246	405,234
1890	8,277,039	3,194	633,238
1900	10,129,677	3,811	854,523
1910	14,347,027	4,845	1,237,251
1920	17,735,553	5,852	1,701,219

his schooling were to rob him of that." They also affirmed those "Catholic parents [that], clearly grasping this essential truth, have undergone great sacrifice and enormous expense to establish and maintain schools which will continue to enlarge the spiritual development of the child . . ." Even though these words were not written until the middle of the twentieth century, they express a conviction felt and acted upon much earlier. In the eighteenth and nineteenth centuries, Catholics who endured the voyage to America landed in a society that, its promise of religious freedom not withstanding, was markedly anti-Catholic. That did not stop them from coming, however, and thus the American Catholic leadership spent much of their time trying to keep abreast of their swelling population. Churches, social service agencies, and not least of all schools had to be built to meet the needs of successive waves of Catholic immigrants. The Catholic hierarchy had encouraged Catholic schooling over public, officially nonsectarian institutions since at least the early nineteenth century, an effort that crystallized in 1884 when the Third Plenary Council of Baltimore ordered the construction of a Catholic school near every church within two years and bound Catholic parents to send their children to these parochial schools. Over the next several decades, American Catholics struggled to actually build and maintain the schools their leaders called for. As Table 1.1 indicates, their efforts were not without success.

Catholic school growth continued so that by 1930 there were 7,923 schools and more than 2.2 million students enrolled.[10] Though each of these schools represents the commitment and hard work of parents, teachers, and administrators, it is also beneficial to see their growth as part of a focused denominational effort to promote religious schooling. In fact, in each of the groups we will look at, the rise in religious schooling was organized by trans-congregational and other parachurch organizations, some voluntary and some more professionalized. These organizations are worth noting in part because they were successful but they also remind us that individual schools are only part of the story. As these efforts reached critical mass the individual schools benefited from cooperation and the collective wisdom of their peer institutions, networked through umbrella organizations. Assembling these resources required supra-local leadership. Additionally, since education itself was increasingly directed by state and especially federal policy, advocates of faith-based schooling saw the need to have a unified voice speaking at the national level as well to defend their interests. Finally, these organizations also served as a driving force in the expansion of religious schooling within each community. Particularly as their schools faced legal and political challenges, it was often these institutions that stepped forward to defend the principles and practices of religious schooling.

In the opening decades of the twentieth century, two different groups emerged as the champions of Catholic education. In 1904 the Catholic Education Association (CEA) was founded essentially as a professional organization for practitioners of Catholic schooling. The CEA (later the National Catholic Education Association) served as a voluntary forum for Catholic educators to come together and discuss issues related to Catholic schooling. As a voluntary organization, the CEA had no real authority over Catholic schools or families. For the most part, the CEA debated matters of curriculum and pedagogy, including topics similar to those commanding the energies of the National Education Association such as progressivism, vocational education, and the length of the school year. The most important issue to face American Catholic schools in the early twentieth century would not be a matter of instruction or even finances, however. Not two decades after the founding of the CEA, the very existence of Catholic schooling would be threatened by the Orgeon school law of 1922. This law, which will be examined in more detail later, made attendance at public schools mandatory, thus eliminating the prerogatives of all private schools, Catholic and non-Catholic alike. The task of defending the very existence of Catholic schools fell to another newly formed organization, the National Catholic War Council.[11]

The massive mobilization of American resources prompted by World War I required considerable effort on the part of the public. The Catholic Church, along with virtually every social institution in America, faced new pressures and opportunities in terms of contributing to the cause. The lack of a national body to direct Catholic efforts created a gap that was temporarily filled by voluntary organizations many of which, like the Knights of Columbus, focused on Catholic men in uniform. Aside from the efforts of the various Catholic societies, it became clear that if American Catholicism was going to rise to the occasion a national organization was necessary. Accordingly, plans were put in motion to create a national war council to direct Catholic efforts. This organization started as a primarily administrative agency directing the recruitment and placement of Catholic chaplains or the redistribution of church resources since the Catholic population shifted geographically when so many soldiers moved to training camps in the south. Material resources such as prayer books and worship manuals had to be moved as well, and a national administrative body was needed to ensure that these resources ended up where they were most needed.

Some American Catholics, such as Father John Burke, had long advocated a national Catholic agency, but it was the war mobilization that made the need for such a body evident. His guiding principle was to ensure the place of the Catholic Church in American life by bringing into existence an organization that could not only direct Catholic efforts for support of the war, but could also represent Catholic interests in the national arena.[12] Over the first several months of its existence, Burke's hopes for the newly formed National Catholic War Council (NCWC) were for the most part realized. In November of 1917, the council came under the control of the archbishops, who in turn established an administrative committee to guide the organization. Various members of the administrative committee had responsibility for the direction of one of five departments: the Department of Press and Publicity; the Department of Laws and Legislation; the Department of Social Action; the Department of Lay Organizations; and the Department of Education. Of course, the members of the hierarchy that chaired these departments all had other responsibilities. The first chairman of the Department of Education, Austin Dowling, was the Archbishop of St. Paul. Thus, within each department there were offices in Washington, DC, with on-site managers and officers that ran the day-to-day operation of the NCWC.

Though the war ended in 1918, the reconstruction of Europe along with the resettling and rehabilitation of veterans in the United States were massive undertakings in their own right. Almost immediately, requests for a permanent national organization were heard from around the nation, some from members of the hierarchy and some from laymen. Advocates of the permanent organization argued that the demobilization of the war machine demanded almost as much effort as had the mobilization, but they also began to speak of the need for a national body to represent Catholic interests in American life. It is worth noting at this point that education was already a key consideration in the development of a national organization. Pope Benedict XV had made it clear that he wished for the American church to focus on the problem of Catholic schooling, and it surfaced again and again in the discussions over whether or not the War Council should continue, and if so, under what conditions.[13] Part of the justification Burke and his colleagues used focused on the increasing federalization already at large in American society. The advocates of a national Catholic organization seized on this to argue that since important political decisions were now being made on a national level, Catholic input into those decisions should be on a national level as well.

Officially, the NCWC Department of Education was the voice of the bishops on matters related to Catholic schooling. In 1921 the Department of

Education opened the interdepartmental Bureau of Education in part to represent Catholic schooling to interested parties, friend, and foe alike. Essentially, the Bureau of Education, like the department more broadly, was charged with promoting an accurate picture of Catholic schooling in America, a role that was endorsed by the CEA at the opening of the bureau. The bureau's four-fold purpose was clearly stated at its founding and repeated in the February 1921 edition of the NCWC's official newspaper, the *Bulletin.*

> The purpose of the Bureau is to serve as: I. A clearing house of information concerning Catholic education and Catholic education agencies—for Catholic educators and students, and for the general public. II. An Advisory agency, to assist Catholic education systems and institutions in their developments. III. A connecting agency between Catholic education activities and Government education agencies. IV. An active organization, to safeguard the interests of Catholic education.

Though the bureau continued to compile statistics and directories on Catholic schooling, its fourth stated purpose, to defend the interest of Catholic education, loomed large on the horizon.

The attitude of the NCWC Department of Education toward American public schools was more nuanced than the mere antagonism of which it is often accused. In fact, the Department of Education claimed to be interested in, and eager to work for, the improvement of all schooling, not just Catholic institutions. Father Burke, the general secretary of the NCWC, suggested that no group in America was more interested in seeing public education extended and improved than were American Catholics. At the opening of the bureau, it was made clear that "[t]he Bureau of Education of the National Catholic Welfare Council believes in public education, and the public school system. It will be ready to cooperate in all desirable movements for the improvement of public schools, provided such movements will not curtail the rights of the people to maintain and patronize private and parochial schools."[14] These sentiments were repeated a few months later.

> The great majority of Catholics agree to the following: They believe that general education for all youths in the United States is necessary for the well-being of the State, and the prosperity, health, and safety of its individuals. They agree that it is the right and the duty of the State to require that all children receive a certain amount of education, the minimum being fixed by State legislative enactment. They believe that the State should maintain free public schools so that this minimum education essential to its well-being will be available to every child whose education is not provided otherwise, and that these schools should be supported from public money raised by taxation or otherwise from all citizens regardless of whether or not they have children attending the public schools.[15]

   Earlier statements not withstanding, the Department of Education asserted that Catholics had never opposed public education.[16] Quite the opposite. Catholics supported the necessity of state-run schools, but held that
it was their right to refuse to send their children to such schools. They
would pay taxes for their support, and work to make state schools better in whatever ways they could, but they would not send their children
to them. Implying that the critics of parochial schooling were guilty of
misleading the public about the truth of Catholic education, the NCWC
leadership claimed that their church "does not oppose and never has opposed a 'Public School System' of education as within the right of and duty
of the Civil Government, and indeed worthy of praise from all classes of
citizens and beneficiaries."[17] Father James Ryan, one of the most influential clerics in America, devoted an entire chapter in his *Civics Catechism* to
explaining the position of American Catholics toward public schools. He
pointed out that Catholics recognized the need for state schools, and supported those schools with their tax money, but opposed the idea that the
state should have a monopoly on something so vital to the population as a
whole.[18]
   The NCWC's role as defender of Catholic schools was secured by the
events culminating in the famous *Pierce* decision by the United States
Supreme Court in 1925. This case, which firmly established the legal right of
private and religious schools to exist in America, was one of the major efforts
of the NCWC during its first decade of existence. On November 7, 1922,
the citizens of Oregon adopted a compulsory school law forcing all children
to attend public schools through either eighth grade or age sixteen. The
measure was adopted by a slim margin, with less than 12,000 votes splitting
the sides out of more than 219,000 cast. No doubt the post-war climate of
patriotic fervor in part motivated supporters of the compulsory attendance
bill, but old-fashioned anti-Catholicism was also a powerful force in support
of the school legislation. Supporters of the bill, including the Ku Klux Klan,
even produced an updated version of the "escaped nun" Maria Monk in the
person of Sister Lucretia who toured the state spreading lurid tales about
what went on at Catholic institutions. The Church was portrayed as attack-
ing the very institution that safeguarded American democracy. *The New Age*,
a Scottish Rite publication, hinted at the existence of plans to abolish public
schools on the part of members of the Catholic hierarchy.[19]
   Supporters of the law also held rallies with invited speakers who ha-
rangued public officials that had not endorsed the legislation. One Ray
McDougall, of Salt Lake City, spoke at an evening rally just four days before
the measure was voted on and urged Oregonians to "send back to oblivion"
any candidate for public office who could not demonstrate 100 percent
support for public schools.[20] They took out ads, complete with pictures of
local schools and classes of students, demanding that they be protected.
Nothing less than the future of the United States hinged on whether or not

the citizens of Oregon would endorse public education by outlawing private schools.

After its passage, the NCWC was quick to respond to the Oregon Law.[21] Archbishop Dowling, Chair of the Department of Education, criticized the measure as an attack on the rights of all American citizens. Almost immediately, the American Catholic hierarchy began searching for an opportunity to test the constitutional validity of the Oregon law. In January of 1923, barely two months after its passage and fully three years before its intended date of enactment, the administrative bishops of the NCWC voted their full support for Oregon's Catholics in their attempt to challenge the law. Describing the sentiments expressed at that meeting, the *Bulletin* declared it the

> ... firm conviction of all present that the Oregon law, drawn up and passed under conditions and by methods almost unbelievable, is a direct and vicious attack upon the fundamental liberty in state and nation, upon liberty of education, parental rights, and rights of children, and property rights. It was also their firm conviction that it is contrary to the constitution of the United States and the spirit and traditions of the country from the Declaration of Independence down to the present time. Furthermore, the opinion was unanimous that true patriotism and public welfare are seriously injured by all legislation begotten of the spirit behind this law.[22]

As a means of raising money for the push to repeal the Oregon law, the NCWC organized the Catholic School Defense League for the purpose of producing and disseminating literature to lawmakers and journalists that would counter the anti-Catholic propaganda coming from supporters of the Oregon law and similar measures in other states. The League was designed to raise money and mobilize national support so that Catholics outside Oregon would not think of this as only a regional matter. In 1923 representatives from the Sisters of the Holy Name of Jesus and Mary, along with those from the Hill Military Academy, filed an injunction to restrain the state from putting the law into effect.

The petitioners held that the real purpose of the law was simply to close the private schools, a claim that proponents of the law never opposed and in fact confirmed in arguments before the Supreme Court. But the legal issues on which the petitioners acted were more varied than that. They argued that, if enacted, the bill would deprive the Sisters of property without due process, impair an existing contract between the state and the Sisters, violate the rights of conscience, and most important, the Act would violate the natural right of parents to control the upbringing and education of their children. The other issues may have had legal merit, and in fact due process concerns were of critical importance to the decision, but the rights of parents animated the discussion and held national attention. On March 31, 1924, the United States District Court issued an injunction against the law, barring the governor from enforcing it. Analyzing the Oregon law following the favorable decision of the district court, William Guthrie, a New York attorney, affiliated with the case, defended parochial education against charges of disloyalty:

> It is surely high time that misrepresentation of the Catholic parochial schools should cease and particularly the false assertion that they are un-American in spirit or object. The splendid record during the World War, in patriotic service and in the army and navy, of the graduates of those schools refuted all the slanders and libels of the past. In the ranks of the army and navy alike were Catholic youths far more than the quota of Catholic citizens would call for. In Catholic schools, patriotism, obedience to the law and loyalty to the Constitution are taught as a religious even more than a civic duty, and the best and highest ideas of American citizenship are exalted. No true American Catholic can be other than a good and patriotic American citizen.[23]

The Attorney General of Oregon appealed to the Supreme Court in June of 1924, and the hearings were held in March of 1925. Most of the same arguments were made before the high court as had been made back in Oregon, and on June 1, 1925, the Supreme Court upheld the injunction, ruling that the law requiring all children to attend public schools was unconstitutional. They did not deny that the state had the right to regulate educational institutions whether public or private, but they held that Oregon had gone too far in seeking to abolish such schools. Arguing for the rights of parents, the court famously declared:

> The fundamental theory of liberty upon which all governments in this Union repose excludes any general power of the state to standardize its children by forcing them to accept instruction from public teachers only. The child is not the mere creature of the state; those who nurture him and direct his destiny have the right coupled with the high duty to recognize and prepare him for additional obligations.[24]

That the NCWC had played a huge role in the Oregon case is clear from the historical record. Oregon's Catholics invited and welcomed the national Catholic body in this struggle. It was the NCWC that coordinated and essentially bankrolled the entire legal proceeding by making it a national issue. They did everything from find the attorneys that argued before the Supreme Court to mediate personality clashes among those defending their schools. NCWC leaders such as John Burke and James Ryan were in constant contact with John Kavanaugh from Oregon and William Guthrie of New York, the attorneys selected to argue the case.[25]

The decision, of course, was heralded by American Catholics. James Ryan called it the beginning of a new era in terms of the state's relationship to education. He decried the "recent" philosophy that identified the state as the supreme institution of man. Instead, Ryan called for recognition of the rights of individuals even if they might have been in conflict with state inter-ests. The *Pierce* decision, he said, was a signal of the court's affirmation of the very principles American Catholics had been arguing for. More than a legal victory, the decision served as an endorsement of the Catholic philosophy of education.

According to their defenders, not only were Catholic schools capable of producing good Americans in terms of civic instruction, but also the very act of establishing their own schools pointed to just how American these institutions and their supporters were. In their view it was their critics that had betrayed American history and principles. Far from being anti-American institutions, then, parochial schools were the very manifestation of a citizen's rights to freedom in America:

> Our Catholic schools are not established and maintained with any idea of holding our children apart from the general body and spirit of American citizenship. They are simply the concrete form in which we exercise our rights as free citizens, in conformity with the dictates of conscience. Their very existence is a great moral fact in American life.[26]

As the major force behind religious schooling at the time, *Pierce* was an enormous victory for American Catholics. It represented the successful outcome, at least in the legal realm, of more than a century of struggle. In subsequent decades other religious communities would benefit from *Pierce* as well, including some whose denominational ancestors decried the decision at the time.

The NCWC remained active in Catholic education for several decades af-ter their 1925 victory, though its focus shifted to maintaining and improving the schools. From 1929–1966 whoever directed the NCWC's Department of Education simultaneously directed the National Catholic Educational Association. In 1967 the entire NCWC was reorganized with the creation of the United States Catholic Conference and the National Conference of Catholic Bishops, which merged into the United States Conference of Catholic Bishops (USCCB) in 2001. Though there have been several organi-zational changes since the *Pierce* years, the work of the NCWC Department of Education continues through the efforts of the USCCB. They continue to advocate on behalf of Catholic parents who, as the "primary educa-tors" of their children are responsible for their spiritual and intellectual development.[27] In continuity with their nearly 100-year history, they also continue to stress the development of citizenship and political responsibil-ity through the schools, a focus that will be explored in subsequent chapters.

THE JEWISH DAY SCHOOLS

A "romance" is how one scholar characterized the relationship between American Jews and America's public schools. Such poetic language well describes the way Jewish immigrants in each successive wave of immigration embraced public education as a way into American society. Reflecting on his own childhood, Milton Himmelfarb remembered his mother saying approvingly, "In Russia the Czar didn't let us go to school. Here they not only let us, they made us."[28]

There is more than anecdotal evidence for this claim. Numerous historians of the American Jewish experience portray the history of Jewish education as shaped largely by the acceptance by Jews of American public schools as the primary institutional means for educating their children. Lloyd Gartner for instance, argued that the death knell for the first all-Jewish day schools was the "definitive establishment of public schools without such sectarian features as prayers, Bible and especially New Testament readings and moralizing . . . A new ideology regarded the tax-supported, religiously neutral, universal public school as the indispensable training ground for American citizenship." He went on to speak of the long "Jewish affinity to the American public school."[29]

Multiple waves of Jewish immigration, for instance the German Jews starting in 1825 and the Eastern European Jews starting in 1880, both embraced the public schools. By the time the German Jews arrived, various forms of public schooling in America were underway, particularly in the major industrial cities where immigrants of all backgrounds tended to settle. The second major wave of Jewish immigration began around 1880 and lasted up through the end of World War I. Most of these immigrants came from the nations of Eastern Europe and brought with them the traditions and institutions of their native lands. As for education, the Eastern European Jews followed the lead of their predecessors and were largely supportive of the public schools.

To be sure, there was always a minority that favored full-time religious schooling, but most Jewish families chose to support public education and supplement it with the study of specifically Jewish topics. The story of Jewish education in America is in large part the story of various supplementary programs aimed at compensating for the inevitable, but understandable, religious shortcomings of nonsectarian public education. The very preponderance of these programs serves to reinforce the conclusion that for the most part American Jews embraced the public schools. As influential nineteenth century American rabbi Isaac Mayer Wise put it in an oft cited remark to the U.S. Commissioner on Education: "It is our settled opinion here that the education of the young is the business of the State, and the religious instruction, to which we add the Hebrew, is the duty of religious bodies. Neither ought to interfere with the other. The secular branches belong to the public schools, religion in the Sabbath schools, respectively."[30]

The widespread acceptance of the legitimacy, even the necessity, of secular branches of learning betrayed in Wise's statement is one of the most significant factors affecting the evolution of Jewish education in America. At least in terms of hours and prominence, religious instruction was marginalized in the lives of American Jews, taking place only in Sunday schools, weekday afternoon programs, and summer camps. Supplementary education came in various forms, from Sunday school programs not too dissimilar from their Protestant neighbors to "heders," privately maintained after-school programs that existed by the hundreds in the immigrant neighborhoods. Another widespread form of supplementary education in America was the Talmud Torahs. These were communal schools, meaning that they were not directly connected to any one synagogue or family, though both synagogues and families were active supporters of their efforts and often underwrote the financial needs of the Talmud Torah. Generally, there was a tuition payment made by each child that provided for materials, space if necessary, and teacher salary. Usually meeting for up to ten hours a week, pupils were instructed in Bible, Jewish history, religious customs, and perhaps Jewish music or art. These supplementary programs provided the vast majority of Jewish education in America, although even they reached only a minority of Jewish children.[31]

The first elaborate survey of Jewish education, conducted by Mordecai Kaplan and Bernard Cronson, focused on New York City. They identified six forms of Jewish education: Talmud Torahs, institutional schools, congregational schools, Sunday schools, Chedorim (heders), and private tutors. This study, conducted a full twenty years or more after the beginning of the 1880 migration, estimated that there were close to 200,000 Jewish children in New York City, with not more than a quarter of them receiving any Jewish education. A later study by Dr. Samson Benderly, the "father of modern Jewish education," reported only minor progress. Still estimating the number of Jewish children in New York to be about 200,000, Benderly estimated that perhaps 40,000 received institutional Jewish education with an additional 10,000 receiving private instruction. Benderly also commented on the lack of preparation for many Jewish educators. Of the 1,400 teachers, "not many could pass a satisfactory examination in both secular and Jewish subjects."[32] Indeed, the multitude of forms of Jewish education coupled with disturbing findings about its efficacy led numerous community leaders to characterize Jewish education in America as "a mild wide and an inch deep."

There had always been a small number of families who sought more intensive forms of Jewish education. Almost from the beginning, there were all-day schools, sometimes called, somewhat imprecisely, Yeshiva.[33] The first 100 years after the Revolutionary War witnessed the rise and fall of many Jewish day schools, constructed under both individual and congregational auspices. Most lasted only a few years, and even some of the more efficacious closed relatively quickly. For instance, in 1842 the B'nai Jeshurun congregation in New York converted its afternoon education program into a day school, enrolling some eighty students. It closed after just

Table 1.2. Growth of Jewish Day School Education in Five-Year Intervals in the United States and Canada[34]

Year	Number of schools	Enrollment	Number of communities
1940–1941	35	7,700	7
1945–1946	78	11,000	31
1950–1951	139	23,100	52
1955–1956	203	38,000	68
1960–1961	265	55,800	95
1963–1964	306	65,400	117

five years. Similarly, an all-Jewish school in Detroit opened in 1850 only to close in 1869 because it could not match the efficacy of public-school education. In Cleveland, the school operated by the Anshe Chesed congregation closed in 1867. Christian missionaries operated a "Hebrew" school in New York in the 1860s, an arrangement that led several Orthodox and Reform synagogues to open another day school just down the street. At one point there were several Jewish schools in Chicago, but by 1874 all had closed. Newark and Philadelphia also witnessed the transition from all-day Jewish schools to widespread embrace of nonsectarian public education by Jews. Most of the Jewish day schools that operated in these early years closed as families opted for the public schools that were growing in stature. Beset by numerous problems such as poor teaching and lack of resources, the Jewish day schools of the nineteenth century could not compete with the secularized, free tuition, and increasingly effective public schools.[35]

It was not until the middle of the twentieth century that day schools took hold among the American Jewish communities. The years 1940–1964 stand out as the beginning of the "Era of Great Expansion" for the Jewish day schools.[36] On the eve of American entry into World War II there were thirty-five day schools enrolling approximately 7,700 students. By 1964 there were more than 300 day schools in the United States and Canada educating more than 65,000 students, the vast majority of which were located in America. Table 1.2 charts the growth of the day school movement by focusing on the number of day schools, approximate enrollment, and the number of communities in which day schools could be found.

Numerous studies conducted during the post-World War II years confirm rapid growth of the movement, though they disagree on specific numbers.[37] That the day schools were taking an increasing portion of the total enrollment of Jewish students in any form of organized Jewish education can be further established by comparing day school enrollment with the total Jewish education enrollment in the United States. In 1942 day-school enrollment was approximately 9,200, accounting for 4.1 percent of the total Jewish school enrollment in America. By 1964 there were some 660,000 students receiving some type of Jewish education, 9.1 percent of which, or 59,900, were in day schools.[38]

The growth of the day schools is indicative of their coming of age as an instrument for Jewish education in America. Although these institutions were controversial, their phenomenal growth demanded more attention from all American Jews, not just those whose children attended day schools. The National Council for Jewish Education recognized as much in a 1961 resolution calling for widespread financial support for the day schools.

> The National Council for Jewish Education notes with deep satisfaction the significant growth of the all-day school and its emergence as a major form of Jewish education in numerical strength and wide-spread appeal manifesting, as it does, the increasing commitment of a substantial segment of American Jewry to Jewish education in a greater degree of depth than that which the predominant supplementary Jewish school can offer. Recognizing the singular contribution of the all-day school to raising the sights and goal of Jewish education and meeting this growing need for more intensive Jewish education, and considering the unique promise it holds for training and providing an intellectual-spiritual leadership for the American Jewish community, and taking into account the American democratic milieu which sanctions legally and morally the fostering and maintenance of such education programs for the perpetuation of the distinctive religious-cultural groups and mindful of the onerous financial burden borne by the groups conducting all-day schools . . . 1. The Conference, therefore, calls upon Federations and Welfare Funds to extend financial support to all-day schools . . . [39]

It is difficult to point to a single organization that became the public face of Jewish day schooling in America in the way that the NCWC did for American Catholics. In part, this is due to the lack of public struggle for the place of Jewish schooling. The debate over Jewish schools raged to be sure, but it was largely an intra-community debate. Further complicating matters, the American Jewish community is not all of one cloth. Portions of Orthodox, Reform, and Conservative Jewry all eventually embraced religious schooling, though at different points in time. That is not to say that there was no national voice speaking out on behalf of day-school education, only that there were a plurality of voices saying similar things at different points in time, speaking to their respective communities.

One important voice came from a former Talmud Torah principal and teacher named Feivel Mendlowitz, who, in 1944, helped found of a new Jewish day school organization, Torah Umesorah. Mendlowitz had also served as a principal and administrator of Yeshiva Torah Vodaath in New York City, where he had moved with his family in 1921. Convinced that the individual efforts of institutions like Torah Vodaath, while noteworthy, were insufficient, Mendlowitz advocated an expanded effort to make the benefits of day school education more available to Jewish children, especially those outside New York City. The purpose of Torah Umesorah was to establish new day schools throughout the country, not at all an inexpensive undertaking. In fact, the main activity of Torah Umesorah was to finance the construction and expansion of day school facilities, and to help ensure the supply of competent teachers for intensive Jewish education. Mendlowitz knew that in order to be successful, he would have to recruit laymen to bankroll his new agency. In a series of meetings in the late spring and early summer of 1944, several influential Jewish businessmen and philanthropists gathered in New York and pledged their support for the first National Convention of Torah Umesorah to be held June 20, 1944, at the Waldorf Astoria. More than thirty thousand dollars was raised at that meeting, and some ten weeks later, on September 6, 1944 Torah Umesorah was officially incorporated in New York State.

What is most interesting about the founding of Torah Umesorah is the language that surrounded it. Both the rabbis who made up the supervisory council and the laymen who made Torah Umesorah a reality spoke of intensive Jewish education as a "survival factor" for Judaism. It would counteract the "Nazi Tyranny" that had attempted to rid the world of Israel's Torah tradition. Even early on, then, we can see that the Hebrew day schools were not intended as just alternative educational arrangements. Supporters of Torah Umesorah, and of Hebrew day school education more generally, saw themselves as ensuring the survival of Judaism itself.

Although most of the significant personalities behind Torah Umesorah were orthodox, the organization itself transcended political and ideological boundaries in pursuing a common goal. Numerous groups, again, mostly aligned with orthodoxy, supported the work of Torah Umesorah. And even if most of their support came from Orthodox Jewry (as did most of the demand for day schools in the early years of the movement), Torah Umesorah's own guidelines specify that they would:

1. help all Day schools regardless of political allegiance or national affiliation,
2. not "sell" a political program to any of its affiliated schools,
3. cooperate with all elements within the Jewish community to set up a Hebrew [Day] School.[40]

There were other organizations working for the expansion of Hebrew day-school education, but most of them were tied to particular religious or political groups. For instance, both American Zionists and the Lubavitcher movements sponsored day schools, and worked for the expansion of more intensive education. Torah Umesorah was the only group not limited to working with only one community however, and it had no purpose other than expanding the day schools. It had no program for supplementary education or any other social service function.

Torah Umesorah's all but official identification with orthodoxy probably limited its appeal to other segments of the American Jewish community. For some time, the day school movement was perceived as the educational prerogative for primarily orthodox Jewish families. That is not to say that orthodoxy was the only support for the day school movement. Both Conservative and Reform Jewry joined in the new venture, although to a lesser extent. In 1951, for example, the Beth El Day School in Rockaway Park, New York was founded as the first day school sponsored by a conservative synagogue. In 1956 the United Synagogue Commission on Jewish Education organized a day school education committee, and nine years later the Association of Solomon Schechter Day Schools was formally structured at the first Conservative day school conference in New York. The association claims that it "pioneered" the use of day schools outside of Orthodox Judaism, and there are now seventy-six Solomon Schechter Day Schools operating in eighteen states and Canada.

Reform Judaism's embrace of day-school education was slower in coming. During the 1950s, when Orthodox and to a lesser extent Conservative day schools were beginning to take off, there were rumblings within the Reform community about the place of day school education in Reform Judaism. A few voices inside American Reform called for day schools, but for the most part supplementary schooling was the established, if not officially sanctioned, policy of Reform Judaism.[41] In fact, in 1953 at the height of the Orthodox movement, Reform leadership specifically encouraged their various congregations through the country to withhold the use of their facilities for day school education. Over the next decade, however, their position softened. In the first half of the 1960s, the Commission on Jewish Education, representing both the Union of American Hebrew Congregations and the Central Conference of American Rabbis, undertook a multi-year study to reexamine their position on day school education. Although the study committee had not come to any conclusion three years later, they made a point of saying that they did not oppose the establishing of day schools with a liberal Jewish outlook.

Protestations aside, some Reform Jews, like both the Orthodox and Conservatives before them, recognized that Reform Judaism would need leaders well-versed in Jewish thinking. This required a more intensive form of Jewish education than the various forms of supplementary education were able to provide. They also argued that day schools were more likely to instill a sense of belonging in students. The public schools, which still moved to the rhythm of the Christian calendar with celebrations of Easter and Christmas, could never do that. In even the most progressive public schools, Jewish children would always be outsiders, but day schools could reaffirm the Jewishness of the child. All were agreed that a more effective program of Jewish education was needed, but critics of the day school approach worried about educational separatism and a self-imposed isolation from American culture. Rabbi Elliot Rosenstock, who, as a member of the Joint Commission on Jewish Education voted against a resolution endorsing the establishment of Reform day schools, argued that the very idea of a separate educational institution was evidence that Reform Judaism had failed in America and called on Reform Jews to lead the efforts to improve public education.[42] The issue of Reform day schools came to a head in November of 1963, during the Union of American Hebrew Congregations forty-seventh biennial convention in Chicago. Rabbi Jay Kaufman, vice president of the Union, and his colleague Rabbi Alexander Schindler, head of the Union's Division of Religious Education, were quoted in the *New York Times* as affirming the role of day school education in Reform Judaism, indicating a shift in position even without a formal policy in favor of day schools. Already on the agenda for discussion, day schools became the hot topic of the meeting. Rabbis Kaufman and Schindler voiced the conviction that the program of Jewish religious education, including the all-day Jewish schools, was the "concern of the total Jewish community, meriting its material support."[43] Although Schindler pointed out that no budgetary request would be made for support of Reform day schools, he and Kaufman did call on wealthy individuals to fund day schools that were Reform, rather than Orthodox, in outlook.

Day schools have continued to grow at an impressive rate, so that by 1999 there were 691 Jewish schools, enrolling more than 169,000 students. Of the twenty-four religious denominations recorded in the National Center for Education Statistics 1999 survey of private schools in America, only four (Catholic, Baptist, Amish, and 7th Day Adventists) accounted for a higher percentage of total religious private schools than Jews. Though American Jewry is still largely supportive of public education, the Jewish day school has emerged as a significant institution in both American Judaism and in religious schooling more broadly.

PROTESTANT SCHOOLING

The relationship between Protestantism and public schooling in America is more complicated than one might assume. Protestant ministers and theologians were often at the forefront of the push for public education, understanding the entire effort as an extension of the Christian civilizing process, as well as a useful tool against Catholicism. Though both Catholic and Jewish advocates of religious schooling identified the public schools as essentially Protestant schools, it is not the case that all Protestants thought them Protestant enough. Throughout the nineteenth century, Protestant denominations built their own schools in America. Some of these were ethnic and old-world enclaves every bit as much as they were religious schools. Indeed, for many communities these sources of identity went hand in hand. Various Lutheran bodies, especially the Missouri Synod, established schools throughout the Midwest. Devoted to religious instruction and the preservation of denominational particularities, these schools were often fairly small, but also remarkably perseverant. A significant aspect of the immigrant experience, religious schools often embraced old-world languages and customs, and were thus an important part of the various immigrant communities' attempts to retain part of their old identity even in their new land. Calvinists, too, built their own schools throughout the nineteenth century, though as with other denominations, the rise of "free," nonsectarian public schools materially impacted their denominational institutions. The Protestant tone embraced by nineteenth-century common schools in America served to minimize the cognitive dissonance some religious groups might have experienced had the government schools been more secular. In this era, public schools were seen by many as contributing to, rather than undermining, Protestant culture in America.[44] Most of the Protestant groups that had established school systems gave at least tacit approval to public education, often lagging behind what was happening in the homes of their members many of whom embraced public schooling.

By the middle of the twentieth century, however, a growing chorus of discontent over the state of public schooling could be heard even by a casual listener to educational conversations. Concerns over the decline in the quality of American education, exacerbated by Cold War tensions with Russia and damning reports such as *A Nation At Risk*, reenergized religious schooling as a self-conscious strategy among conservative Protestants in the latter half of the twentieth century. The perceived academic decline in the public schools was a larger part of the justification for why some Protestants fled the public institutions more so than in either the Catholic or Jewish experience earlier in the century. Particularly since the middle of the 1960s evangelicals, especially, have been active in establishing alternative educational settings for their children.[45] In the last four decades there have been two distinct exoduses from public education on the part of conservative Protestants. First, and more heavily documented, a number of evangelical and fundamentalist Protestants built their own schools starting in the 1970s. The second wave, Christian homeschooling, emerged more slowly but by the 1990s was a full-fledged movement on its own accord. The homeschool movement has been less analyzed and thus will be the focus of our analysis. While it is not coterminous with the Christian day school movement by any means, there are a number of similarities that are of particular relevance to the present study (most notably the controversy over its place in a democratic society).

Between 1971 and 1981 the number of students in Christian schools rose from 140,000 to as many as 450,000. James Carper estimated that by the middle of the 1980s, two decades after the general renewal of this strategy in Protestantism, there might have been as many as 11,000 schools enrolling a million or more students.[46] This is not to say that all of the families whose children went to such schools were conservative Protestants. Still, it was during this same time period that more conservative churches recorded impressive growth, a phenomenon that surprised many observers who thought that religion would have to negotiate with, more than resist, modern life. The reasons for this period of dramatic growth in Christian day schooling are varied, but certainly it cannot be separated from the reemergence of conservative Protestantism in society more broadly.[47] One of the most dramatic and often commented on trends in late twentieth-century American religion is the growth of more conservative churches and denominations, even as mainline groups declined. Given the place of schooling in American life it was inevitable that this movement would have ramifications for education. Leaders of this conservative Protestant resurgence, including nationally prominent figures such as Jerry Falwell and Tim LaHaye, specifically addressed the issue of education as part of their mission. Political and legal decisions that disallowed practices such as prayer and Bible reading in the public schools drew attention to the growing rift between some devout believers and their local schools. The public schools were seen as incubators for a litany of what conservatives saw as pressing social problems, from drug use to rampant teenage sexuality.[48] Additionally, there were several curricular skirmishes between conservative Protestant families and various public school systems across the country. The headline garnering battle between Vicki Frost and the Hawkins County School Board in Tennessee is a case in point. Complaints about the curriculum's hostility to Christian belief and practice erupted into a sustained legal and social drama, and was dubbed by some commentators as Scopes II (a title other battles over public schools have been saddled, or rewarded, with as well).[49]

As in the cases of both Catholic and Jewish schooling, the rise in conservative Protestant day schooling occasioned, and in turn was reinforced by, the emergence of national organizations advocating for their cause. The largest of these (there are state, regional, and other national associations as well) is the Association of Christian Schools International (ACSI), now headquartered in Colorado Springs, Colorado. The result of a 1978 merger between three other associations (The National Christian School Education Association, The Ohio Association of Christian Schools, and the Western Association of Christian Schools), ACSI has more than 5,300-member schools in some 100 countries around the world. As of June of 2007, ACSI had 3,885-member institutions in the United States, educating almost 747,000 students.[50] ACSI's mission is both to represent Christian schooling in various forums and to serve individual member schools. They offer accreditation services, additional self-study opportunities, and advice such as the STAR program designed to enhance an institution's own efforts at improvement (in keeping with the Bush administration's emphasis on assessment, outcomes, and accountability in all of education), teacher certification in several disciplines, and even student assessment services such as the Stanford

Achievement Tests. In terms of representing Christian schooling, ACSI has joined other pro-family advocacy groups in a variety of causes mostly related to religious freedom. In March of 2007, for instance, ACSI urged federal lawmakers to add a religious freedom amendment to legislation aimed at improving Head Start. They also monitor legislation in individual states and lobby on behalf of Christian schooling at all levels of government. More so than their counterparts in Catholic or Jewish schooling, ACSI is also focused on providing resources for children through instructional materials and other ministries.

These schools have been the subject of several studies and are certainly a major part of the story of faith-based schooling in America.[51] They are not, however, the only, or even the most recent, example of evangelical and conservative Protestants embracing the concept of faith-based education. Alongside this renewal of institutional religious schooling has been the equally noteworthy but less understood phenomenon of Christian homeschooling.[52]

Homeschoolers themselves, however, see their history going back much further than just the last few decades. They do not see themselves just as an offshoot of the Christian school movement, though they clearly have much in common with these immediate predecessors. In their view, the primary educative agency in human history was, and should be, the family, an insight they think guided earlier generations of Americans. In their view, the history of education is the story of the usurpation by the state of the God-given right and duty to direct the moral, spiritual, and intellectual formation of their children.

Estimating the size of the home education phenomenon is not easy. Since it is largely a decentralized movement, there is no single office one can call for dependable numbers. The various state departments of education that do keep records do so in different ways, and have often developed new methodologies or reporting requirements themselves over the last two decades, making it difficult to track the movement's growth. Government statistics are sometimes doubled by other estimates, making even consensus figures hard to come by. The U.S. Department of Education, for instance, estimated the number of homeschooled children in 1999 to be 850,000, a number specifically disputed by National Home Education Research Institute President Brian D. Ray as too low. He estimated that by 1999 the figure was closer to 1.5 million, nearly double the Department of Education figure.[53]

What everyone does agree on is that, specific numbers aside, the movement has experienced remarkable growth. It is estimated that in the late 1970s there were perhaps 12,500 children being schooled at home.[54] That number grew throughout the 1980s, particularly as the practice caught on among conservative Protestants.

Table 1.3. Modern Homeschooling[55]

Year	Number of homeschooled children
Late 1970s	10,000–15,000
1983	60,000–125,000
1988	150,000–300,000
1990	250,000–350,000
1995	700,000–750,000
1997	Up to 1,000,000 (based on annual growth rate)

The National Home Education Research Institute's estimates are considerably higher. President Brian D. Ray has argued that by 1999 there were closer to 1.5 million children in homeschools, surpassing the combined public school population of Wyoming, Vermont, Delaware, North Dakota, Alaska, South Dakota, Rhode Island, Montana, and Hawaii. More recent estimates put the number at between 1.7 and 2.1 million for the 2003–2004 academic year. Yearly growth is estimated at 7–12 percent, making it one of the fastest growing trends in education.[56]

While the numbers are impressive in their own right, one should note that homeschooling emerged as part of a larger cultural matrix that favored local initiative, deregulation, and a return to the home as the center of life. It has long been observed that the bureaucratization of society during modernity meant that many of the functions formerly carried out by the family in the home were taken over by the state and wider society. For example, industrialization took workers outside the home and moved them to factories, which then became the center of economic production. Simultaneously, and not at all unrelated, other activities of the family were also gradually taken over by outside agencies thus reinforcing the "statist" model of family policy. By the end of the twentieth century, however, that trend showed signs of reversing. Virtually every activity necessary for modern life can now take place entirely within the confines of home. Paychecks can be direct deposited, bills can be paid on-line, and more and more people now work out of their home. Even entertainment in the home can now rival going out for an evening as cable stations, satellites, and 'surround sound' turn every television into a potential cinema. Jonathan Gershuny, writing in the late 1970s, identified two services that at that point had resisted the shift toward home, medicine, and education. This is not the place to go into the dramatic growth of home health care as an industry. Suffice it to say that the rise of home health care in the late 1980s and 1990s was significant enough to make home health care workers one of the fastest growing aspects of modern health care. Even neighborhood drug stores carry oxygen canisters for home-based patients now. As for education, the growth of homeschooling is one of the most remarkable movements in education in the last two decades.[57]

This growth is all the more remarkable given the movement's unusual trajectory. Homeschooling in America is hardly uniform, though it is widely identified with conservative Protestantism. Thirty years ago that would have been hard to predict. The anti-establishment left were the ones talking about "deschooling" society at that point—men like the "radical humanist" Ivan Illich argued that the school system in the United States reinforced and reproduced the hierarchical social structure they purported to level. The very certificate of graduation and accomplishment that schools award perpetuated the stratification schooling was supposed to combat. He advocated removing the self-appointed monopoly that controlled the dissemination of knowledge in America.[58]

Among Illich's contemporaries was an American education critic named John Holt. More influential among the progressive wing of the homeschool movement, Holt carried out much of the intellectual groundwork that later homeschool advocates capitalized on. After a string of disappointing teaching positions at various schools Holt published How Children Fail in 1964, inaugurating a twenty-year career as one of the leaders in the cultural and political left's attempt to reform education in America. Holt charged that schools were too focused on the presentation of a predigested body of knowledge that to children could not but have appeared stale and depressing. Since they were required to be there, however, the quest for students became how to get by without actually engaging the material. As an antidote Holt advocated a system in which teachers would guide children through lessons that the children themselves wanted to learn. Education would be based on interest, and would therefore differ for each child, making mass, institution-based schooling all but impossible.[59]

But how did a movement whose early leadership was largely from the left end up being dominated by conservative Protestants? For that answer, we must turn our attention to Raymond and Dorothy Moore. They began their criticism of public education not because they saw the schools as hotbeds of agnosticism, but because they believed that schooling was simply started too early in America. They were advocates of delayed schooling, a philosophy that argued that children were not emotionally and developmentally prepared for the social context of what they called out-of-home education until between the ages of eight and ten. That most children were leaving their homes well before this age, either for preschool or the early primary grades depending on the family, the Moores saw as disastrous not just for the children but for society at large.

The Moores argued that the home was designed as a place of protection and familial attachment, and thus all but the very worst homes were still better than even the best out-of-home facilities. They recognized that certain children, for instance the developmentally disabled and the underprivileged, might need institutionalized help before others, but they advocated in-home care even for these children until the family situation was no longer capable of meeting the needs of the child. In a series of books and articles in the early 1970s the Moores gained national attention as critics of several aspects of public schooling. It was not a particularly long jump from their advocacy of delayed schooling, with its focus on the superiority of the family and the importance of attachment between parent and child, to homeschooling. The obvious importance they attached to the family resonated with the emerging pro-family religious organizations like Focus on the Family, and, in fact, the Moores' later books were praised by Dr. James Dobson and other leaders of the conservative Christian movement.

Though the Moores would eventually be eclipsed by a new generation of leaders in the Christian homeschooling movement, they are still credited with popularizing homeschooling in the Christian community. Their emphasis on attachment and securing in learning form the backdrop for many of the ideas that Christian homeschoolers still hold dear. For the Moores, the best environment for learning was the home, and thus homeschools were presented not just as a Christian alternative to public schools, but as the best option for all children, Christian or not. The burden of proof, they insisted, should be on the state to prove the superiority of public education since the evidence is, in their view, overwhelming in favor of delayed schooling and keeping children with their parents. Their decline in terms of leadership was directly related to the emergence of a more distinctly Christian approach to homeschooling popularized by men like Greg Harris (a former Moore employee) and Michael Farris.[60]

In March of 1983 two homeschooling fathers who also happened to be attorneys, Michael Farris and Michael Smith, founded an organization originally designed as a legal coop to defend other homeschooling families from government intrusion or criminal prosecution. Farris and Smith met at a 1982 homeschool rally in Santa Monica, California. Smith, who lived with his family in Sacramento, had been homeschooling since 1981 and was already active in the Christian Home Educators Association of California (CHEA). Farris, now the acknowledged leader of the Christian homeschooling community in America, and his wife had decided to homeschool their daughter. At the time, homeschooling was an obscure practice, and families who engaged in it were virtually certain to face critical questions from friends and extended family. At times, the questions came from the educational bureaucracy and could, if not resolved, result in legal entanglements. According to Smith, Farris was actively looking for someone to found the organization with him, and one of the other leaders of CHEA suggested he contact Smith. The two men agreed that an organization was necessary to fulfill their goals (both were already involved in legal proceedings regarding homeschooling families) and thus the Homeschool Legal Defense Association (HSLDA) was created. Farris recalled that by the end of the first year there were some 200-member families. That number had grown to 3,600 by the spring of 1987.[61]

Smith and Farris both volunteered their time for the first few years of HSLDA's hectic existence. In 1984, attorney Jordan Lawrence was hired by HSLDA as a part-time legal advocate (he also worked part time for Concerned Women for America). Attorney Chris Klicka, who had previously interned with the Rutherford Institute in Charlottesville, Virginia, where he studied the various state laws regarding home education, joined the staff in 1985 as the first full-time legal staff member. Farris (who had earlier represented Vicki Frost) and Smith did not take full-time positions until 1986 and 1987 respectively.

HSLDA is the largest homeschool lobby in the country. Each family pays a set fee ($115 in 2007) and for that price is guaranteed legal defense for any issues related to the education of their children. With tens of thousands of member families, HSLDA has an annual budget in the millions of dollars and an impressive suite of offices located in Purcellville, Virginia, on the campus of Patrick Henry College (founded by Farris and dedicated to homeschool families). According to their Web site, the mission of HSLDA is "to preserve and advance the fundamental, God-given, constitutional right of parents and others legally responsible for their children to direct their education." In this, they rely on two "fundamental freedoms" in their legal arguments: parent's rights and religious freedom.[62] These are the cornerstones of their legal defense, and as we will see in Chapter 4, they have been very active in securing these rights for homeschooling families.

Since the mid-1980s, a series of legal and legislative victories has largely secured the right to homeschool in America. Farris himself has noted that no HSLDA member has ever been convicted and sent to jail for their actions, though some have been convicted and paid fines. That is not to say that HSLDA is closing down. Its successes have allowed the organization to shift its focus from defending the basic rights of parents to homeschool to fending off intrusive legislation that would regulate the activities of parents in the home. These include things like mandatory testing for graduates, curfews, and now working to pass the American Sovereignty Amendment that would prevent international law (treaties) from "trumping" domestic law (the Constitution). They are also heavily involved in leadership development and civic awareness for homeschooling families.

As we saw earlier, public schooling is the de facto educational establishment in the United States. Some 90 percent of school-age children in America attend public institutions. But alongside the public schools there remain private religious institutions, also an important part of America's educational landscape. Though they do, in fact, predate public education as we know it today, given the superior position of the public schools one might have expected the entire enterprise of faith-based schooling to eventually fold. And, to be sure, many specific institutions have closed as public schooling grew. Religious schooling as a whole, however, has thrived. Not only have individual parents continued to choose faith-based schooling for their children, but also entire religious communities that at one point in their history opposed the idea of separate institutions have come to adopt them. Why that would be the case is the focus of the next chapter.

NOTES

1. On the evolution of compulsory school laws see David Tyack, "Ways of Seeing: An Essay on the History of Compulsory Schooling," *Harvard Educational Review* 46 (August 1976): 355–389. See also Charles Burgess, "The Goddess, the Schoolbook, and Compulsion," *Harvard Educational Review* 46 (May 1976): 199–216; and Michael Katz, *A History of Compulsory Attendance Laws* (Bloomington, IN: Phi Delta Kappa Educational Foundation, 1976).

2. These figures are from the National Center on Education Statistics Annual Report entitled *Digest of Educational Statistics*, 2001, available online from the NCES, publication number 2002130.

3. The religion promoted in the common schools was not one all of kind, and there was considerable opposition to the very idea of nonsectarian education even among some Protestant groups. See Charles Glenn, *The Myth of the Common School* (Amherst, MA: University of Massachusetts Press, 1988).

4. See the NCES *Digest*, 2001.

5. *Homeschooling in the United States*, National Center for Education Statistics (2003), available online from the NCES, publication number 2001033.

6. Of course, not all private schooling is carried out under religious auspices, but the vast majority is religious in origin. On the importance of religion as a motivation for private schooling, see Otto Kraushaar, *American Non-Public Schools: Patterns of Diversity* (Baltimore, MD: Johns Hopkins University Press, 1972). He estimated that as much as 85 percent of private schooling is religious in origin. Recent studies by the National Center for Education Statistics confirm that only about 15 percent of all private schooling is nonsectarian. See *Private School Universe Survey, 1999–2000*, available online from the NCES, publication number 2001330.

7. Catholic educational history in America has been the subject of numerous studies, so much so that it is difficult to say anything new on this topic when trying to write in broad themes as I am here. My own interests are in the ways in which certain aspects of the Catholic school experience were replayed by later religious communities, and thus I have tried to present the information on Catholic schooling with that in mind. Nevertheless, the Catholic-themed material presented here and in subsequent chapters might be familiar ground to some readers. The literature on Jewish day schools and Protestant schooling, especially the homeschooling variety, is less extensive. Among the excellent histories of Catholic education in America are Harold Buetow, *Of Singular Benefit: The Story of Catholic Education in the United States* (New York: Macmillan, 1970), and Timothy Walch, *Parish School: American Catholic Parochial Education from Colonial Times to the Present* (New York: Crossroad Publishing Company, 1996). For an account of the early relationship of Catholic schools to their common-school counterparts, see Diane Ravitch's excellent *The Great School Wars* (New York: Basic Books, 1974).

8. See the 1950 letter from the American Catholic hierarchy, "The Child: Citizen of Two Worlds," in *Catholic Education in America: A Documentary History*, edited by Neil McCluskey (New York: Teachers College, 1964).

9. See Harold Buetow, *Of Singular Benefit: The Story of Catholic Education in the United States*, previously cited.

10. See *Directory of Catholic Colleges and Schools*, National Catholic Welfare Council, (NCWC) Washington, DC: Department of Education, 1932.

11. In subsequent years, the National Catholic War Council became the National Catholic Welfare Council to signify its continuing mission after World War I ended. In 1922, it changed names again, substituting the word conference for council to indicate its relationship to other councils in the Catholic hierarchy.

12. On Burke and the national effort, see Elizabeth McKeown, *War and Welfare: American Catholics and World War I* (New York: Garland Publishing, 1988).

13. There was some consideration as to whether or not a national organization was canonically permissible. In fact, the Vatican suppressed the NCWC in 1922 in part because well-placed leaders in the American church feared that it would interfere with their own diaconal administration. After a hearing, the council was affirmed by the Consistorial Congregation in June of 1922 and then continued the work it had already been doing for some time.

14. On the opening of the interdepartmental Bureau of Education, including Burke's comments on the relationship between the CEA and the NCWC, as well as the overall mission of the NCWC's initiative, see National Catholic Welfare Council, "Opening of the NCWC Bureau of Education," *NCWC Bulletin* (February 1921): 9ff.

15. A.C. Monahan, "Work of the N.C.W.C. Bureau of Education," *NCWC Bulletin* (June 1921): 14ff.

16. Several decades before, New York City bishop John Hughes had been more critical of the public schools, but as they had become dominant, later Catholic leaders moderated their stance. For more on Hughes, see Chapter 3.

17. This was the same basic position taken by a representative of the United States Bureau of Education at the opening of the Board of Education of the NCWC in 1921. Commissioner Claxton had affirmed the right of parents to choose their children's school, but also insisted on support for public schools regardless of whether one's children patronized them. See "Opening of the NCWC Bureau of Education," previously cited. See also National Catholic Welfare Council, "Administrative Bishops of N.C.W.C. Hold Important Meeting," *NCWC Bulletin* (February 1923): 5ff.

18. James Ryan, *Catechism of Catholic Education* (Washington, DC: Bureau of Education of the National Catholic Welfare Council, 1922).

19. On the relationship between the Klan and the Masonic orders, see David Tyack, "Perils of Pluralism: The Background of the Pierce Case," *American Historical Review* (October 1968): 74ff. See also Lloyd Jorgenson, "The Oregon School Law of 1922: Passage and Sequel," *Catholic Historical Review* (1968): 455–466.

20. "Speaker for School Bill," *Oregon Statesman*, November 3, 1922.

21. There was considerable opposition to the Oregon law. National newspapers, the U.S. Commissioner of Education, the American Jewish Committee, and the Seventh Day Adventists, all opposed the bill. Jorgenson also shows that the secular press, including *The New York Times* and the *Chicago Tribune*, opposed the law as well.

22. National Catholic Welfare Council, "Administrative Bishops of N.C.W.C. Hold Important Meeting," previously cited.

23. National Catholic Welfare Council, "Eminent Catholic Lawyers Successfully Defend Rights of Private School," *NCWC Bulletin* (June 1924).

24. *Pierce v. Society of Sisters*, United States Reports volume 268, Government Printing Office, Washington, DC (1926).

25. Kavanaugh argued the case before the District Court, while Guthrie took over in Washington. There is some evidence that this was a matter of contention among the Catholic hierarchy, and that this division of labor was basically a compromise between Oregon's hierarchy and the NCWC. On the involvement of the NCWC, see Thomas Shelley, "The Oregon School Case and the National Catholic Welfare Conference," *Catholic Historical Review*, 75(3) (1989) 439–457.

26. Bishops 1919 Pastoral Letter available online at Catholic Social Teaching Web site: http://www.osjspm.org/majordoc_us_bishop_statement_pastoral_letter_1919. aspx.

27. In the early twenty-first century there is much more of an emphasis on empowering parents to direct the education of their children than there was in earlier periods when the church largely instructed parents as to what they should do. The stress on parental involvement, while changing in emphasis, is a consistent feature of religious schooling and will be explored more in Chapter 2.

28. Milton Himmelfarb, "Reflections on the Jewish Day School," *Commentary* (July 1960): 29.

29. See Lloyd Gartner, *Jewish Education in the United States: A Documentary History* (New York: Teachers College Press, 1969). See also Hyman Grinstein, *The Rise of the Jewish Community of New York: 1654–1860* (Philadelphia: Jewish Publication Society of America, 1945); Nathan Glazer, *American Judaism* (Chicago, IL: University of Chicago Press, 1972); Naomi Cohen, *Jews in Christian America: The Pursuit of Religious Equality* (New York: Oxford University Press, 1992).

30. See Lloyd Gartner, *Jewish Education in the United States: A Documentary History*, 1969, previously cited, 86.

31. Grinstein estimated that in 1880 there were between forty and fifty thousand Jewish children in the United States (up to twenty thousand of which were in New York City) with perhaps fifteen thousand receiving any sort of Jewish education nationwide. See Hyman Grinstein, "In the Course of the Nineteenth Century," in *A History of Jewish Education*, ed. Judah Pilch (New York: American Association for Jewish Education, 1969).

32. See Meir Ben-Horin, "From the Turn of the Century to the Late Thirties," in *A History of Jewish Education* ed. Judah Pilch (New York: American Association for Jewish Education, 1969). Bernard Steinberg argues that one of the noteworthy features of Jewish education in this period was the switch from congregational to communal responsibility, thus expanding educational opportunities to those families not affiliated with a particular congregation. The Jewish community had always provided for the education of poor children, but now the education of all Jewish children took on new significance for the entire community. Thus, the children of even middle-class Jews who had perhaps neglected to provide Jewish education were welcomed in the Talmud Torahs and other supplementary programs. See Bernard Steinberg, "Jewish Education in the United States: A Study in Religio-Ethnic Response," *Journal of Jewish Sociology* 21(1) (1979): 5ff.

33. *Yeshiva* was the term given to academies of higher Jewish studies in the Old World that in America came to refer to any all-day Jewish school regardless of the level

of student achievement. See Leo Honor, "The Impact of the American Environment and American Ideas on Jewish Elementary Education in the United States," *Jewish Quarterly Review*, xlv (1955).

34. Table 1.2 is adapted with gracious permission from Schiff, *The Jewish Day School in America*, (New York: Jewish Education Committee, 1966), 49.

35. See Alvin Schiff, *The Jewish Day School in America* (New York: Jewish Education Committee, 1966); Eduardo Rauch, "Jewish Education in the United States, 1840–1920," Unpublished doctoral dissertation in the School of Education, Harvard University (1978). Grinstein, previously cited, relates the story of the Christian "Hebrew" school and the Jewish community's response.

36. This is Schiff's term.

37. See, for instance the summary report by Alexander Dushkin and Uriah Engelman, "Jewish Education in the United States," *Jewish Education* 30 (Fall 1959): 14–23; 33. See also Joseph Kaminetsky "Evaluating the Program and Effectiveness of the All-Day Jewish School," *Jewish Education*, 27 (Winter 1957): 39–49. There is some disagreement about the exact number of day schools in any given year because the criteria for reporting what counts as a day school is not uniform. Different organizations count them in different ways. Schiff, who authored the most in-depth study of the movement, uses the figures reported by Torah Umesorah, a day-school advocacy organization founded in 1944, and various other sources. Sometimes junior high programs and senior high programs are listed as two different schools, when in reality they were closely connected, perhaps even housed together. Some reports also included all-day preschool programs, or counted extension programs sponsored by one school as two different institutions.

38. Schiff, *The Jewish Day School*, previously cited, 72.

39. Originally written as a resolution, the text here has been rendered in paragraph form. For the entire resolution, see National Council for Jewish Education, "Resolution on Community Support for Day School Education," *Jewish Education*, volume 32 (Winter 1961): 123.

40. On the founding of Torah Umesorah, see Doniel Kramer, *The History and Impact of Torah Umesorah and Hebrew Day Schools in America*, unpublished dissertation, Yeshiva University, 1976, 32.

41. See Daniel Syme, "Reform Judaism and Day Schools: The Great Historical Dilemma," *Religious Education* 78/2 (1983): 153–181.

42. Elliot D. Rosenstock, "The Case against a Reform Jewish Day School," *Dimensions*, (Summer, 1969): 37–39.

43. Irving Spiegel, "2 Reform Rabbis Back Day Schools," *New York Times*, November 17, 1963.

44. On the efforts of various denominations to build and maintain their own schools, see James Carper and Thomas Hunt, *Religious Schooling in America* (Birmingham: Religious Education Press, 1984.) See also their *The Dissenting Tradition in American Education*, (New York: Peter Lang Publishers, 2007).

45. David Sikkink has shown that not all Protestant groups embrace religious schooling with the same enthusiasm. He finds that Pentecostal and charismatic traditions are more likely than others to feel alienated from the public schools. Evangelicals, he argues, are often supportive of public education. Sikkink's work has been invaluable in my own research, but his conclusions rely on self-identification for religious identity, which makes comparing groups difficult. Additionally, breaking up

Protestants into multiple categories, while theologically and sociologically justified in many cases, risks missing the overall embrace of the faith-based schooling strategy by conserving Protestants in the twentieth century. David Sikkink, "The Social Sources of Alienation from Public Schools," *Social Forces,* 78(1) (September 1999): 51–86.

46. James Carper, *Religious Schooling in America,* previously cited. See also "A Case for Moral Absolutes," *Time Magazine* (June 8, 1981): 54–56.

47. On the general strength of conservative churches consult Dean Kelley, *Why Conservative Churches Are Growing* (New York: Harper and Row, 1962). On the emergence of the Christian Right in America, see Steve Bruce, T*he Rise and Fall of the New Christian Right: Conservative Protestant Politics in America, 1978–1988* (Oxford: Clarendon Press, 1988).

48. See William Reese, "Soldiers for Christ in the Army of God: The Christian School Movement in America," in *Educational Theory* 35(2) (Spring 1985): 175–194.

49. See Stephen Bates, *Battleground: One Mother's Crusade, The Religious Right, and the Struggle for Control of Our Classrooms* (New York: Poseidon Press, 1993). The growth of Christian schooling was also spurred on as part of the reaction to forced integration of public education. In parts of the South, independent schools were founded, sometimes with the cooperation of religious bodies, as a means of defending segregationist ideas. Later advocates of Christian schooling have disavowed this part of the overall legacy. See Reese, previously cited.

50. These figures were provided to me by ACSI (Association of Christian Schools International) personnel in November of 2007 and reflect their pre-membership drive numbers.

51. See, for instance, Susan D. Rose, *Keeping Them Out of the Hands of Satan: Evangelical Schooling in America* (New York: Routledge, 1988). See also Alan Peshkin, *God's Choice: The Total World of a Fundamentalist Christian School* (Chicago: University of Chicago Press, 1986).

52. The relationship between Christian homeschooling and Christian day schooling is complex. They share many of the same concerns regarding secular humanism in the public schools, and utilize some of the same resources in terms of textbooks and other materials. Both groups are pro-family, but homeschoolers tend to be more anti-institution in general than their day school counterparts. As later chapters will show, they have been subject to very similar charges in terms of the political functions of schooling.

53. Most discussions of the size of the homeschool population refer at some point to the work of Patricia Lines of the Department of Education. Her 1991 paper, "Estimating the Home School Population" is widely cited for both its estimates and its methodology. Lines has released more recent estimates as well and is still the leading expert on the size of the movement. See Patricia Lines, "Estimating the Home School Population" (Washington, DC: U.S. Department of Education Office of Educational Research and Improvement, 1991).

54. See Brian D. Ray, *Home Schooling on the Threshold: A Survey of Research at the Dawn of the New Millennium* (Salem, OR: NHERI Publications, 1999).

55. These numbers come from various estimates by Lines. They have been widely reported in both scholarly literature and the media. See her 1998 paper "Homeschoolers: Estimating Numbers and Growth" produced for the U.S. Department of Education, available online at http://www.ed.gov/offices/OERI/SAI/homeschool/index.html.

56. Brian D. Ray, "A Home School Research Story," *Home Schooling in Full View*, ed. Bruce Cooper (Greenwich: Information Age Publishing, 2005).

57. Jonathan Gershuny, *After Industrial Society: The Emerging Self-Service Economy* (Atlantic Highlands, NJ: Humanities Press, 1978). For more on the return of the home see Krishan Kumar, "Home: The Promise and Predicament of Private Life at the End of the Twentieth Century" in *Perspectives on the Grand Dichotomy: Public and Private in Thought and Practice*, ed. Krishan Kumar and Jeff Weintraub (Chicago, IL: University of Chicago Press, 1997).

58. On Illich see Erich Fromm's introduction to Illich's *Celebration of Awareness: A Call for Institutional Revolution* (Garden City, NY: Doubleday and Company, 1970). See also John Elias, *Conscientization and Deschooling: Friere's and Illich's Proposals for Reshaping Society* (Philadelphia, PA: Westminster Press, 1976).

59. Holt's influence can hardly be overestimated, particularly as it is felt in what is now the smaller segment of the homeschooling community. Studies of the home-schooling population tend to divide practitioners into two groups. The initial distinction put forward by Jane Van Galen was between pedagogues and ideologues influenced many early studies of homeschoolers. Pedagogues believed that they could simply provide a better education for their children than could a teacher already stretched too thin by a room full of other students. Ideologues cared more about the transmission of values to their children. They based their decision to homeschool on conviction rather than expediency. The problem with Van Galen's dividing line is that the majority of homeschoolers are, at least on some level, moti-vated by ideological concerns, but often these concerns differ from family to family. Recently, Mitchell Stevens offered a different dividing line for the homeschooling population: believers and inclusives. Inclusives are the ideological descendents of the alternative movements of the 1960s and 1970s, while evangelical and funda-mentalist Christians comprise the much larger believers camp. The sharp ideolog-ical distinctions among homeschoolers have prompted some observers to suggest that we ought to speak of two movements, or more. See Jane Van Galen, "Ideo-logues and Pedagogues: Parents Who Teach Their Children at Home," in *Home Schooling: Political, Historical, and Pedagogical Perspectives*, previously cited. See also Mitchell Stevens *A Kingdom of Children* (Princeton, NJ: Princeton University Press, 2001).

60. On the relationship between the Moores and the rest of the Christian home-school leadership see Mitchell Stevens, *Kingdom of Children*, previously cited.

61. The numerical strength of the organization represented here are estimations made by Farris and Smith themselves in a feature article on HSLDA's Web site. See www.hslda.org/about/history/good-bad-inspiring.asp.

62. There is no single case that defends the right to homeschool the way the *Pierce* decision did for private religious schools. Many of the most influential cases have been decided on the state level, and many states have laws specifically to protect the rights of parents to teach their children at home.

2 The Place of Schooling in Religious Communities

H aving seen that the majority of private schooling in America is religious in origin, and that this practice transcends particular religious communities, one question that needs to be asked is why should this be the case? Why do religious communities in America endure the bureaucratic headaches, controversy, and, not least of all, expenses, when tax-supported public schools are available in virtually every neighborhood? This is not the same as asking why individual parents choose the educational setting they do for their children. It is related to this question, but not identical. Although a number of studies have examined the motivations for homeschooling, there are surprisingly few more general studies of why people choose the schools they do for their children. Costs and academic performance are obviously important factors in such a decision, but again these apply more to the individual or familial level. With regard to the decision to homeschool, other motivating factors include safety concerns, the flexibility of the curriculum and options for specific courses of study, proximity of other alternatives to the home, and the parent's own experiences from back when they were in school. The number one concern, however, is the desire on the part of parents to guide the formation of their children's values. It is not unreasonable to assume that similar motives apply to parents who choose other forms of religious schooling.[1] Indeed, what evidence we do have confirms that religion is one of the key determinants of where parents choose to send their children for school. A 1996 survey of families in the Millard Public School District in Omaha, Nebraska, found that religion was by far the most commonly cited factor in school selection. Families with strong ties to their religious community are more likely to sense tension between their religious values and those of the supposedly value-free public schools.[2]

While we should not be surprised by the fact that religion is an important influence on whether or not parents send their children to a religious school, posing the question this way assumes the existence of alternative arrangements to public schooling. That is, this question presents schooling choices as one set of options that individual parents must simply make a decision on, rather like what summer camp to go to or which house to buy. Faith-based schools are the supply side of an economic equation: individual parents demand alternatives to public education, so religious communities make schools available. While there is probably some truth to this on the level of particular schools, I contend that religious schooling itself is more than just the sum total of individual decisions by parents. It is best understood as a social space in which the truths and demands of religious life are enacted.[3] In this space, the worldview embraced by parents and religious leaders is not set aside or presented as a quaint reminder of the past, but rather it undergirds the entire institution. Likewise, behaviors that are at best accommodated in public institutions are weaved seamlessly into the school day. Prayers, dietary restrictions, and religious holidays are not just tolerated or treated as curiosities, but expected and affirmed. Thus, though often defensive in origin (meaning that it was problems with the public schools that led to their founding), religious schooling also serves positive functions for religious communities and their constituent families as well. In this sense, faith-based schools are an important part of any religious community's attempt to maintain boundaries from the society that surrounds them. They have the added benefit, too, of reinforcing community-specific behaviors. Both boundary maintenance and community-specific behaviors have been shown to increase the vitality of religious communities more broadly, making faith-based schools doubly attractive.[4]

Although the specific motivations for each group differ with historical and social circumstance, two themes that resurface in the history of religious schooling will occupy us here. The first is an epistemological claim about the source of knowledge and the religious community's privileged access to truth. The second theme revolves around a divinely sanctioned social order in which parents are responsible to God for bringing their children up in the faith. On the issue of access to truth, advocates of religious schooling have stressed the divine underpinnings of all knowledge. Any education that fails to recognize the divine origins of what humans know, or similarly that fails to contextualize what we know in a larger, divinely created and maintained universe is inadequate, even false. Religious traditions, as guardians of this divine revelation, often construct their own educational systems to safeguard this knowledge and to guarantee its transmission to subsequent generations. There is an element of self-preservation here, to be sure. Continuity in the religious community is, after all, impossible if the next generation is raised without a strong attachment of the community's worldview. There is always a concern on the part of religious school advocates that sending their children to secular schools will stunt their religious development, either by presenting an alternative worldview that undercuts the religious tradition, or by more direct proselytization on behalf of a different worldview.

With regard to the second theme, advocates of religious schooling believe that the family is the fundamental unit of society, and that parents have a divine obligation for their children's education. They are instructed to, in the words of the Hebrew Proverb, "bring up their children in the way that they should go, so that when they are old, they will not depart from it."[5] Sending one's children to a religious school (or taking those responsibilities on one's self in the case of homeschooling), then, can become an act of piety on the part of parents. It is the discharging of a religious duty.

Before examining these two themes, a word on the goal of this chapter is in order. Having already explained that I am not trying to produce an equation that predicts a parent's decision as to where they educate their children, I should also point out that I am not trying to develop a full-fledged philosophy of religious schooling for each community. Indeed, there are significant differences in the ways in which these communities represented themselves and organized their schools. Leaders of the Jewish day school movement, for instance, often asserted that their schools were not cut from the same cloth as the Catholic parochial institutions. They likened their own schools more to the public institutions than to some other private religious schools. Nevertheless, there are some common themes that surface in each religious community as they evaluate building and maintaining their own schools. To identify these points of contact, I have relied on religious schooling advocates from each community active in the time period in which their schools emerged. Thus, the voices represented here come from both different religious communities and different time periods. What is striking, however, is not how different they are, but how similar.

ACCESS TO TRUTH

It is too easy to say that all advocates of religious schooling share a common set of epistemological considerations that mandate their particular educational arrangements. Indeed, this story would be much easier to construct if there were some major sticking point, for instance, the primacy of revelation over empirical observation as a source of knowledge, which all advocates of religious schooling since the middle of the nineteenth century have shared. The truth is that except on the very broadest level, no such consensus exists, either across religious traditions or even within particular religious communities across time. There are several middling positions on the relationship between reason and revelation, and like religious voices more broadly advocates of religious schooling are not all of one mind.

Additionally, the attempt to identify one issue would likely be too heavily influenced by the struggles of a particular era. Observers of contemporary Christian homeschooling, for instance, might assume that all advocates of religious schooling were motivated by a concern over the question of human origins since that issue is frequently mentioned as a point of contention between evangelicals and public schools. That assumption, however, ignores the fact that Catholics and Jews did not leave the public schools because of the content of a science lesson. Catholics, for instance, left more because of Protestants than Darwinists! It is simply not the case that the question of faith-based schooling is always a religious versus secular issue.

Still, there are common themes related to the pursuit of knowledge that recur in the history of religious schooling. Advocates of religious schooling believe that their institutions have access to a source of truth that other school systems lack. To be sure they do not all have access to the same truth, and even within faith-based schooling some institutions deny the legitimacy of the very foundations that animate other institutions. Christian home-schoolers, for instance, do not agree with the theological ideas espoused by supporters of the Jewish day schools, still less with leaders of the fledgling Muslim school movement. They do, however, share the idea that knowledge and wisdom have a source other than the natural world. Advocates of religious schooling stress certain ideas about the divine origin, unity, and acquisition of knowledge, and these ideas are an important part of the rationale for religious schooling.

To say that truth is united and divine in origin is to say that all branches of knowledge from the mathematical to the historical will ultimately lead back to God as the architect of the universe.[6] In fact, the pursuit of knowledge is largely understood in religious schooling as the exploration of the how's and why's behind God's creation. As the title of Arthur Holmes' 1977 book puts it, *All Truth is God's Truth.*[7] This is the necessary consequence of theism, or more specifically monotheism. For example, consider the Christian tradition, for which Holmes is instructive:

> Theism gives us a point of reference in thinking about truth. That point of reference is neither human knowledge in general nor science in particular, nor anything in creation. It is the transcendent, unchanging, and omniscient God. He knows everything about every conceivable topic regarding himself, his creation, and things that are possible but that he never created. He knows it all perfectly, everything past and present, and every future possibility. He knows everything in every one of our disciplines, every possibility for creative art, creative thought, and human technology... God's own knowledge, all-inclusive, perfect, and unchanging, is the ultimate locus for truth.[8]

Though Holmes is writing in the Protestant Christian tradition, the implications of monotheism for knowledge are more expansive than his own attempts to construct a Christian worldview.[9]

To the extent that all truth comes from one source, and that education is the pursuit of truth, it also follows that moral and spiritual truths cannot and should not be segregated from other ideas. Near the end of the nineteenth century, Cardinal James Gibbons, only the second American to be made a cardinal, in addressing himself to the school question on behalf of American Catholics expressed sentiments many advocates of religious schooling could endorse: " . . . it is not enough for children to have a secular education; they must receive a religious training. Indeed, religious knowledge is as far above human science as the soul is above the body, as heaven is above earth, as eternity is above time." Education that imparts knowledge without moral and spiritual direction is not just incomplete, but dangerous:

> The religious and the secular education of our children cannot be divorced from each other without inflicting a fatal wound upon the soul. The usual consequence of such a separation is to paralyze the moral faculties and to foment a spirit of indifference in matters of faith. Education is to the soul what food is to the body. The milk with which the infant is nourished at its mother's breast feeds not only its head, but permeates at the same time its heart and the other organs of the body. In like manner, the intellectual and moral growth of our children must go hand in hand; otherwise their education is shallow and fragmentary, and often proves a curse instead of a blessing.[10]

All faith-based school systems value moral education, not just the learning of facts and figures. For most religious communities, the greatest moral truths are contained within the religious tradition, so any education that cannot appeal to that tradition, by definition, cannot be complete. In his catechism on Catholic education, James Ryan argued that the public schools can offer, at best, an ineffective presentation of the natural virtues. The "highest motives, which are spiritual and religious," could only be found in religious, in his case Catholic, education.[11]

Other religious communities echo Ryan's thinking on this matter. With many secular philosophers of education, they believe that morally neutral education is impossible, adding to this general indictment a conviction that their own tradition has privileged access to divine truth and morality. Only a system that flows out of this divine truth can truly educate. To the extent that education may be understood as the transmission of values from one generation to the next, homeschooling activist Christopher Klicka, a Home School Legal Defense Association's (HSLDA) attorney, agreed that neutrality in education is impossible. The values transmitted will always have their roots in religious and moral visions of the good life. The contest over public education, then, is a contest between those who know that all knowledge is rooted in God's revelation, and those who believe that humankind is the measure of knowledge. For Klicka and his audience, the exclusion of explicitly religious teaching in the schools, coupled with the inflated elevation of humankind's natural potential, was disastrous. In fact,

Klicka charged that most of the problems in public education can be traced to the influence of humanism and the abandonment of God in the schools.

Although they take this in different directions, advocates of religious schooling cite approvingly numerous historical affirmations about the inseparability of education, good character, and religious instruction. Ryan's 1922 catechism, for instance, cites figures such as George Washington and George Bernard Shaw to the effect that religious principle is essential for good character, a widely recognized goal of education. Shaw wrote in 1921 that "[I]f you will have people legislating without any religious foundation, you will get the sort of thing we had from 1914–1920. The only remedy for war is conscience and you will not have that until you have religion carefully taught and inculcated."[12] For many advocates of faith-based education, the logic is fairly straightforward. All branches of learning reveal the divine design of the universe just as surely (if not always as plainly) as the study of sacred texts. Education that fails to capitalize on this insight is at best incomplete, at worst heretical and dangerous. True education, then, has a religious dimension.

But the inverse is also true. Religion has an educative dimension. Learning is instrumental to the life of all religious communities. As one Jewish scholar put it,

> It is a positive commandment of the Torah to study the Torah . . . therefore every Jewish person is so obligated, whether rich or poor, healthy or sickly, youthful or venerable; even a door to door beggar or a husband and father. He must fix a time for Torah study, day or night . . . and one who is completely incapable of study shall assist others who do study and it will be reckoned for him as though he himself has studied. Until when is a man obligated to study? Until the day he dies . . . [13]

The sacred texts that animate the world's religions almost uniformly praise knowledge and study. The Hebrew scriptures contain several exhortations to study and learn, from the examples set by prophets such as Ezra and Isaiah to more general reflections on the superiority of knowledge over foolishness like those found throughout Psalms and Proverbs. Similarly, New Testament figures praised study and learning as acts of religious devotion and piety. Paul encouraged Timothy to study as a means of pleasing God. Outside the Judeo–Christian tradition learning and study were valued just as much as in the communities that came to dominate the West. As we will see in Chapter 6, Islam praises knowledge and learning as the prelude to right living. The first command received by Muhammad was to "Recite" that which the angel Gabriel revealed to him. His words were then written down by early converts and became the basis for meditative reflection and religious study for generations of Muslims around the world.

Aside from scriptural exhortations, learning and study have been an integral part of the formation of religious communities. The rites and rituals, as well as the commands and precepts, of organized religion are learned behaviors. From monastic communities in the Middle Ages to current-study Bibles and devotional guides, study and learning have long been a part of religious life. At a 1960 honorary dinner of Torah Umesorah Rabbi Immanuel Jakobovits captured the importance they attached to their mission in his keynote speech. Reflecting on the biblical story of Esau and Jacob, twin brothers raised in the same household who undertook very different paths in life, Jakobivits upheld Jacob as a model of Jewish life, whereas Esau is synonymous with idolatry and abandonment of Jewish living. The difference is explained by a single sentence in Genesis, chapter 25, verse 7: "So long as they were small, they could not be recognized by their deeds... but when they became thirteen years of age (i.e. 'grew up') one turned to houses of learning, and the other to (places of) idolatry."[14] Good homes, he argued, are not enough, as Esau's story plainly shows. Good schools are needed to preserve and promote the ideals of the religious community.

Given the importance of learning to religious communities and their conviction that truth and knowledge are from a single source, one recognized and safeguarded by their own tradition, any school outside their tradition will be seen as flawed at best, but more likely hostile, regardless of the offending party's statements to the contrary. Advocates of religious schooling often saw public, supposedly nonsectarian, schools as anything but neutral. Even if a truly nonsectarian education was possible, advocates of religious schooling refused to marginalize their community's access to truth by either eliminating it from the curriculum or compartmentalizing it as appropriate for some subjects, but not for others. Even setting it alongside other explanations is unacceptable. Indeed, merely presenting competing explanations of the world could unleash what Peter Berger has called a "cognitive contamination" that in the minds of religious school advocates not only undercuts the authority of the tradition, but borders on violating the laws of God.[15] It is disintegrative of the community and deleterious to children. Religious communities have a distinctive understanding about the relationship between education and parental responsibility, and subjecting the youngest members of the community to thousands of hours of potentially corrupting influence is simply not an option.

Beyond a general objection to the possibility or desirability of neutral education on the epistemological level, there was often the perception that the public schools were actually agents of proselytization.[16] Children from particular traditions that perceived themselves as a minority, or at least out of power, were assumed to be under attack, sometimes subtly and sometimes very direct. Catholics made it clear that it was the very notion of common schooling they found objectionable. Thus, even if the public school society's schools were truly nonsectarian, they would still not meet with the approval of the Catholic Church. Education without religion was impossible, the Church reasoned, and religion is not something you leave to vagaries, for each child to make up his or her own mind: "The Catholic Church tells her children that they must be taught their religion by AUTHORITY. The Sects say, read the [B]bible, judge for yourselves. The [B]bible is read in the public schools, the children are allowed to judge for themselves. The Protestant principle is therefore acted upon, slyly inculcated, and the schools are Sectarian."[17]

Isaac Leeser made a similar argument in the debate over Jewish children and the supposedly nonsectarian schools of his day. Leeser, warning against the influence of Gentile teachers over Jewish children, noted that Jewish children would still

> hear prayers recited in which the name of a mediator is invoked; they hear a book read as an authority equal if not superior to the received word of God;... Besides all this, we are in a great error if we suppose that Christian teachers do not endeavor to influence actively the sentiments of their Jewish pupils; there are some, at least, who take especial pains to warp the mind and to implant the peculiar tenets of Christianity clandestinely... [18]

Religious communities, especially religious minorities, are often threatened by the promotion of a creed antagonistic to their own, and thus their schools become a means of preserving their community. The most obvious example of this was the expansion of the Jewish day schools in America, which some advocates presented as a response to the Holocaust. Day schools were "survival factor" for Judaism. It would counteract the "Nazi Tyranny" that had attempted to rid the world of Israel's Torah tradition.

This same sense of beleaguered defensiveness surfaces, albeit without the Nazi references, in the rhetoric of other religious school advocates. Homeschool advocate Greg Harris told the story of an elementary school teacher, popular with his students, who in a warm and tender way announces to his impressionable students that he knows there is no God. Stories like this abound in Christian homeschool folklore, and are meant to serve as an indictment not so much of the teacher as an individual, but of the whole system that tolerates, even encourages, these moments while disallowing prayer in schools. Harris went on to relate several stories of antireligious sentiment and student persecution, all of which reinforce the already agreed upon notion that the public schools are antagonistic to religious faith. He cited approvingly the well-known work of New York professor Paul Vitz on the content of textbooks. Vitz argued that a systematic program of censorship from school textbooks has excluded the voices of morally restrained and politically conservative factions of American society. This program of exclusion makes the liberal, secular positions familiar to students not just by open advocacy, but by neglecting conservative, religious alternatives altogether so that they always appear to come from the reactionary fringe.[19]

Chris Klicka made a similar argument. Citing Vitz and others, Klicka tied the removal of any reference to religion, increasing disciplinary problems, drug trafficking, and rampant sexuality into one package and argued that given the humanistic basis for public education, these indications of decline are inevitable. Klicka related his own horror stories, including tales of sexual and physical abuse, which are, in his view, a foreseeable consequence to humanistic philosophy: "Knowing the immoral philosophy embraced by many public school teachers today and the immorality which is encouraged in the public school curricula, we should not be at all surprised that so many public school teachers would practice this immorality on the students."[20]

Also condemned are any sort of values clarification programs that are not based directly on the Judeo–Christian tradition, along with the hard to identify but supposedly pervasive New Age and Occult influence. Klicka raised red flags against practices that, in his eyes, encourage channeling or meditation. Usually billed as self-esteem programs or imagination games, these programs and curricula are presented as widespread and well established, even if not readily visible to the casual observer.[21]

The criticisms made by Harris and Klicka are echoed in the list of reasons given by parent educators as to why they chose to homeschool. This is one of the most common research questions in homeschool scholarship, and a number of studies have reported similar findings. Two of the most oft-given answers to the question of why homeschools are to achieve more academically, and for parents to have more control over value transmission. Hope for increased academic achievement may include a belief in the superiority of individualized learning or a better teacher/student ratio, but regardless of the specific motivations, it is clear that academic achievement is an important part of the decision to homeschool. The same is true for value transmission, usually included under the larger topic of socialization. Here, home educators have turned the tables on the critics. Instead of trying to prove that homeschooled children are not socially inept, home education advocates have themselves criticized the notion that age-segregated peer groups outside the home should be the dominant reference for developing a value system. While they also cite a substantial body of research that suggests that homeschooled children score at least as well on measures of affective development, in recent years their response has evolved into a question posed back to the advocates of public education about the wisdom of age-based peer groups.[22]

Not all the communal concerns were based on outright hostility. Religious schools enveloped children in the total worldview of the tradition, and therefore, it was argued, provided a more developed and more deeply instilled sense of the community's truths. The Jewish community, for instance, argued that supplementary Jewish education does a disservice to the idea of Jewish identity by making it seem less important, less privileged, than public education. Day schools overcame this handicap by placing Jewish education on par with general education topics like math and science. Furthermore, in the day schools, much Jewish learning can be accomplished informally because the whole atmosphere is designed to reinforce the tenets of Judaism. And, of course, in the day schools many more hours are devoted to Jewish subjects than the supplementary programs can possibly provide. This insight was used across religious traditions whenever the idea of parochial or faith-based schooling was questioned. Intensive religious education was often seen as the more holistic means of introducing the next generation to the faith.

Of course, this aspect of religious schooling is a source of contention as well. Basing education, as faith-based schoolers do, on particular creedal commitments and a desire to root the child in a specific worldview and community is open to the charge of indoctrination. Some critics hold that religious schools, rather than opening minds, actually curtail learning by setting preexisting limits beyond which a student's intellectual journey must not pass. This is one of the most common objections to religious schooling, having been made against Catholics in the nineteenth century and virtually every group since then. The image is always of a school more concerned with instilling a preset series of absolutes as opposed to encouraging debate and critical thinking. Alan Peshkin, for instance, in his ethnographic study of a fundamentalist Christian school, labels Bethany Baptist Academy a "total institution," a sociological term for any institution that seeks complete control over the outlook, experiences, and worldview of its members. What exactly is meant by indoctrination is unclear, but the implications are always negative.[23] But, as advocates of religious schooling themselves have replied, all educational programs are committed to some ideals. They charge the public schools with indoctrinating students, and claim that surely religious communities have the same rights to promote their ideas and commitments as the supposedly nonsectarian public schools.[24] In short, they prefer to have their own beliefs taught to their children rather than a supposedly neutral set of ideas they often experience as hostile to their claims. Indoctrination, its pejorative connotations aside, is precisely what religious schools are trying to do, if by that we mean raising children with a firm commitment to the ideals of a religious community. Rather than a criticism, to some extent the advocates of religious schooling see this as a responsibility based on their understanding of how God has designed the social order.

PRIMACY (AND PIETY) OF THE FAMILY

In 1948 the General Assembly of the United Nations proclaimed and adopted the Universal Declaration of Human Rights. Article 26 of that document affirms the "prior right" of parents to choose the type of education their children receive, while also declaring that that education should be free and compulsory.[25] Two decades before the UN Declaration, the United States Supreme Court recognized a complementary right in the 1925 *Pierce* decision, overturning Oregon's mandatory public school attendance law and ruling, in a famous and often quoted passage, "the child is not the mere creature of the state." The decision went on to recognize that parents have both a right and a responsibility to prepare their children for what the court called "additional obligations." Recognizing and affirming rights is part of the court's purpose, but this notion of a responsibility, a "high duty" in the language of the *Pierce* decision, is critical for understanding religious schooling. Advocates of religious schooling from a variety of religious traditions understand what they do as the discharging of a God-given responsibility to raise their children in the faith. In this sense, religious schooling is an act of piety on the part of parents. Exercising this piety, however, can be a source of conflict with the wider society in that any institution that threatens, or even competes with, the ability of parents to live up to this obligation can appear as a challenge to the divinely sanctioned social order. This conflict between parents and other social institutions is exacerbated in the modern world because of the sheer number and scope of agencies that now shoulder responsibilities formerly left to the family. While some families may be glad to have outside agencies easing their burden, others are increasingly frustrated by these interventions. Institutional differentiation and bureaucratization mean that these agencies are less responsive and more autocratic in their dealings with families, and accordingly parents may be more likely to see them as unwelcome and hostile. Institutions like religious schools that seem to affirm family life or provide a means through which parents can reclaim some of their authority have found an increasingly receptive audience for their message.[26]

On the broadest level, the Abrahamic faiths all recognize the family as the basic unit of society. Christianity, Judaism, and Islam all affirm marriage as the heart of the family and the wider social order as well. Aside from issues of companionship and fulfillment (more modern concerns), they also present marriage as a socially recognized and enforceable pact, one that comes with rights and duties for all parties. Indeed, it is not too much to say that marriage is a duty in most of the world's major religions. Children, too, though seen in different ways even within a single tradition, are an expected part of family life and bring with them obligations for support and nurture.[27]

Among advocates of faith-based schooling, family and religion overlap so much that to try and separate them is almost nonsensical. Religion empowers the family as the primary group in a believer's life, and the family itself is largely shaped by the religious tradition and serves as the entry point for most young believers. Children attend worship with their parents and the expectations and practices of the religious community are reproduced in the home. Religious schools are often presented as the educational option that will not undermine what the family and home seek to accomplish, namely raising faithful members of the community. Instead, they reinforce those attitudes and practices that make up the community's distinctiveness.

The 1829 Pastoral Letter appealed to Catholic parents for their support of parochial schooling along just these lines:

> How would your hearts be torn with grief did you foresee, that through eternity those objects of all your best feelings (children) should be cast into outward darkness, where there is weeping and gnashing of teeth! May God in His infinite mercy preserve you and them from the just anticipation of any such result! But, dearly beloved, this is too frequently the necessary consequence of a neglected or an improper education ... Believe us: it is only by the religious education of your children that you can so train them up, as to ensure that, by their filial piety and their steady virtue, they may be to you the staff of your old age, the source of your consolation, and reward in a better world ... In placing them at school, seek for those teachers who will cultivate the seed which you have shown; for of what avail will it be, that you have done so much, if the germs which begin to put forth, shall not be stifled or eradicated; and should tares be sown where you had prepared the soil?

And then, toward the end, the bishops suggested the proper course of action:

> How well would it be, if your means and opportunities permitted, were you at this period to commit your children to the care of those whom we have for their special fitness, placed over our seminaries and our female religious institutions? It would be at once the best mode of discharging your obligations to your children, and of aiding us in promoting the great object which we have already endeavored to impress upon your minds.

The letter went on to remind Catholic parents that it was not just affection that should prompt concern for appropriate training, but "duty requires of you to be vigilant in securing the spiritual concerns of your offspring."[28] The Third Plenary Council likewise praised the home and Church as educational agencies that fostered religion, but decried the public school's lack of attention to religion and called upon Catholics to support those schools that would cooperate with the Christian home.[29]

Supporters of the Jewish day schools, too, presented their schools as a means of discharging a parental responsibility. Education is a communal responsibility in Judaism, with some observers noting that for two millennia Jews have pioneered the concept that the entire community is and should be involved in the education of each new generation. Joseph Lookstein noted a Talmudic image that portrayed God as teaching little children to argue that all Jews should, as part of their attempt to follow God's example, educate their children. He went so far as to call this the first compulsory education law in history. This commitment to communal responsibility is a source of strength and pride in Judaism, but even advocates warn that it can go too far if parents use it to abdicate their own responsibility. The Mishnah itself recognizes the duty to train one's child in the Torah as a legal obligation incumbent upon parents.[30] The family is seen as the most important setting for all learning in Judaism, so that by the late 1970s there were "family education" programs designed to help Jewish families "Judaize" their home life.[31] Raising their children in the faith was part of the motivation for the various supplementary education programs that make up so much a part of the history of Jewish education in America. Thousands of Jewish families went to any number of lengths, some more onerous than others, to ensure that their children received some sort of religious training.

Just as the Jewish day schools were beginning to grow in influence, some educators called for the "reawaken[ing] of the conscience of our people along the lines of greater responsibility of each parent for the education of children, and for each adult for his or her own educational advancement."[32] In their 1959 study of Jewish education in America, Alexander Dushkin and Uriah Engelman called on parents and community leaders to provide a more conducive atmosphere for Jewish living if any form of Jewish education, supplementary or full time, were to succeed. When supplementary education proved ineffective, some families embraced the more intensive day school model as a means not only of reinforcing their child's connection to Judaism, but as providing leaven for the entire community. Rabbi Samuel Segal, for instance, argued that the actions of those parents that found supplementary religious instruction inadequate, and therefore opted for day schools, were providing the future rabbis, teachers, and social workers needed for the Jewish community to thrive.[33] Day schools were also praised as a location in which the efforts of the family would not be undermined the way they might be in public institutions. Joseph Kaminetsky, the one-time director of Torah Umesorah, likened day schools to the sort of culture Abraham and Sarah created for their own children in that it reverenced and preserved the traditions at the heart of Jewish life.[34] Day school education was both means of taking one's parental duties seriously and simultaneously ensuring the survival of a rich Judaism.

Conservative Protestant advocates of religious schooling sounded similar themes, both in the Christian day schooling movement and the later Christian homeschooling movement. This sentiment goes back further than the most recent movements. Even while American Catholics were the dominant story in religious schooling in this country, J. Gresham Machen was arguing (with them) against a federal role in education and calling on Protestants to oppose the public schools' continual usurpation of parental authority. Both as a means of preserving liberty and promoting the Christian religion, Machen actively endorsed religious schools as a check against public institutions.[35] Though the circumstances were not identical, Machen, like other advocates of conservative Protestant schooling, saw himself as besieged by liberalism and secularism, and turned to Christian schools as a means for ensuring that religious parents could faithfully discharge their God-given duties. More recent advocates of Christian day schools also framed their efforts in terms of parental rights and responsibilities as part of a defense of the "traditional family" that motivated a large part of their resurgence.[36] Jerry Falwell, for instance, praised the National Pro-Family Coalition for asserting the primacy of the family in education and repudiated state efforts to interfere with this "sacred" realm. He also promoted Christian schools (and homeschooling) as a means of securing America's future.

For Christian homeschoolers, and really for all religious school advocates, education is a sacred trust. Children themselves are both blessings and responsibilities. Combining certain biblical references with lessons from the history of Israel in the Old Testament, homeschool advocates Greg Harris and Chris Klicka both argued that state-run education is tantamount to abdicating God-given responsibilities for raising children. The embrace of homeschooling by "Bible believing Christians" is not just a reaction to the failures of the public school, though that may have served as a catalyst for the reemergence of homeschooling in the last three decades of the twentieth century. Instead, Christians rediscovered the divine plan for education that up until the advent of state schooling they had practiced anyway.

Harris identified the biblical insight that parents were divinely called to educate their children as the basis for the entire Christian homeschooling movement. "The first thing that becomes clear when we look at education in light of God's Word is that it is *parents* who are called by God to train their children."[37] Harris retold the biblical story of Moses' leadership of Israel and the giving of the law in Deuteronomy as the basis for how Christians, as the inheritors of God's revelation, should educate their children. In Deuteronomy 4–6 Moses delivered the commands of God, including the Ten Commandments, to the people of Israel, instructing them to "keep these words that I am commanding you today in your heart. Recite them to your children and talk about them when you are at home and when you are away, when you lie down and when you rise. Bind them as a sign on your hand, fix them as an emblem on your forehead, and write them on the doorposts of your house and on your gates.[38]

Chris Klicka also found biblical prescriptions for homeschooling. Like Harris, Klicka cited the Deuteronomy passages, but the primary biblical texts he worked with come from the book of Psalms. For Klicka, the Bible clearly teaches that children are a gift from God, given to parents for a sort of temporary stewardship. Over and over again the Old Testament referred to children as the "work of the Lord's hands," a phrase Klicka interpreted as an indication of divine ownership. The fact that that stewardship is temporary means that parents are not free to raise their children however they see fit. Children, the scriptures make clear, should be raised to love and fear the Lord, and be made aware of God's law. The public schools, which do not teach such things, are likened to an idolatrous system that denies God his rightful prerogative in the raising of his children.

Both Harris and Klicka made extended use of a biblical metaphor, also from the Psalms, in which children are likened unto arrows in the hands of a warrior: "Sons are indeed a heritage from the Lord, the fruit of the womb, a reward. Like arrows in the hand of a warrior are the sons of one's youth. Happy is the man who has his quiver full of them. He shall not be put to shame when he speaks with his enemies in the gate."[39] The question that troubled both men was what sort of arrows Christian parents were preparing. The kind that fly straight? Crooked? "Have we personally guaranteed our 'arrows' are the most carefully crafted and have the sharpest point, or did we hire some stranger ignorant of the way the Creator demands that arrows be made? Are we training our children to be the best prepared warriors for God? What kind of 'arrows' are the public schools crafting? These are questions we must ask ourselves as we raise our children—the never-dying souls whom God has entrusted to us."[40]

Ultimately, the choice as to how to provide for the education of children comes down to a simple question. Can any amount of parent correction counteract six to seven hours per day of humanistic instruction from the public schools? Answering in the negative, Harris and Klicka taught that Christian parents who take seriously the scriptural commandments about their responsibility and authority should educate their children at home. Even sending Christian children into public schools with a missionary mentality was not sufficient to outweigh the risks of public education. Klicka likened this mentality to sacrificing children in an effort to save souls, a noble sounding idea, but an abdication of God-given responsibility.

Some parents, because they believe they had a divine responsibility for their children's upbringing, have also insisted on the right to direct their education. This is one aspect of a larger conviction they have that the family, as the foundational social institution, should be essentially inviolable. In some analysis, though, the primacy of the family is under threat in America through the colonization of private life by public forces, usually the state. Dana Mack's 1997 book, *The Assault on Parenthood: How Our Culture Undermines the Family* is a case in point. Mack describes a number of ways in which the rights and authorities of parents have been trampled by public forces, both ideological and institutional. Ideologically, ideas like "the best interests of the child" came to dominate reasoning about child development, while on the institutional level a number of agencies from courts and social welfare offices to schools claimed the power to determine where and under what conditions children should be raised. Mack credits the rise of alternative schooling, including homeschooling, to part of the backlash against this assault. Though this decline in the social recognition of the family is a long-term process, the decades on either side of the turn of the twentieth century, the heyday of progressivism, were particularly dramatic. The absolute authority of parents, and more particularly fathers, had over their children, extending as it did to control over their education and access to

their wages in the case of child laborers, gave way to the state. The public, through policies such as compulsory attendance laws and child labor
reform, asserted its place in family life, and importantly, also took over the
obligation and means of educating children.[41]

The primacy of the family is also challenged by the claim that "the family"
need not be treated as in indivisible unit. Some hold that the rights of
parents should be weighed not against the position of the state, but *by* the
state *against* the rights of children. Of course, in doing so these critics place
the public good as recognized and defined by the state in a position of power
over and against families, something advocates of religious schooling reject
from the start. In a society like ours that values moral autonomy and the
rights of an individual to make his or her own decisions, religious schools,
and indeed any institution that advocates a position on major questions
rather than presenting a series of options and then enabling a choice, can
seem anachronistic.[42] Religious schools are assumed to violate a student's
right to liberty and uncoerced intellectual formation.

At the bottom of this argument is a two-fold assumption about the relationship between children, families, and the state. First, advocates of children's
rights argue that the right to full citizenship for all competent members
of a society has implications for children's education. For an adult to, for
instance, have the right to autonomous decision making requires that as
a child that individual cannot have been coerced to think a certain way.
Stanford philosopher Rob Reich has pointed out that homeschooling is
uniquely susceptible to this charge because it is the only form of education in America that gives parents total control over the content of their
children's education. Not only content, but pedagogy and other opportunities for socialization can all be manipulated by parents so that their own
authority is respected without examination. Reich calls this the "freedom
argument," and bases it on the idea that in liberal societies (by which he
means those that favor individual freedom over other ends) the rights and
interests of students are separate from, and potentially in conflict with,
those of parents. The state, in Reich's view, ought to regulate education to
prevent parents from rendering their children incapable of life in a liberal,
pluralist society.[43] In practice this means that if some children leave the
religious communities embraced by their parents, so be it. This is a reality
that some hold to be an inevitable part of life in a liberal society but that
is surely anathema to many parents themselves.[44] Secondly, advocates of
children's rights argue that the state is in a position to act on behalf of children if their rights are violated. James Dwyer, for instance, charges that the
federal and state governments have "abandoned" the children in religious
schools, but that assumes the government had certain responsibilities, in
this case the responsibility to educate, in the first place. Indeed, after a litany
of ways that religious schools (Catholic and fundamentalist in his analysis)

harm students, including intellectual coercion, the purposeful suppression of critical thinking skills, the imposition of intolerance, and a host of emotional maladies, Dwyer argues that the state must consider whether or not to "eradicate" religious schools in the same way it would eradicate the physical branding of children. Taking what he calls "the perspective of the state," Dwyer goes on to find the case for religious schooling wanting.[45]

Practitioners of religious schooling, on the other hand, do not cede primacy to the "perspective of the state." Homeschool advocate Chris Klicka considers this very idea to be evil. The root of his objection is that humanism teaches that the state is good in its own right and has responsibility for, and therefore ownership of, the children within its borders. They exist to serve the state. This violated the sanctity of the family, to be sure, but more importantly for Klicka it violated the system of order God established in the world. In God's order, families are primarily responsible for education. For Klicka, state control over education resulted in, at best, a fake neutrality on matters of ultimate truth, an arrangement he called "Satan's lie."[46] Though not all advocates of faith-based schooling go this far, in general they do oppose what they see as state intervention into family life. In this sense, they advocate what Amy Gutmann calls the "state of families" as opposed to the "family state." In a state of families, predominance is given to the parents in terms of raising and educating their children. The state ensures their freedom to pursue, within limits, their own course of action. This does not necessarily mean parents must do the educating, but that it is their intents and purposes that would guide decision making. Based sometimes on the facts of human reproduction and sometimes on more enigmatic principles, in the state of families parents direct their own children's upbringing. The family state, on the other hand, rests on the firm conviction that a harmonious social order is desirable and possible and that the unity we normally associate with familial life is in fact a social good available across individual family units. Educational authority lies outside the family itself because the social order has so great a stake in producing publicly minded citizens.[47]

The issue of parental rights and responsibilities in education has traction outside the debate over religious schools themselves. Advocates of school voucher programs often support their proposals by appealing to the idea of empowering families, particularly those of more limited means, to have more of a say in where their children attend school. Inner-city families could send their children to suburban schools, which often have superior facilities and greater per-pupil expenditures. Others would promote even greater choices by allowing families to opt for private, even religious schooling. Proposals for how to pay for such a scheme range from privatizing all education and collecting less tax (presumably so that families could keep part of their income and use it to pay for the schools they choose) to issuing vouchers out of the public purse that parents could then direct to various schools. Vouchers are probably the most publicly discussed of these proposals.

Not all voucher programs are the same. Some think vouchers should be available to all school children. Others favor them only in areas where the public schools are underperforming. Exactly how funds are dispersed is controversial, even within the pro-voucher camp. While not all advocates of religious schooling favor gaining access to public money, either through vouchers or other means, all do share a certain logic with such proposals. Parents should be able to choose what schools their children attend, and that empowering parents to make such decisions will actually improve education for everyone because poor schools will be forced to improve or go out of business.[48]

Religious schools (or homes, in the case of homeschooling) are physical entities. But the social space they occupy goes beyond their address. The religious school is an extension of the church and home. It provides for harmony between these three influences. In these schools, reality is seen through the lens of religious doctrine and commitment. It may be specific issues such as the debate over human origins that motivate a particular community to build their own school. Or it may be a more general sense of moral decadence in the schools that is both a cause and consequence of a larger cultural decline that prompts some advocates of faith schools. And to be sure, the purpose and motivations for religious schooling can change over time. The critical point is that these schools serve as locations in which the truths of the religious community are affirmed, not undermined. Religious behaviors valued by the family and the community are expected, not suspected.

The next two chapters will take up the case for and against religious schooling in a democratic society. To some extent the notion of parent's rights over and against those of the public sphere, or more recently children themselves, is part of that debate. Certainly the Supreme Court linked these issues in the precedent setting the *Pierce* decision, but a more vocal political battle has occurred over the place of these schools in American society. If the public schools are means of creating *E Pluribus Unum* (Out of Many, One), then faith-based schools can be seen as disintegrative of both the institution that was supposed to build a United States of America, and subsequently of America herself.

NOTES

1. There were several studies published on why parents chose Jewish day schools, but most were based on very small samples. See, for instance, David Kapel "Parental Views of a Jewish Day School," *Jewish Education*, 41 (Spring 1972): 28–38; Louise Adams, Judith Frankel, and Nancy Newbauer, "Parental Attitudes Toward the Jewish All-Day School,' *Jewish Education*, 42 (Winter 1972): 26–30.

2. John Crawford and Sharon Freeman, "Why Parents Choose Private Schooling: Implications for Public School Programs and Information Campaigns," *ERS Spectrum* (Summer 1996): 9–16. This study was conducted by officials from the Millard public schools in an effort to improve public education and the public relations of the school district. On homeschooling, see Brian Ray, *Home Schooling on the Threshold*, previously cited. On the general lack of examination of this topic, as well as an analysis of some of the relevant characteristics for who sends their children to private institutions, see Philip Yang and Nihan Kayaardi, "Who Chooses Non-Public Schools for Their Children?" *Educational Studies*, 30(3) (September 2004): 231–249.

3. On this notion of social space, see David Martin, "The Evangelical Upsurge and its Political Implications," *The Desecularization of the World: Resurgent Religion and World Politics*, edited by Peter Berger (Grand Rapids, MI: Eerdmans Publishing, 1999).

4. Boundaries and participation in community-specific behaviors have long been part of the sociological study of group life. For a thorough development of these themes, see Christian Smith, *American Evangelicals: Embattled and Thriving* (Chicago, IL: University of Chicago Press, 1998).

5. Proverbs 22:6.

6. I have followed Rodney Stark's practice of always capitalizing "God" when referring to the deity of the monotheistic religions examined in this project.

7. Arthur Holmes, *All Truth is God's Truth* (Grand Rapids, MI: Eerdmans, 1977). Holmes' work is a distinctly Christian expression of this idea.

8. Arthur Holmes, *Contours of a World View* (Grand Rapids, MI: Eerdmans, 1983) 129.

9. On the importance of monotheism for intellectual progress, see Rodney Stark's *For the Glory of God: How Monotheism Led to Reformations, Science, Witch-Hunts, and the End of Slavery* (Princeton, NJ: Princeton University Press, 2003). Stark has championed the view that Europe's success in terms of intellectual, technological, and social progress should be credited to Christianity. Though in other places he specifically rejects the idea that Islam, for instance, could also embrace science and the progress that comes with it, it is important to note that he is writing about the *origin* of science. His claim is that science and social progress took off in Europe because of, not in spite of, the influence of Christianity. Practitioners of religious schooling from the late nineteenth century have tended to see their own tradition as both benefiting from and contributing to scientific progress. There are, of course, significant points of disagreement between the monotheistic, and even the Abrahamic, faiths. Their own understandings of the implications of theology also led to different historical trajectories. See also his *The Victory of Reason: How Christianity Led to Freedom, Capitalism, and Western Success* (New York: Random House, 2005).

10. See Cardinal Gibbons' speech, "Should Americans Educate Their Children in Denominational Schools," in *Denominational Schools* (Topeka: Kansas Publishing House, 1889), 5.

11. James Ryan, *Catechism of Catholic Education*, previously cited.

12. Quoted in Ryan, *Catechism of Catholic Education*, previously cited, 53.

13. See Lloyd Gartner, "Jewish Education in the United States," in *The Jewish Community in America*, ed. Marshall Sklare (New York: Behrman House, 1974), 227.

14. Immanuel Jakobovits, "The Strengths of the Yeshiva Movement," *The Jewish Parent:* (February 1961): 4. Parenthesis in the original. This should not be understood as downplaying the importance of the home and family, which were at the center of Jewish living.

15. Berger develops this notion as part of his model of secularization and the legitimacy of plausibility structures. See his *The Sacred Canopy* (New York: Doubleday, 1967). See also his *A Far Glory: The Quest for Faith in an Age of Credulity* (New York: Random House, 1992).

16. The identity of the proselytizers changes from case to case. Catholics saw the schools as agents of Protestantism, Jews saw them as agents of Christianity, Protestants as agents of secular humanists, and as we will see in Chapter 6, Muslims see them as agents of westernization, usually meaning either secularism or Judeo–Christian identity.

17. See Diane Ravitch, *The Great School Wars*, previously cited, 45.

18. In Lloyd Gartner, "Temples of Liberty Unpolluted: American Jews and Public Schools, 1840–1875," in *A Bicentenniel Festschrift for Jacob Rader Marcus*, ed. Bertram Wallace (Waltham, MA: American Jewish Historical Society, 1976): 167.

19. See Paul Vitz, *Censorship: Evidence of Bias in Our Children's Textbooks* (Ann Arbor, MI: Servant, 1986).

20. Christopher J. Klicka, *The Right Choice: Home Schooling* (Gresham, OR: Noble Publishing Associates, 1995): 63.

21. Klicka points to the *Impressions* curriculum, the "Developing an Understanding of Self and Others" program, and the SOAR curriculum (otherwise unidentified) as evidence of widespread corruption in the public schools, but he fails to provide evidence for how many schools are actually using these programs. Words like "widespread" and "prevalent" are the only indicators for any numbers or empirical research.

22. Psychologists interested in children and self-esteem have focused on the socialization experiences of homeschooled children. They usually assume that homeschooled children miss out on an important part of adolescence; namely, contact with peers. Parents and professionals alike have expressed concern that these children are out of touch with their own generation and accordingly suffer emotional consequences as the price for homeschooling. However, empirical work in the field suggests just the opposite. John Taylor found that homeschooled children score significantly higher than public school children on the *Piers-Harris Children's Self Concept Scale.* See his 1986 article "Self-concept in home-schooling children," *Home School Researcher* 2 (2): 1–3.

Sociologists and education researchers spill much ink attempting to construct a list of the reasons people choose to homeschool. Most of these lists include concerns over the transmission of values, declining academic standards, individual attention, and parental responsibility. These concerns, along with the increasing expense associated with private education, make homeschooling a more attractive option for many families. On the motivations for homeschooling, see Ray's 1999 overview, *Home Schooling on the Threshold* (previously cited) as well as Maralee Mayberry, J.G. Knowles, Brian Ray, and Stacy Marlow, *Home Schooling: Parents as Educators* (Thousand Oaks, CA: Corwin Press, 1995).

Since the most common reason offered by homeschooling families concerns the transmission of values, one would not be surprised to learn that this area is well researched. And indeed, particular attention has been paid to the Christian portion of the movement. Commenting on ideology and motivation among the believers, researchers have noted that homeschool advocates "found and espoused Biblical and religious rationales" and served as the "ground of and for ideological, conservative, religious expressions of educational matters, which symbolized the conservative right's push towards self-determinism." See Gary Knowles, Stacey Marlowe, and James Muchmore's 1992 article, "From Pedagogy to Ideology: Origins and Phases of Home Education in the United States, 1970–1990," in *American Journal of Education* 100: 195–235.

23. On the pitfalls of indoctrination as a criticism of religious schooling, see Elmer J. Theissen, *In Defence of Religious Schools and Colleges* (Montreal, Canada: McGill-Queens University Press, 2001).

24. Kariane Mari Welner has shown that homeschooling families are well aware of the indoctrination charge and that they see the public schools as doing the same thing. See her March 2002 Occasional Paper from the National Center for the Study of Privatization in Education, "Exploring the Democratic Tensions Within Parents' Decisions to Homeschool," available online from the National Center.

25. It is worth noting that these provisions of the Declaration can be construed in such a way as to compete with one another, primarily because education is largely undefined. Parents have the right to provide whatever type of education they deem appropriate for their children, but some form of education is compulsory. They do not, then, have the right to refuse their child an education, an issue that would surface in the United States in the 1970s when Amish families in Wisconsin won the right to take their children out of the public schools after the eighth grade.

26. On the conditions of modern family life, see Brigitte Berger, *The Family in the Modern Age: More than a Lifestyle Choice* (New Brunswick, NJ: Transaction Press, 2002).

27. On the role of the family in the world's major religions, see *Sex, Marriage, and Family in World Religions*, eds. Don S. Browning, M. Christian Green, and John Witte, Jr. (New York: Columbia University Press, 2006). See especially the introduction to the entire volume, which lays out a series of connections between the major world religions in terms of marriage and family. There is, of course, considerable difference between the religions as well, and even within single religious traditions there is wide variation in opinion and practice when it comes to family related issues.

28. 1829 Pastoral Letter. "Provincial Councils of Baltimore," in *Catholic Education in America: A Documentary History*, ed. Neil G. McCluskey (New York: Teachers College, 1964), 53–55.

29. Catholic statements about religious schooling in this era focused less on empowering the parents to make their own decisions and more on promoting adherence to the hierarchy's policies. Nevertheless, the Church endorsed parental as opposed to public authority and certainly saw providing religious instruction as part of a faithful parent's duty.

30. Joseph Lookstein, "The Goals of Jewish Education," *Tradition: A Journal of Orthodox Jewish Thought*, 3(1) (Fall 1960): 34–43.

31. See Jack Wertheimer, "Jewish Education in the United States: Recent Trends and Issues," *American Jewish Year Book* (New York: American Jewish Committee Publications, 1999).

32. Salo Baron, "Communal Responsibility for Jewish Education," *Jewish Education*, 19 (Spring 1948): 7.

33. Samuel Segal, "Evaluation of the Jewish Day School," *Jewish Education*, 25 (Winter 1955): 46–62.

34. Joseph Kaminetsky, *Hebrew Day School Education: An Overview* (New York: Torah Umesorah, 1970).

35. See the essays collected in J. Gresham Machen, *Education, Christianity, and the State* (Hobbs, NM: The Trinity Foundation, 1995).

36. See William J. Reese, "Soldiers for Christ in the Army of God: The Christian School Movement in America," previously cited.

37. Greg Harris. *The Christian Home School* (Brentwood, CA: Wolgemuth and Hyatt, 1988), 66.

38. This passage, and others like it from both Old and New Testaments, form the biblical basis for Christian homeschooling because they command believers to teach their children, which advocates of homeschooling take quite literally. See Deuteronomy 6: 6–9. See, for example, Deuteronomy 4 and Ephesians 6, which figure prominently in homeschool literature.

39. Psalm 127: 3–5.

40. See Chris Klicka, *The Right Choice*, previously cited, 103.

41. Dana Mack, *The Assault on Parenthood: How Our Culture Undermines the Family*, (New York: Simon and Schuster, 1997).

42. Chapters 3 and 4 take up the case for and against religious schooling in a democratic society. Philosophers and legal theorists often advance arguments about the rights of children as part of the case against religious schooling, but given that this project is more focused on the public place of the schools themselves I have opted to treat the issue of children's and family rights as part of the rationale for religious schooling in the first place. The children's rights argument, while political, is not ultimately the same charge about the place of the religious schools in American society.

43. Rob Reich, "Why Home Schooling Should be Regulated," in *Home Schooling in Full View: A Reader*, ed. Bruce Cooper, (Greenwich, England: Information Age Publishing, 2005). Reich argues that abolishing homeschooling would be unjust, but he does favor government regulation in a way that many in the homeschooling community would reject. See also his "Testing the Boundaries of Parental Control in Education: The Case of Homeschooling," in *Moral and Political Education*, eds. Stephen Macedo and Yael Tamir (New York: New York University Press, 2002).

44. On this point, see Meira Levinson and Samford Levinson, "Getting Religion: Religion, Diversity, and Community in Public and Private Schools," in *School Choice: The Moral Debate* (Princeton, NJ: Princeton University Press, 2003).

45. James G. Dwyer, *Religious Schools v. Children's Rights* (Ithaca, NY: Cornell University Press, 1998).

46. Klicka, *The Right Choice: Home Schooling*, previously cited, 95.

47. Amy Gutmann, *Democratic Education* (Princeton, NJ: Princeton University Press, 1987).

48. Until fairly recently discussions of school vouchers centered on the constitutional question. That public money could go to pay for private, possibly religious, schooling seems to many people a clear violation of the separation of church and state. The U.S. Supreme Court however has ruled that at least some voucher programs are constitutionally permissible. In 1989 the state of Wisconsin enacted the first voucher program in the country. Aimed at improving educational opportunities

for poorer families, the original program disallowed participants to attend faith-based schools. A later revision of the law opened up faith-based schools as options for participants and, importantly, changed the mechanism of payment. Checks were sent from the state directly to the selected school, but were issued in the name of the parents and could only be endorsed over to the school (thus, money could not be taken and spent for other purposes). State funds went to the school "indirectly" in that the parents technically received the money and directed it as they saw fit, having already chosen which participating (and approved) school their children would attend. Though the issue went back and forth in Wisconsin courts, that state's supreme court eventually upheld the voucher program and the U.S. Supreme Court refused to hear an appeal. In the mid 1990s Ohio started a voucher program that was put to use in the city of Cleveland's troubled public school system. This case made it all the way to the U.S. Supreme Court, which ruled in *Zelman v. Simmons-Harris* that voucher programs can be constructed in such a way as to not violate the Establishment Clause. That is not to say that all voucher programs will pass consti-tutional muster, but the court has opened the door for further voucher programs. The literature on school choice and vouchers is voluminous. For a discussion of the Wisconsin and Ohio programs, see Michael Coulter, "School Vouchers in America," in *Church and State Issues in America Today, volume 2*, eds. Ann W. Duncan and Steven L. Jones (Westport, CT: Praeger Press, 2008). For analysis on the role of choice in education, see especially the essays by Nancy Rosenblum, Charles Glenn, and Meira and Sanford Levinson in *School Choice: the Moral Debate*, ed. Alan Wolfe (Princeton, NJ: Princeton University Press, 2003).

3 Religious Schools and the Undermining of Democracy

The First Amendment's prohibition against governmental establishment of religion was written on the assumption that state aid to religion and religious schools generates discord, disharmony, hatred, and strife among our people...[1]

So said Justice Hugo Black in his dissenting opinion in *Board of Education v. Allen* in 1968. Contrary to Black's advice, the Supreme Court upheld a New York Court of Appeals decision sustaining the provision of textbooks to private, religious schools. The specifics of this case aside for the moment, the suspicion that religious schools promote social discord is a longstanding feature of American political and educational thought. In order to uncover the logic of this criticism, it is first necessary to briefly explain the connections between a society's schools and its political order. Institutionally, schools do not build and maintain themselves. They are provided for and staffed by members of the society. Of course, then, they will reflect that society. But as part of their very purpose, they will also shape that society through the molding of future generations. In short, education must begin with the end. That is, societies must ask what sort of person they are trying to shape and produce *before* education can begin.[2]

Social scientists as well as philosophers have this plain. Emile Durkheim recognized that education always and inevitably reflects, and then shapes for the next generation, a particular people's experience and understanding of the good life. He held this to be unavoidable, even desirable: "For us too the principal object of education is not to provide the child with a greater or lesser degree of items of knowledge, but to create within him a

deep lying disposition . . . of the soul which orients him in a definite direction. . . ."[3] American educational theorists and leaders agree. John Dewey
made explicit the connection between political theory and educational theory by conceiving of education in its broadest sense as the transmission of
culture. It made no sense to formulate the content of education, or even
to think of education in general, until we know what sort of society we are
trying to construct and inhabit. Schools serve as controlled environments
in which children gain experience into the preferred way of life for their society. For Dewey, the sort of society we envision will shape the sort of schools
we build, thus making a clear vision of social order a necessary precursor to
any sort of educational system.[4]

To say that education is always political is not to say that education should
be partisan. Rather, by "political" I mean to refer to those consequences of
education that are related to the ordering of public life.[5] In this analysis, the
acts of some social institutions are almost entirely political in that their very
reason for existence is the shaping of the public sector. Parties or lobbies are
clearly political in this sense of the term. But there are other institutions,
the schools not least among them, which while not engaged in the daily
grind of influencing legislation are no less political. As Lawrence Cremin
recognized, education is unavoidably political because it has ramifications
for the future character of the state.[6]

The link between education and the formation of the citizenry has implications beyond the individual level. Education is part of the very real task
of state formation. Ernest Gellner, in his influential work on nationalism,
argued that the state's ability to monopolize schooling is essential for its
formation, even more than its ability to legitimately monopolize violence,
long considered a crucial aspect of state power. Schooling, he held, is critical to a nation's internal development.[7] Commenting on the historiography
of American education, Andrew Green pointed out that public education
was in fact a decisive break with what had come before, precisely because
it did not reinforce small group particularities the way private education
did. Instead, it stressed large group, usually national, interests.[8] Political
formation through schooling, then, does more than extend citizenship to
new segments of the population. It extends the state's authority over an increasingly diverse population. The state's interest in developing a common
culture is magnified in complex societies precisely because familial socialization is too limited. A more differentiated polity requires widespread,
common, and therefore nonfamilial socialization. State schooling is an institutional means for this process: "A state-authorized educational system, by
structurally and symbolically removing actors from their constituent groups
and relating them directly to the corporate structure, confers on its graduates the political identity of corporate agents as legitimate members of the
state."[9] Removing actors from their constituent groups may be good for

society on some level, particularly when the way of life espoused by those groups may be antithetical to society's continuation.[10] However, the key to political development is not found in just weakening previous attachments, but in supplanting them with a sense of belonging and loyalty to the larger political unit.

"Deep lying disposition of the soul," "future character of the state," "legitimate members of the state"—given all that is apparently at stake, it is notable that for many Americans the presence of nonpublic schools in or near their neighborhood is not too alarming. Even those without any personal experience with private schooling probably know someone who attended Catholic schools, Jewish schools, etc. Earlier in American history, however, the very presence of religious schooling generated considerable debate, something akin to the kind of attention that is now paid to issues like school vouchers. Politicians, clergymen, and community leaders, for instance, had to take a stand on the "school question." This is no longer the case. Vouchers and other privatization efforts command significant attention, true, but the existence of private and religious schools is, at least by the public at large, taken for granted. This is not to say that the debate is over. It is not. Rather, the place of private and religious schools in American life is now the subject of primarily academic treatises as opposed to public forums. And yet, in many ways, the debate is unchanged from when it was a more public spectacle. To be sure, both the critiques and defenses are more sophisticated in presentation, but the root issues remain the same. Who has the right and responsibility to educate children? And for what ends? Depending upon the level of detail one wants to explore, there are almost innumerable possible criticisms that have been made of private and especially religious schools along just these lines.[11]

Though there are many different ways of constructing and elaborating these arguments, two broad themes can be identified as particularly pressing. First, once public schools achieved a de facto monopoly on all formal schooling in America, alternatives to public education have been seen not just as competition for, but also as a threat to, the public institutions. That is, private institutions are seen as undermining public ones. They leave less capital, both economic and social, for the public institutions, which are usually portrayed as already strapped for cash and in need of more public support. Second, not only are the schools themselves undermined, but the social purposes they serve are also imperiled by private and especially faith-based schooling. Religious schools have been seen not just as alternative educational institutions, but as road blocks to the larger social good of cultivating a *United* States of America. They are repositories of old-world or subnational loyalties, promoting exclusiveness and isolation at the expense of the supposedly broad-minded, inclusive, benevolently assimilative public schools.

THE RESOURCE DRAIN ARGUMENT

With regard to the first problem, critics charge that the exodus from public schooling associated with the build-up of religious institutions drains the public schools of necessary resources. The most recent statements of this objection come from professional educational theorists often in reference to homeschooling, but the basic logic applies to most all private and religious schools, regardless of orientation. It was certainly present in the nineteenth-century conflict between the Free School Society (later the Public School Society) in New York and the various church schools that sought a share of the tax money earmarked for education. New York City's public schools were run by the Free School Society with the self-appointed task of educating children that were not already enrolled in a church or private school. Officially nonsectarian, the schools operated by the society still ratified a largely Protestant worldview through Bible readings, hymns and prayers, and the religious identity of the teachers themselves. Thus, Governor William Seward's 1840 recommendation for the establishment of schools in which children could be taught by members of their own faith, speaking their own language, was a direct challenge to the emerging model of public education in New York City.[12]

Though most often connected to the history of Catholicism in America, the Free School Society's conflict with religious schools started not with Catholics, but with Baptists! In 1820 Bethel Baptist Church opened a non-denominational school for the education of all neighborhood children. The next year, the Bethel school received a portion of the state education fund. With the infusion of money into their school coffers, Bethel Baptist Church began to expand their educational programs by building new schools, which in turn prompted other churches to open schools as well. All these competed with the Free School Society's schools, and were thus worrisome to the Society, who appealed to the legislature to repeal Bethel's funding. In doing so, the Free School Society took the position that no public money should be given to a religious school, and should instead be reserved for nonsectarian institutions. Up to then, it was not uncommon for denominational schools to receive a portion of the state funds for education, and even some Catholic schools received some state aid.[13] The city sided with the Free School Society, and thus their position on the use of public money for religious schools carried the day. Denominational schools would no longer be eligible for public money, thus securing certain financial advantages for the officially nonsectarian, but still largely Protestant schools of the Free School Society.

Sensing an opportunity to further cement their position, the Society determined that more schools were needed to meet the educational needs of the growing city. In changing their name to the Public School Society in 1826, the Society also experimented with alternative ways of funding their operations, eventually settling on a property tax, the proceeds of which were to be earmarked for the support of the public schools. By public schools, the society meant their own supposedly nondenominational institutions. New York City's Catholic population had a different idea. They filed a petition with the city government requesting a share of the tax monies for their schools. Their claim was based on the idea that since Catholic schools educated the children of the poor, they should have access to the same public funds as the Public School Society. Since they were taxed for education, it was a violation of their rights that all the tax money should go to schools that they in good conscience could not support. They claimed that their appeal for a share of the tax funds was made on the same basis on which they were taxed in the first place—as citizens. New York's fiery Bishop John Hughes often remarked that when the tax was levied, Catholics were considered citizens, but when the funds were distributed, they counted only as Catholics! The end result of this conflict was a mixture of victory and defeat for advocates of faith-based education. The state legislature stripped the Public School Society of much of its power and status, but also disallowed further expenditures of public money for denominational schooling. Eventually, other states followed New York's decision that only public, nonsectarian schools could receive public money, thus forcing advocates of religious schooling to fund their own schools over and above what individual parents paid in taxes for the public institutions. The benefits reaped by public schools because of this arrangement went beyond the already important fact that public schools had access to considerable sums of money. Taxation essentially diverted monies that might have been spent on private efforts, thus weakening, and in some cases eliminating, the competition.[14] As part of the public school's rise to prominence, religious schools came to occupy the periphery of the American educational landscape.

Though access to tax monies is no longer the crucial issue, updated versions of this criticism have been leveled against later advocates of faith-based schooling. Just as Jewish day schools were beginning their dramatic growth, Alexander Dushkin of the New York Board of Jewish Education acknowledged that the general logic of this criticism applied to all private schooling. A "general universal extension" of religious and other private schools could undermine public education, a claim he backed up by pointing to the Catholic school's appeal to public funds.[15] More recently, some have argued that since public schools receive state money on the basis of enrollment, the absence of religious schoolers from the system means that public schools see their budgets dwindle. Similarly, the withdrawal of committed parents from the system means that public school teachers no longer have access to some of the most dedicated parents that could be a help to the entire classroom. Michael Apple has criticized homeschooling along just these lines. He holds that a widespread mistrust of government agencies, felt mostly by conservatives and definitely held by Christian homeschoolers, has led to a resistance movement struggling against what they perceive as the illegitimate encroachment of the state into familial life. The public school, as the state agency most in contact with the daily lives of most Americans, is naturally the first casualty in this conflict over government intrusion. In his view, homeschoolers fear the imposition of moral sentiments from those unlike themselves, the "real Americans" ("patriotic, religious, and moral"). Apple suggests that homeschoolers could next refuse, for instance, to pay taxes that support the public schools. The lowered revenue would, of course, be damaging to the already financially strapped education system and would only serve to further America's perpetual educational crisis. Thus, the disadvantaged segments of society that depend on public services like education are harmed, while the already elite segments of society that have more than one educational option benefit.[16]

A feature article in *Time* magazine raised exactly this concern. Noting that the number of homeschoolers in America has grown dramatically, the authors concluded that although more attention is given to charter schools and vouchers, homeschooling is the real story in American education. They argue that homeschooling is a threat to the very idea of public schooling because as parents pull their children out of public schools, local districts lose millions of dollars in per-pupil funding, not to mention the lost confidence the schools must endure. The authors point to Maricopa County, Arizona, which lost $35 million when seven thousand children were pulled out of the public schools.[17] Similarly, a 2004 report entitled "Dereliction of Duty" by People for the American Way argued that lax regulations in states like Florida actually led to public monies directly supporting private and homeschooling, which aside from the constitutional prohibitions once again further siphon needed resources away from public institutions.[18]

Financial costs are not the only resources drained from public schools. Like Apple, *Time*'s journalists also focused on resources other than money. Homeschooling parents are usually affluent and educated. Their withdrawal from the schools is felt by teachers whenever chaperones, or any form of parental aid, is necessary for class projects. How much better off would the schools be, they asked, if parents who currently homeschool put their children back in the public system, bringing with them increased time, commitment, and energy, making public school education better for all involved?

Schools need capital to thrive, both financial and human, in the form of time and energy. All of this is lost when people support private institutions instead of public ones. It is well established that higher levels of familial and communal involvement increase the overall effectiveness of education thus benefiting the whole society.[19] As increasing numbers of parents decrease their level of participation, the potential reservoir of extra-institutional support shrinks. Thus, by the act of withdrawing from the public schools, religious schoolers automatically lower the level of available resources to schools, rendering them less effective and potentially increasing the educational inequality between public and private schools.

This drain affects not just the educational mission of the school, but the democratic mission as well. Chris Lubienski has argued that in exiting the public schools homeschoolers deny society the opportunity for a democratically decided course of remedy. Leaning heavily on Albert Hirschman's distinction between exit and voice as alternative strategies available to those dissatisfied with a given firm's product, Lubienski charged that homeschoolers have opted to "vote with their feet" with regard to the challenges facing public schools.[20] In the realm of education, voicing one's criticism is associated with the willingness to pursue a course of action aimed at improving the schools, and assumes that the political mechanism of democratic deliberation and citizen (consumer) activism will bring about change. Public education is organizationally designed to respond to voice. Part of the promise of local control is that parents and other interested parties could bring about change. Homeschoolers, and by extension anyone who practices faith-based or other private schooling, have given up on the attempt to improve the schools, opting instead to withdraw from them altogether. This exit is problematic because public schools are one of the primary institutional locations for the necessary public debate about what constitutes the good life and what sort of people "we" ought to be. Knowing that education is unavoidably political, Lubienski argued that homeschooling limits the public debate because it removes so many participants. The fact that their voices go unheard, even if their flight from the discussion is self-imposed and voluntary, means that the end of that discussion is not truly representative. This, in turn, guarantees conflict and more flight from the public sphere for generations to come. Vital to any democratic state is the commitment on behalf of contenders to maintain their commitment to the processes and institutions of democratic life, even when they lose in the give-and-take of political struggle. In short, religious schooling as an exit strategy is simply not democratic. It does not allow for the possibility of sustained dialogue and deliberation, closing channels of communication instead of opening them.[21]

The basic thrust of this argument is that the public schools are dependent upon public support. They receive their funding, and no small percentage of their tremendous manpower needs, from the citizenry at large. Any initiative that redirects some of those resources to other institutions imperils the system itself, and harms other aspects of social life to which the school system contributes. In this sense, the argument here is about the elevation of private goods over public goods. Lubienski is instructive on this point as well. Education is a public good, that is, it serves the general public interest. This is part of the justification for supporting schools with publicly collected tax dollars. Lubienski holds that there is a general trend, of which homeschooling is "the epitome," of middle-class parents paying lip service to educational equality, but sacrificing that value on the altar of their own child's well-being. This is the educational equivalent of the NIMBY (Not In My Back Yard) syndrome. Everyone wants affordable energy, but no one wants a power plant just across the property line. In this formulation, advocates of religious schooling, and really all private schooling, are abdicating the responsibilities of citizenship. They are selfish, plain, and simple, and in their selfishness they do harm to the rest of society. We will have occasion in the next chapter to see how advocates of religious schooling answer these charges.

THE SOCIAL DIVISION CHARGE

In the United States, one of the guiding political principles upon which the schools have been built is *E Pluribus Unum:* Out of many, one. The well-worn Latin phrase that decorates our national seal is more than a motto, though. It is one of the cornerstones of American political conviction. That a substantial amount of homogeneity among the population is necessary for political and social order has long been a taken-for-granted assumption in America. The idea that schools could produce such homogeneity has an equally long history. Even today, as Americans have embraced a relatively new appreciation of diversity, it is still true that we value a certain amount of homogeneity as a source of social and political order. In the 1996 Survey on American Political Culture more than 90 percent of the population affirmed the importance of teaching children about America's role as the great melting pot out of which one nation, one people, would arise. Similarly, the 2000 survey found that more than three-quarters of the population believed America would be better off if we could all live by the same basic moral principles, and a majority (56 percent) held that we would be better off if all children attended public schools.[22]

Given the conviction that public schools contribute to social unity it is not surprising that religious schools are often accused of promoting social discord. Indeed, these are two sides of the same coin. If public schools bring people together across their particularities to create a general culture, then schools organized around one of those particularities inevitably undermine the mingling public schools are designed to promote.[23] They will exacerbate, rather than heal, social fissures. This is the most prominent and recurring issue in the debate over religious schools. In earlier years, this charge was wrapped up in the language of patriotism versus old-world loyalty. Immediately after the American Revolution, for instance, numerous statesmen and leaders in the new society saw common schools as a means of fashioning a new people out of the complicated mix of old world ethnic groups. Concerned first with training citizens in the patterns and habits of self-government, and thus avoiding tyranny, founders like Thomas Jefferson, Benjamin Rush, and Noah Webster also saw in education the opportunity to cultivate a sense of attachment to the new nation in the hearts and minds of the youngest Americans.[24]

Dr. Benjamin Rush, from Pennsylvania, was perhaps the most vocal of the early patriots with regard to the need of this thoroughly domestic education. Rush believed that the war for independence, though it changed the form of government, was only the initial stage in a much larger social and political revolution. As he argued in 1786, the greater challenge was to fashion a people that could sustain this new type of polity: "The business of education has acquired a new complexion by the independence of our country. The form of government we have assumed has created a new class of duties to every American. It becomes us, therefore, to examine our former habits upon this subject, and in laying the foundations for nurseries of wise and good men, to adapt our modes of teaching to the peculiar form of our government."[25]

Rush believed that the schools would help to establish a common core of values and sentiments that would surpass older loyalties. Surveying his beloved Pennsylvania, Rush saw all the social diversity of Europe compressed into one state. A uniform system of schooling, he held, would produce a homogenous people, one better suited to peaceable self-government. Rush, in common with most of the early republican theorists of education, held that for freedom to thrive a certain level of self-control had to be encouraged and developed among the population. There is, of course, a certain paradox here. To avoid the evils of either anarchy or tyranny, citizens must be molded, at an early age, into "republican machines" that will make it possible for them to "perform their parts properly in the great machine of the government of the state." The "wills of the people must be fitted to each other by means of education before they can be made to produce regularity and unison in government."[26] Pupils would be taught that they were "public property," and that while a certain love for family was appropriate, they should be willing to "forsake and even forget them when the welfare of his country requires it."

Noah Webster is most commonly associated with education in the founding era, and for good reason. The founder of Amherst College and before that a schoolmaster, Webster spent his career advocating and contributing to American education. His legacy in the field of education stems less from his own presence in the classroom than from his attempts to guide the activities of other teachers through the publication of numerous textbooks, most notably his three-part work entitled *A Grammatical Institute, of the English Language, Comprising, an Easy, Concise, and Systematic Method of Education, Designed for the Use of English Schools in America* originally published between in stages between 1783 and 1785. An American classic, the most interesting thing about Webster's famous speller is the motivation behind it. Webster's concern was less with correcting errors in spelling per se than it was with establishing common rules for spelling that would distinguish the

American language from its European counterparts. What he sought was a peculiarly American expression of the English language to coincide with the new American nation that was separate from the Old World. This was part of his attempt to instill his own intense patriotism into America's youth. Webster wanted more than a common language. He wanted an American language.

The rest of his *Grammatical Institute* gives evidence of the same concern. In the 1800 edition of his reader he revealed the guiding principle behind his selections:

> In the choice of pieces I have been attentive to the political interests of America. I consider it as a capital fault in all our schools, that the books generally used, contain subjects wholly uninteresting to our youth; while the writings that marked the revolution, which are perhaps not inferior to the orations of Cicero and Demosthenes, and which are calculated to impress interesting truths upon young minds, lie neglected and forgotten. Several of those masterly addresses of Congress, written at the commencement of the late revolution, contain such noble, just and independent sentiments of liberty and patriotism, that I cannot help wishing to transfuse them into the breasts of the rising generation.[27]

So concerned was Webster with what young American minds would learn in the schools that he desired the history of the United States to be the very words with which a child learned to speak: "He should rehearse the history of his own country; he should lisp the praise of liberty and of those illustrious heroes and statesmen who have wrought a revolution in her favor."[28]

Horace Mann, the nineteenth-century architect of public education in America echoed the sentiments of the founding generation, and specifically criticized religious schools for promoting social discord.[29] Mann was convinced that education could provide the moral elevation necessary for self-government. In his Tenth Annual Report, written in 1846 to the Massachusetts Board of Education, Mann argued that self-government was only possible if a certain level of moral education had taken place. Since self-government was still a relatively new practice for people, Mann held that the schools alone could provide the moral knowledge and respect for law necessary to sustain social order. Mann was awed by the pluralism of the early nineteenth century, but typical of his day his awe was also characterized by concern. Like others before and after him, Mann believed in the necessity of a common value system that might undergird American political stability. In fact, Mann's entire quest for common schools was an attempt to construct a sense of community out of the myriad of cultural traditions already present in America.[30]

With regard to recent immigrants, Mann held that the very virtues that sustained social order in the Old World, like servitude and obedience to authority, would threaten social order in a society in which the people must govern themselves.

In order that men may be prepared for self-government, their apprenticeship must commence in childhood. The great moral attribute of self-government cannot be born and matured in a day; and if school children are not trained to it, we only prepare ourselves for disappointment, if we expect it from grown men. Everybody acknowledges the justness of the declaration, that a foreign people, born and bred and dwarfed under the despotisms of the Old World, cannot be transformed into the full stature of American citizens, merely by a voyage across the Atlantic, or by subscribing to the oath of naturalization.[31]

Mann specifically addressed the potential of the Common Schools to overcome social divisions in his First Annual Report as the secretary of the Massachusetts Board of Education, written in 1837. Discussing the problems that private schools pose for the Common Schools, including loss of financial and community resources as well as an early example of "brain drain," Mann argued that most private schools resembled the old educational institutions of England, "where churchmen and dissenters, each according to his own creed, maintain separate schools, in which children are taught, from their tenderest years to wield the sword of polemics with fatal dexterity. Of such disastrous consequences, there is but one remedy and one preventive. It is the elevation of the common schools."[32] In these few lines Mann articulated the basic charge that advocates of religious schooling have had to answer ever since. Their schools promote discord over unity.

Mann's Common School crusade highlights other features of this debate as well. In Massachusetts and elsewhere, administrative centralization was part and parcel of the Common School movement. In fact, part of the rationale for the very Board of Education that Mann directed was to counteract the inefficiencies of local control. If the local districts and townships could not be trusted to act in the interest of education rather than taxpayers, Mann was prepared for the state to step in and assume responsibility for, and therefore at least some measure of control over, the common schools. Matters as important as education simply could not be left to individual, perhaps unsuited, parents that might make educational decisions that would bring about something other than the social utopia Mann believed his schools could promote.

Later periods of educational reform give evidence of the same political concerns that inspired Rush, Webster, and Mann. On the heels of Mann's accomplishments came the rise of compulsory attendance laws, which, like the spread of schooling itself, was at least partly concerned with the production of good, loyal Americans. Post-Civil War and early twentieth-century America was still adjusting to the comprehensive set of social changes brought about by industrialization. The increase in the number of power-consuming factories made more exploration and mining a necessity, thus introducing industry into previously untouched rural areas. Of course, all of these changes required a different sort of education as occupational specialization demanded specific skills.

This period is also marked by increasing levels of immigration from the Old World as those people near the bottom of the socio-economic ladder in Europe sought increased opportunity in America. Most of these immigrants migrated to the already overcrowded cities and in large part formed the population of the city slums that social reformers decried as harmful to the family. The prospect of thousands of uneducated, unsupervised children roaming the streets of the city each day played no small part in the vision of the school as a place where children would be not only under adult authority, but also transformed from an unruly mass to constructive citizens.

In fact, it was fear of unruly children in the cities, many of them immigrants, which formed part of the support for the idea of compulsory attendance laws. Increased social complexity and variety in the cities, and the social changes that always accompany communities in flux, prompted renewed attention to schools as agents of social control and assimilation.[33] These conditions were perceived as detrimental to the very fabric of American society. Something was needed to provide the necessary direction and socialization for immigrant children so that they could become useful, productive citizens. That something was the school, and compulsory attendance laws ensured that the immigrant children would not escape the long arm of public socialization.[34]

The political promises of public schooling continued to feature prominently in American education throughout the twentieth century as well. For instance, in the 1930s there was great concern about the spread of radical, subversive elements supposedly influenced by foreign ideologies such as communism. The schools, supposedly, were simultaneously a hotbed of subversion as communists sought to mold the minds of young Americans, and a bulwark of defensive activity against these threats. Teachers swore loyalty oaths to American ideals, and national organizations such as the Daughters of the American Revolution and especially the American Legion saw the schools as both the battlefield and the prize in the West's confrontation with the Russians.[35]

The Educational Policies Commission (EPC), an initiative of the National Education Association, was formed in the 1930s to study American education and to make recommendations for its improvement. Over and over again during the thirty-plus years of the Commission's existence, they issued reports and recommendations stressing the role of the schools in maintaining and promoting American democracy.[36] The commission's 1955 report entitled *Public Education and the Future of America* makes this clear. Acknowledging their debt to Lawrence Cremin for his intellectual leadership, the commission argued that American society was becoming increasingly complex, and that the schools were the one social agency that could prepare children with the "know how of ordinary living" necessary for American life.[37] The same report, in listing the accomplishments of the public schools, gave primacy of place to the assimilation of "more than thirty million immigrants into American life."[38] The EPC went on to argue that the public schools have "helped to create a sufficient unity among all classes and groups and regions in America to keep a far-flung people in a vast and varied country united." They cited as evidence for this claim the fact that

> no major, enduring political party has been organized on strict religious or ethnic or class or regional lines. Rather, there have been Catholics, Jews, and Protestants; Italian-Americans, Polish-Americans, Irish Americans, and French-Canadian Americans; owners and workers; liberals and conservatives within every major political camp. Each major political party in the United States appeals to "all the people"—a people welded together by a common school in which children of all backgrounds have met and mingled and learned.[39]

Finally, the EPC praised the way the public schools have nurtured loyalty to the American way of life by "pointing to American achievements and, indeed, shortcomings that need remedying, public schools have alerted the young to the privileges and responsibilities of citizenship." By stressing and instilling the "essential American values" the public schools had "inspired in the young not a narrow unreasoned patriotism that could easily be abandoned in crisis but rather a mature devotion that can withstand subtle propaganda and repulse the most direct challenge."[40]

Turning to the future of public education in the United States, the EPC identified the need for increased attention to democratic citizenship through the schools. It renewed calls for national unity through the schools. Citing increasing population pressures and "insidious" forces that would "array American against American, the EPC warned of a potential national disaster: "The American tradition, whether expressed in cultural or political or education terms, emphasizes a voluntary unity that allows for diversity within the encompassing framework of common values. Such a unity, resting upon cultural pluralism, does not arise automatically in a society as diverse and far-flung as is America."[41] This unity, the report held, would have to be the conscious goal of American citizens who were willing to work, presumably through the schools, for its achievement. Although the EPC's 1951 report admitted that private religious schools were a rightful part of America's educational enterprise, it nevertheless praised the public school's ability to promote religious values and to therefore create a place for religion in general in American society. That report, too, suggested that if all the religious bodies in America should build their own schools, the "indispensable contribution to unity and common loyalties" made by the public schools would disappear.[42]

As this brief review shows, Americans have been conscious of social unity as a goal, and have worked toward that goal through the schools especially. Understanding American education is impossible without proper attention to the political functions it served in American history. Throughout the history of American public schooling, the idea of promoting attachment to the national political community and its values played an important role in every period from the founding generation on through to today. It is simply part of America's educational landscape that the public schools turn "them" into "us." But that transformation was not always greeted with enthusiasm.

On the one hand, the attempt to integrate people groups into the political life of the state need not be seen as a form of coercion, or cultural homicide. Teaching people unfamiliar with the demands of American democratic life to participate fully as citizens is a noble endeavor. Self-government is, after all, a coveted political ideal, and certainly a minimum amount of civic and political knowledge enhances each citizen's right to meaningfully partic-ipate in the life of his or her society. Schools are an obvious avenue for conveying this knowledge through civics and history classes that familiarize all students with such basic citizenship rights as freedom of speech, associa-tion, or religion. Essentially, schools can and do teach the how's and why's of political participation in their society. On the other hand, political inte-gration is not entirely benign. The same classes that teach students about the right to vote also reinforce a certain "we/they" dichotomy to students, with "they" encompassing all those outside the political community. Those students that do not pass though the institutions that transform "them" into "us" risk a certain political stigma that threatens their place as legitimate actors in a public life.

THE RELIGIOUS SCHOOL PROBLEM

Every system of faith-based education has faced criticism not only about the academic potential of their arrangements, but also about the political implications of their efforts. Scholarship on this issue has tended to see the criticism as a question of the ability of religious schools to turn out partic-ipating citizens. In the face of this concern, recent studies have pointed out that the privately schooled are in fact very active citizens, outscoring their publicly schooled counterparts on standard measures of civic engagement such as voting, contact with legislators, and even patronage of public facili-ties other than schools.[43] This research has been heralded as evidence that the long-held fears about private schooling's political ramifications were unfounded. The debate, some argue, is over. Religious schools produce good, meaning active citizens. While this recent research is important in its own right, and a welcome empirical contribution to what had been a largely rhetorical debate, I contend that it has overlooked an important part of the political objection to religious schooling. The charge was not just that the privately schooled would be uninvolved in public affairs, but that they would be unintegrated into the national political community. Even if they were politically active, the privately schooled would still pose a threat to

political order. This explains why high levels of participation further an-
tagonized the critics of faith-based education rather than silencing them.
For instance, when Bishop John Hughes organized a political ticket and
brought New York City Catholics to the polls in the 1840s on behalf of
Catholic schooling, it was seen as proof for the supposed plot by Catholics
to take over America, rather than as reassurance that advocates of Catholic
schooling would still discharge the responsibilities of citizenship.

Having already seen that their expected ability to unite people across
creedal lines was part of the public school's triumph in America, we can
turn now to two of the specific ways this hope became a criticism of religious
schools. First, critics have charged religious schools with undermining the
legitimate expectation of the state that citizens would be loyal to the nation.
Second, some hold that religious schooling promotes intransigence on the
part of graduates. Regarding this question of national loyalty, it is worth
noting that this is not just an academic debate. Violent arguments have
broken out precisely because at stake here is where and how parents will
educate their children, and how those children will get along in their society.
This is a volatile issue, and it has roots in the rough and tumble world
of local politics as much as it does in the ivory tower. For instance, in a
debate with Bishop John Hughes, public school advocate Hiram Ketchum
worried aloud that a foreign potentate would have a say in the curriculum of
America's public schools. Ketchum specifically called for Hughes and other
immigrants to give their heart to America first, dissolving the partialities the
Catholic schools promoted.

The same charges surfaced some four decades later at a debate held at
the 1889 meeting of the National Education Association. At that meeting,
the critics of Catholic schooling framed the issue specifically as one of
loyalty to the state. Dr. Edwin Mead took as his point of departure an
article from the 1883 edition of *A Catholic Dictionary* about the purpose
and methods of Catholic education. The Catholic position held that any
interest the state had in education was secondary to that of the parents and
the church. Mead noted that other Catholic authorities had characterized
the struggle for parochial schools as a conflict between the state and the
family, a position he rejected as connived and dishonest. Catholic teaching,
in requiring families to support parochial schools, was not honoring the
"liberty of conscience" for families either. Mead argued that this was really a
church and state issue. More specifically, this was an issue about the church's
interference with the state's effort to cultivate loyal citizens, striking Mead
as a "poor piece of special pleading by one not making an earnest effort to
reconcile great conflicting claims and establish sound and useful general
principles, but laboring to weaken men's allegiance to the state and the
reverence of families for the state . . . "[44]

Mead characterized the state as the "ground and reinforcement of all
other legitimate authority" because the state accepted everyone in the

society. "Every man belongs to the state" regardless of what religion they profess, including the profession of no religion at all. Mead charged the church with promoting anarchy as opposed to order, and argued that it was really the church that violated individual liberty by demanding allegiance to parochial schools. This form of coercion was unacceptable according to Mead, especially since the coercion originated in Rome. "The policy of the church as to American schools, let it be remembered, as well as to other things, is determined at Rome, and the bishops here [in America] have simply to fall into line."[45] Mead called any attempt by the church to enforce parochial education on American citizens a claim to temporal power by an ecclesiastical body. It was "the last poor exhibition of the hoary old claim of the priest to empire and the sword."

And who would protect the citizenry from Roman attempts to gain power? The state.

> Against all this stands the modern state, the people, jealously respecting the rights of every religion and the sane scruples of every man within its body . . . leaving with strict impartiality to every sect the religious training of its own children; permitting private schools, with howsoever much etiquette and tone, or with prayers many and catechisms many, to any who desire them and will keep them to the standard which the state proscribes; but insisting that every child shall be well educated in those things which belong to the good education of all citizens alike; providing schools in which this education shall be given, and insisting that every child shall have the privilege of attending these schools.[46]

No exceptions could be made; else the public schools themselves would be threatened. Public support for faith-based education threatened the "confusion and debasement, and then the destruction of the public school system."[47] The public schools served democracy by increasing understanding across classes and people groups. "I find in most of the Catholic utterances on education no sense of obligation to the whole, no civic breadth, no thought of any children but their own."[48] The "insular" schools of parochial education would only reproduce the ghetto menace of yesteryear. In short, parochial education was a threat to the very fabric of American society. "This thing [parochial education], I say, is not proper in America, and this thing cannot be permitted in America. It is a flagrant violation of the rights of citizenship, as citizenship is conceived in this republic . . . the Roman Catholic citizens of America, because they are citizens of America as well as members of the Roman Catholic Church, are entitled to be freed from this coercion."[49]

Public school advocate John Jay's remarks at the same event were more stereotypical than Mead's. He held that no foreign power should be recognized in the United States, and warned of the plot to convert America to a Catholic nation. He praised "loyal American Roman Catholics" that supported the public schools. Jay relied on the Americanization arguments made earlier in the century to paint a picture of public schools as benevolent instructors of the benefits of American living. Only the schools could help the "tidal wave" of immigrants overtaking America's cities. The schools would forge these untrained elements into "loyal citizens of an undivided republic."[50]

Speaking on the role of education in America, Jay was emphatic on the question of allegiance.

> The aim of the American public school and of the Roman parochial school are as antagonistic as the constitution and the syllabus, as the doctrine of popular sovereignty and the dogma of papal supremacy. The duties of the American citizen for which the public school is intended to fit him, are those of a sovereign ruler. He is to be independent of the world, and especially of every foreign prince or potentate; he is to be governed by allegiance to the Republic . . . The public school, if faithfully maintained as established by our fathers, teaches not only the elements of education, but teaches personal responsibility, freedom of conscience and of thought, loyalty to American principles and constitutions, love of country, and duty to our fellow-men.[51]

The parochial school, on the other hand, aimed to "form a subject of the pope, and not an independent citizen of the American Republic, and the character of the education is admirable fitted for this purpose. The "intelligent," Roman Catholic, by which he meant those that supported public schooling,

> desire[d] his sons to speak in the manly tones of an American citizen, and not as Taine describes it, "the infantile and snuffling tone of the Middle Ages." But above all he desired his children to have the characteristics of the country to which they have come, while as Dr. Brownson declares of the parochial schools: "These schools must be taught chiefly by foreigners, or if not by foreigners, at least by those whose sympathies, connections, tastes, and habits are un-American, because what is wanted by their founders and supporters is not simply the preservation of orthodoxy, but the preservation of the foreignisms associated with it."[52]

Amazingly, Christian homeschoolers at the end of the twentieth century faced similar criticisms. Although they did not have the taint of being foreigners under the control of a trans-Atlantic despot, they were lumped in with other subversive elements bent on overthrowing America's government. The most public statements of this concern have come from popular media, and while largely unsustained, were quite dramatic. For instance, in the wake of the 1995 Oklahoma City bombing by Timothy McVeigh, much attention was focused on antigovernment elements of the population. Concerns were raised over radical elements that seek to separate themselves from the American mainstream. Militias and other paramilitary organizations were the first to face scrutiny, but coupled with them were homeschoolers. Homeschoolers have been linked with other "far right" segments of conservative thought, along with conspiracy theorists, tax protestors, and second-Amendment activists (gun owners). According to *Time* magazine, this coalition was a force in the 1994 Republican victories and represents just the sort of "paranoid, violent thinking within our borders" that set off the "grisly mix of fertilizer and hatred" in Oklahoma.[53]

Also based on the idea that religious schools promote discord is a second criticism. Religious schooling is seen as promoting intransigence on the part of graduates. The suspicion here is that the religious schools insulate students within the boundaries of their own religious community, thus rendering them incapable of working with those outside their own group. Alan Peshkin, in his in-depth look at fundamentalist Christian schooling, concludes that the instructional program at Bethany Baptist Academy (the school he studied) is, and means to be, divisive rather than pluralistic. For Peshkin, this is the result of both institutional and epistemological features of religious schooling. Fundamentalist Christian schools promote uniformity and strict adherence to their doctrines as outgrowth of their claim to truth, but the lack of alternative voices results in a more strident tone to these lessons, thus reinforcing certainty at the expense of curiosity and open-mindedness. Peshkin sees this as particularly problematic given what he calls his preference for pluralism as a value and feature of American society.[54]

Just as anti-Catholic forces worried that the schools would shield children from "American" values, so too do contemporary critics of religious schooling charge practitioners with a too narrow exposure to the America praised by public schools. This is not to say that contemporary critics are modern day "Know Nothings" bent on persecuting ideological dissenters. Rather, it points to the persistent view that the public schools promote American identity, even as that identity changes. Thus, when Protestantism, broadly conceived, was an assumed part of American identity, fans of public schooling saw an opportunity to expose Catholic children to this part of America. In the same way, pluralism is now a significant part of America's public identity, and pro-public school agencies see religious schooling as a means of shielding children from this aspect of what it means to be an American. For instance, The National Association of Elementary School Principals, although now advocating cooperation with homeschoolers when possible, also criticized homeschooling precisely because it isolates students from other social groups. In both cases, advocates of public schooling saw religious schooling as un-American because it shielded children from that which they thought was central to American identity. It is worth noting again that the cultural identity of the pro-public school voices has changed over the last century and a half. The groups that, at one point, spoke of the public schools as "ours" are now more likely to suspect those same schools because of "secular" influence.

Michael Apple argued that the insularity of homeschoolers is part of a larger conservative restoration in America troubling to him on a number of fronts.[55] He compares homeschooling to gated communities, as places of physical and ideological security where the threat of encountering "the other" is minimized. The problem here, of course, is that as American society becomes more diverse, movements like homeschooling contribute to what Apple sees as the increasing segmentation of American life on the basis of residence, race, income, creed, and the like. It produces communities of specialized interests that cut across local geography, further weakening neighborhoods already near the brink of collapse. A longtime advocate of reform in public education, Apple admitted that American public schools are not without their problems. But homeschoolers, he charges, are not trying to just escape the troubles of public education. They are altogether rejecting the idea of the cultural and intellectual diversity the schools should embody. Homeschoolers, as part of the conservative restoration Apple decried, shun encounters with anything that does not already fit their religious worldview. This purposeful embrace of insularity, cocooning as he called it, is not an unfortunate byproduct of home education. According to Apple, it is the very goal of homeschooling.

Expanding this criticism beyond homeschooling, political philosopher and president of the University of Pennsylvania Amy Gutmann made a similar charge against anyone who would argue, as most advocates of religious schooling do, that educational authority should rest in the hands of parents. Of particular concern are those parents who would "predispose their children, through education, to choose a way of life consistent with their familial heritage."[56] Less an exposition of specific legal precedents, she develops a philosophical argument that distinguishes between the right of parents to have a say in their child's education and the right of parents to "insulate their children from exposure to ways of life or thinking that conflict with their own."[57] Excessive shielding, according to Gutmann, may allow parents to render their children incapable of the rational deliberation necessary in a democracy. It will certainly predispose their children to favor one way of life over another, thus making real freedom to choose one's own course of life impossible. Frances Patterson echoes these concerns in her critical examination of textbooks used in private Christian and homeschools. She argues that these books are biased against anything but a conservative Protestantism, well suited for communal memberships and identity, but bad for democratic life in a pluralist society.[58]

Even in the debate over Jewish day schools, a largely intracommunity affair, these concerns were present. For day school critics, consideration of the day school question called for a wider view of the purpose of education. The "extraordinarily myopic" view that day schools should be evaluated primarily with reference to Jewish education was unsatisfactory. Mordecai Grossman held that any alternative educational arrangement must be measured by the same standard one would use to evaluate the public schools.

> In the total scheme of education, the ideas denoted by such phrases as "Jewish otherness," "Jewish religion," "Jewish civilization," "Hebraic culture," Yiddish culture," and "Palestine-centeredness" can legitimately have only a secondary place. What should be controlling are such inclusive purposes as a common culture equally accessible to all the people; a common country in which both Jews and non-Jews feel at home; a cooperative society without the social cleavages based on class, religion, race, or ancestry; human beings with broad human sympathies; and the kind of mentality which is equal to the task of coping with the problems imposed by a world in transition.[59]

Joseph Blau agreed.[60] He admitted that if the goal of education were just to "keep Jews Jewish" then day schools were the best solution, but he argued the Jewish community had a vested interest in going beyond such narrow purposes. Thus, not only their ability to teach particular subjects, but their contribution to democratic vitality (of which the public schools were a central part) must be considered in any evaluation of the day schools. And on this score, the critics found them lacking.

Recognizing that the Supreme Court had affirmed the right of non-public schools to exist in the *Pierce* decision, Jewish day school critics argued that legality and beneficence were two different things. Parochial schools, no matter how protected by the court, would serve only to segregate children from one another on the basis of difference. This segregation, the critics argued, might make them first-class Jews, but it will make them second-class Americans. Parochial schools necessarily produce individuals whose "denominational loyalties will be supreme in the total hierarchy of loyalties."[61] Support for Jewish day schools, or any form of faith-based education, was labeled unpatriotic because it places the immediate needs of the group above those of the nation. Only the public schools hold forth the promise of increasing open-mindedness and cooperation. Only widespread embrace of the public schools will result in a "more unified America than we have at present; whereas the parochial school points to a sect-divided, indoctrinated, narrow-minded and conflict-ridden America."[62]

No one really wanted a return to the old-world ethnic ghetto, but that is precisely what day schools would do. Blau charged the day schools with failing to inform Jewish children what it meant to live in America. Day schools would never, could never, teach Jewish children to get along with people from a variety of backgrounds with competing, maybe even mutually exclusive, ways of thinking and living. This idea of "getting along" is crucial to Blau's concept of American life. In fact, he called it the "spirit of American democracy" and charges the segregated day schools with destroying it:

Learning to manage this, the valuable kind of "together-ness," is an important part of the educational process in a free and democratic society. Just as the basic argument for co-education is that men and women cannot learn the techniques of working together by being trained apart, by being segregated, so the basic argument against *any* form of segregated educational program is that it fails to meet this first essential need of education for democratic citizenship.[63]

Similarly, Isaac Berkson argued that any educational system in a democracy must express the variety of forces in the community. Schools, if they are to be democratic, must be administered and supported by all the groups under one state authority. If the schools are segregated then the students themselves cannot gain the experience of working with difference so vital in a democratic society.[64]

So no matter how efficacious the education received turned out to be, if it only made better Jews it was ultimately failing. Again, Blau is instructive: "[I]f, as I maintain, self-segregation would, in the long run destroy healthy life in a democratic society, then it would destroy the very conditions under which Jewish life has flourished and can continue to flourish in America. It would not be self-defense, but suicide."[65] To some extent, mid-century critics like Blau and Grossman were restating objections made fifty years earlier. Samson Benderly, the one-time head of the Board of Education of the New York Kehillah (an early Jewish community organization) lamented the very idea of Jewish day schools as early as 1908:

This plan even if it was practical otherwise, should be banished from our minds. In spite of the fact that isolation in the midst of a Christian environment greatly contributed to our preservation in the past, we have paid dearly for this isolation. What we want in this country is not Jews who can successfully keep up their Jewishness in a few large ghettos, but men and women who have grown up in freedom and can assert themselves wherever they are. A parochial system of education among the Jews would be fatal to such hopes.[66]

Beyond the impact on the Jewish community, the critics also held that the widespread embrace of parochial education would seriously undermine American democracy more broadly precisely because it would destroy the institution that in large part built democracy, the public school. Samuel Dinin held that the common schools were worthy of support even while he recognized the legal right of day schools to exist. Though he admits day schools are more effective with regard to Judaism, he also held that the interests of democracy and liberal religion (two unqualified goods in his mind) were best served by improving the quality not of day schools, but of public schools. To the extent that the Jewish community's welfare depended upon a strong commitment to democracy on the part of the general public, anything that undermined that commitment, for instance, threats to public education, was ultimately self-defeating.[67]

The basic thrust of the social division argument is that religious schooling entails withdrawal from the primary institutional setting in which future citizens gain exposure to mainstream America. It bars graduates from effective participation in a public sphere in which "the other" is a necessary dialogue partner. Importantly, not only does it rob children of exposure to other ways of life, it also robs society of its chance to bring up future generations in which mutual respect and tolerance, based on exposure, are assured. As W.D. Hawley noted, in the future American society will need the collaborative efforts of a diverse population, and thus any option that promotes privatized education exposes the nation to social and political risk.[68]

Each time a religious community established their own schools, critics arose to advance some version of these arguments. At stake is the very possibility of a *United* States of America, with the divisions being along creedal lines. Successive generations of public school advocates each saw the schools as the place where the values they think of as integral to American identity, whether Protestant, more broadly Christian, or even secular, are instilled in the next generation, and thus religious schools were seen as attacks not just on the public institutions, but on the society that was reproduced through them.

NOTES

1. *Board of Education v. Allen,* 392 U.S. 236 (1968).

2. See Anne Michael Edwards, *Educational Theory as Political Theory* (Brookfield, WI: Avebury, 1996).

3. Emile Durkheim, "The Development of Educational Systems" in *Emile Durkheim: Selected Writings,* ed. Anthony Giddens (Cambridge, MA: Cambridge University Press, 1972), 207–208.

4. John Dewey, *Democracy and Education* (New York: Free Press, 1916). This is not to say that Americans are always comfortable with these connections. On the aversion to mixing politics and education in America, see Thomas Eliot, "Toward an Understanding of Public School Politics," *American Political Science Review* 53 (December 1959): 1032ff. See also V.O. Key, *Public Opinion and American Democracy* (New York: Alfred A Knopf, 1961). Though Americans are well aware of the connections between education and political life, they do not always think of their schools as political institutions. In 1986 the annual Gallup poll on public education, released every year in *Phi Delta Kappan,* revealed that more than half of those polled identified job and finance reasons as the chief motivation for educating their children. Less than 10 percent cited political objectives such as the desire to produce good citizens or make a public contribution as important motivations for education. More recent polls suggest that preparation for citizenship has gained popularity as a motivation for education. The 2000 Gallup poll finds that responsible citizenship is the most important purpose for education, followed closely by economic self-sufficiency. Importantly, though, the format of the question changed between 1986 and 2000. In the 1986 survey the question was open-ended and merely asked people for the reasons they want their children to get an education. Only a small portion

(6 percent) thought of citizenship. In the 2000 survey, the questioner provided a list of reasons for education, and, perhaps not surprisingly, when asked to rank these reasons on a 10-point scale, people identified citizenship as important. See Alec Gallup, "The 18th Annual Gallup Poll of the Public's Attitudes toward the Public Schools," *Phi Delta Kappan* (September 1986): 43ff; Lowell Rose and Alec Gallup, "The 32nd Annual Phi Delta Kappa/Gallup Poll of the Public's Attitudes toward the Public Schools," *Phi Delta Kappan* (September 2000): 41ff. For analysis on why Americans sometimes argue that their schools are not political institutions, see Frederick M. Wirt and Michael W. Kirst, *The Politics of Education: Schools in Conflict* (Berkeley, CA: McCutchan Publishing Corporation, 1982).

5. See David Easton, "Function of Formal Education in a Political System," *The School Review* 65 (1957): 304–316.

6. See Lawrence Cremin, *Popular Education and its Discontents* (New York: Harper and Row, 1990). On the primacy of the political interpretation of schooling, see R. Freeman Butts, "Assaults on a Great Idea," *The Nation* (1973): 553–557; R. Freeman Butts, "Public Education and Political Community," *History of Education Quarterly* 14 (Summer 1974): 165–183. See also Diane Ravitch, *The Revisionists Revised* (New York: Basic Books, 1978); James D. Hunter, *Culture Wars: The Struggle to Define America* (New York: Basic Books, 1991).

7. Ernest Gellner, *Nations and Nationalism* (New York: Cornell University Press, 1983).

8. Andrew Green, *Education and State Formation: The Rise of Education Systems in England, France, and the USA* (New York: St. Martins, 1990).

9. John W. Meyer and Richard Rubinson, "Education and Political Development," in *Review of Research in Education*, ed. Fred Kerlinger (Itasca, IL: F.E. Peacock, 1975): 153.

10. See Amy Gutmann, *Democratic Education*, previously cited.

11. Readers looking for a fuller discussion of these issues would do well to consult Elmer J. Thiessen's *In Defence of Religious Schools and Colleges*, previously cited. Though Thiessen ultimately defends such schools, he identifies at least eight critiques made against them, most made up of multiple perspectives.

12. See Vincent Lannie, *Public Money and Parochial Education: Bishop Hughes, Governor Seward, and the New York School Controversy* (Cleveland, OH: The Press of Case Western Reserve University, 1968). See also Diane Ravitch, *The Great School Wars* previously cited. I am indebted to both of these excellent works for their examinations of this controversy.

13. See James Burns, *The Principles, Origin and Establishment of the Catholic School System in the United States* (New York: Arno Press, 1969).

14. Robert Everhart, "From Universalism to Usurpation: An Essay on the Antecedents to Compulsory School Attendance Legislation," *Review of Educational Research* 47(3) (Summer 1977): 499–530.

15. Alexander Dushkin, "The Role of the Day School in American Jewish Education," *Journal of Jewish Education*, 20(1) (November 1948): 5–52. Dushkin ultimately defends day schooling in the Jewish community and argues that the general position of public schooling is so secure in American society that there is no real threat posed by private and religious education.

16. Michael Apple, "Is Social Transformation Always Progressive? Rightist Reconstructions of Schooling Today," in *Social Reconstruction Through Education*, ed. Michael

James (Norwood, OH: Ablex Publishing, 1995). See also Apple's *Cultural Politics and Education* (Buckingham: Open University Press, 1996) and "The Cultural Politics of Home Schooling," *Peabody Journal of Education* 75 (2000): 256–271.

17. John Cloud and Jodie Morse, "Home Sweet School" *Time* 158 (August 27, 2001): 46–54.

18. People for the American Way, "Dereliction of Duty" 2004. Online at www.pfaw.org.

19. James Coleman and Thomas Hoffer, *Public and Private High Schools: The Impact of Communities* (New York: Basic Books, 1987).

20. See Albert Hirschman, *Exit, Voice, and Loyalty* (Cambridge, MA: Harvard University Press, 1970). Hirschman's work explored the potential benefit to both economics and political science in utilizing concepts and tools from one another. He notes that exit, as a strategy, is normally associated with economics, while voice, usually thought of as "messier" by economists is more political. He further notes that exit, when used in the realm of politics, is often called "treason." Exit may serve as a motivation for improving the schools, but unfortunately, those most concerned with improvement will have already gone.

21. Chris Lubienski, "Whither the Common Good: A Critique of Home Schooling," *Peabody Journal of Education* 75 (2000): 207–232.

22. For the 1996 figures, see *Survey on American Political Culture*, "The State of Disunion, Volume II: Summary Tables" (Ivy: In Medias Res Educational Foundation, 1996). For the 2000 installment of this survey, see "The Politics of Character," volume 3, of *Survey of American Public Culture*, Institute for Advanced Studies in Culture, University of Virginia.

23. James Coleman called this the political integration of society, and further identified two versions of integration: vertical and horizontal. Vertical integration through education attempts to cross the rich-poor gap and allow students at the bottom of the socioeconomic ladder the opportunity to fully participate in economic opportunities that would be denied them without education. More importantly for my purposes, Coleman also spoke of horizontal integration. This is education that provides the common elements of social identity, thus producing something of a *culture generale*. See James S. Coleman, "Introduction: Education and Political Development," in *Educational and Political Development*, ed. James S. Coleman (Princeton, NJ: Princeton University Press, 1965).

24. Several historians have explored the educational programs of the founding generation, with Thomas Jefferson, Benjamin Rush, and Noah Webster being treated as a sort of triumvirate in terms of early educational leaders. See David Tyack, "Forming the National Character: Paradox in the Educational Thought of the Revolutionary Generation," *Harvard Educational Review* 36 (1966): 29–41.

25. Benjamin Rush, "Thoughts on the Mode of Education Proper in a Republic," in *Essays on Education in the Early Republic*, ed. Frederick Rudolph (Cambridge, MA: Harvard University Press, 1965): 9.

26. Rush, "Thoughts on the Mode of Education . . . ," in *Essays on Education in the Early Republic*, previously cited, 18.

27. Noah Webster, *An American Selection of Lessons in Reading and Speaking: Calculated to Improve the Minds and Refine the Taste of Youth, and also to Instruct Them in the Geography, History, and Politics of the United State*, 12th edition (Boston, MA: Thomas and Andrews, 1800): vi.

28. Noah Webster, "On the Education of Youth in America," in *Essays on Education in the Early Republic*, ed. Frederick Rudolph (Cambridge, MA: Harvard University Press, 1965). Educational historian Lawrence Cremin characterized the moral of Webster's three-volume work as the "inseparability of cultural and political independence" and noted that for the five decades after the *Grammatical Institute*'s publication this theme surfaces again and again in Webster's writings. Believing that the very language one spoke would help form American national character, Webster argued that it was ridiculous for America to imitate the language and habits of foreigners. Only the extension of education to every American would serve to eradicate the traces of foreign influence and produce the required conformity necessary for the young republic. See Lawrence Cremin, *American Education: The National Experience, 1783–1876* (New York: Harper and Row, 1980).

29. On Mann, see especially Charles Glenn, *The Myth of the Common School*, previously cited. See also Lawrence Cremin's edited compilation of Mann's reports: *The Republic and the School: Horace Mann on the Education of Free Men* (New York: Teachers College Press, 1957). Lloyd Jorgenson has shown how the common school movement more broadly was connected to evangelical Protestantism, anti-Catholocism, and the attempt to build a state monopoly in education. See his *The State and the Non-Public School: 1825–1925* (Columbia, MO: University of Missouri Press, 1987).

30. See Lawrence Cremin, "Horace Mann's Legacy," in *The Republic and the School: Horace Mann and the Education of Free Men*, previously cited.

31. Horace Mann, "Ninth Annual Report," in *The Republic and the School*, 58.

32. Ibid., 33.

33. See Michael Katz, *A History of Compulsory Education Laws*, previously cited.

34. It has long been held that part of the explanation for compulsory schooling lay in the desire to prevent the abuses of child labor. While not denying the relationship between opposition to child labor and support for compulsory attendance laws, Everhart did not see this as a sufficient explanation for the sudden upsurge of support of mandatory attendance laws toward the end of the nineteenth century. First of all, compulsory attendance laws were largely ineffective until after 1890, but the number of child laborers was declining as early as 1870. Furthermore, Everhart argued that the compulsory attendance laws only made official what was already in fact the case. Namely, most children were already in school. Numerous cities reported schools that were overrun with children, some having to be turned away for lack of space. Finally, though Everhart does not stress this point, compulsory attendance laws were aimed largely at the children who were running through the streets, totally unsupervised. Thus, the targets of compulsory attendance laws were not the children in the shops so much as the children with no place to go. See Robert Everhart, "From Universalism to Usurpation: An Essay on the Antecedents to Compulsory School Attendance Legislation," previously cited. See also Joseph Kett, "Juveniles and Progressive Children," *History of Education Quarterly* 13 (Summer 1976): 191–194.

35. On loyalty oaths and the general atmosphere of the schools, see Robert Iverson, *The Communists and the Schools* (New York: Harcourt Brace, 1959).

36. Educational Policies Commission, *The Unique Function of Education in American Democracy* (Washington, DC: National Education Association, 1937). See also Educational Policies Commission, *Learning the Ways of Democracy: A Casebook in Civic*

Education (Washington, DC: National Education Association, 1940); Educational Policies Commission, *Policies for Education in American Democracy* (Washington, DC: National Education Association, 1946); Educational Policies Commission, *The Central Purpose of American Education* (Washington, DC: National Education Association, 1961).

37. Educational Policies Commission (EPC), *Public Education and the Future of America* (Washington, DC: National Education Association, 1955): 86.

38. EPC, *Public Education and the Future of America*, 1955, 67.

39. Ibid., 68–69.

40. Ibid., 75–76.

41. Ibid., 92.

42. Educational Policies Commission, *Moral and Spiritual Values in Public Schools* (Washington, DC: National Education Association, 1951): 5.

43. Christian Smith and David Sikkink, "Is Private Schooling Privatizing," *First Things* (April 1999): 16–20; William Galston, "Political Knowledge, Political Engagement, and Civic Education," *Annual Review of Political Science* 4 (2001): 217–234.

44. Edwin Mead, "Has the Parochial School Proper Place in America," in *Denominational Schools* (Topeka, KS: Kansas Publishing House, 1889): 20.

45. Ibid., 30.

46. Ibid., 32.

47. Ibid., 33.

48. Ibid., 38.

49. Ibid., 34.

50. John Jay, "Public and Parochial Schools," in *Denominational Schools* (Topeka, KS: Kansas Publishing House, 1889): 49.

51. Ibid., 57.

52. Ibid., 58. The "Dr. Brownson" cited by Jay is presumably Orestes Brownson, a well-known convert to Catholicism who argued publicly for a version of Catholic faith tailored to the American experience. At one point an opponent of parochial education, Brownson later changed his tune and became an ardent supporter of the Catholic schools.

53. Philip Weiss, "Outcasts Digging in for the Apocalypse," *Time* (May 1, 1995): 48.

54. See Alan Peshkin, *God's Choice: The Total World of a Fundamentalist Christian School*, previously cited.

55. While Apple and Lubienski (both previously cited) are critical of homeschooling in general, they both also single out Christian homeschoolers as the majority of the movement and the segment that raises the most troubling questions. Apple, for instance, argues that traditional and fundamentalist religious values drive a large part of the homeschooling movement and focuses on this group in his critique. Lubienski identifies a number of homeschool advocacy groups, virtually all of which are clearly identified with the Christian wing of the movement. Thus, while their critique of homeschooling as pedagogy is not limited to one branch of homeschoolers, their political objections do focus on the religiously motivated families and organizations.

56. Gutmann, *Democratic Education*, previously cited, 28.

57. Ibid., 29.

58. See Frances R.A. Paterson, *Democracy and Intolerance: Christian School Curricula, School Choice, and Public Policy* (Bloomington, IN: Phi Kappa Delta Educational Foundation, 2003).

59. Mordecai Grossman, "Parochial Schools for Jewish Children: An Adverse View," *Jewish Education* 16 (May 1945): 20–25.

60. Joseph Blau, "The Jewish Day School," *The Reconstructionist* (November 14, 1958): 29–32.

61. Grossman, "Parochial Schools for Jewish Children: An Adverse View," previously cited, 23.

62. Ibid., 22.

63. Blau, "The Jewish Day School," *The Reconstructionist* (November 14, 1958): 31.

64. Isaac Berkson, *Theories of Americanization: A Critical Study* (New York: Arno Press, 1920).

65. Blau, "The Jewish Day School," *The Reconstructionist* (November 14, 1958): 32.

66. In Alvin I. Schiff, *The Jewish Day School in America* (New York: Jewish Education Committee, 1966), 206.

67. Samuel Dinin, "The All-Day Jewish School," *The Reconstructionist* (October 5, 1945): 11–20.

68. W. D. Hawley, "The False Premises and False Promises of the Movement to Privatize Public Education," *Teachers College Record* (Summer) 96(4) (1995): 735–742.

4 Religious Schools and the
Fulfillment of Democratic Freedom

I s private schooling un-American? Its critics say yes. Non-public institutions "rob" the public schools of needed resources, rendering them
less effective in both their educational and social missions. Religious
schooling, especially, is seen as incompatible with American democratic
life because it strengthens subcommunity ties in a way that disintegrates
national unity. These criticisms have not gone unanswered. On both empirical and philosophical grounds, advocates of religious schooling have
denied that their efforts undermine public education, criticized those very
institutions, and denied that their own schools are somehow subversive of
America's democratic character. More than just defending themselves, successive generations of religious school advocates have attempted to show
that their educational arrangements are in fact uniquely American. Their
schools are an exercise in freedom and dissent, both valued aspects of America's political heritage. Additionally, there is a positive democratic case to
be made for religious schooling as a means of denying the state's monopoly
on education.

THE RESOURCE DRAIN ARGUMENT

Advocates of faith-based schooling are well aware of how they are perceived by those in what they often call the "public school establishment,"
but they deny that their actions undermine public schooling by taking away
necessary resources. As we have seen, this criticism occurs on at least two
levels, financial and social. Taking up the question of school finances first,
is it the case that private education, the majority of which takes place under

religious auspices, decreases the coffers of the public schools? No, say defenders of faith-based schooling, and in another historical irony it is the
victory of the Public School Society that makes it so. They point out that
since public education is tax supported, rather than tuition based, all families in America, whether their children attend public schools or not, already
contribute to the financial support of public education. Thus, the total pot
of monies available for public education does not change with school enrollment. It is distribution, not collection, which is impacted by the number of
students. So, while increased numbers may mean more money for specific
schools or districts, it also means less money available for all students across
the tax region because the total available revenue will not change. Policy-
makers would either have to raise taxes or lower per-pupil disbursements
to accommodate the influx of students. Additionally, if millions of students
currently enrolled in religious schools "went public," districts and cities all
around the country would have to build more schools, or at least hire more
teachers, again driving up costs without increasing the available revenue.
The idea that private and homeschooling actually saves money for taxpayers
has also been advanced. Funds that would be distributed to various schools
are eligible for reallocation in either educational or other public projects.
The National Home Education Research Institute claims that homeschooling saves American taxpayers billions of dollars annually. More broadly,
the Council for American Private Education, whose member organizations
include Catholic, Protestant, and Jewish day school associations, estimates
that private schools save taxpayers more than $48 billion a year.[1]

Some critics have held that the real problem is the possibility that religious and other private school advocates could stop paying those taxes that
support public education. This could be particularly damaging on the local
level, since it would not take too large a number of families before their
impact would be felt in the community. Historically, however, advocates of
religious schooling have not moved in this direction, and to do so would
require a significant break with their past. Ever since the Public School
Society's partial triumph in New York that set the precedent for religious
schools being ineligible for public funds, advocates have stressed the extra
burden they take on, essentially supporting two school systems. They have
not, however, seriously advanced the notion that they should not have to pay
taxes to support public schools. Bishop John Hughes, for instance, routinely
pointed out that Catholic citizens bore a double burden for educating their
children. If anything, then, they were meeting the responsibilities of citizenship without availing themselves of the corresponding rights. As Hughes
argued:

> In the operation of that system [the Society's schools], Catholics felt them-
> selves virtually excluded from the benefits of education. Very shortly after that
> construction of the law was adopted, they felt themselves obliged to proceed in

the best way that their poverty would allow for the education of their children. And whilst they have been taxed with the other citizens, up to the present hour they have received no benefit from the system supported by that taxation; but on the contrary, after having contributed what the law required, have been obliged to throw themselves back upon their own resources, and provide, as well as they might, the means of educating their children . . . [2]

Defenders of the Jewish day schools, too, labored to show how their schools did not, in fact, threaten public schools. Even at the height of the day school movement, Jews constituted less than 3 percent of the American population, and even that minority was geographically spread out in several population centers. Even if all Jewish children pursued day school education, the advocates reasoned, this posed no real threat to the public institutions, which are the educational destination for some 90 percent of American children.[3] Others pointed out that by the time the Jewish day school movement was underway, the public schools were well established in the American landscape. As long as the public schools were tax-based rather than tuition-based, advocates of faith-based schooling have reasoned that private education, in whatever form, poses no threat to the finances of public education. After detailing the ways in which Jewish day schooling could never threaten public education, Alexander Dushkin, the executive vice president of the Jewish Education Committee in New York, dismissed the "bugaboo" of "undermining the public school."[4]

Further refuting the charge that their arrangements tap public school funds, some advocates of religious schooling have argued for more publicly minded action on the part of the private school community with regard to resources and funding. For instance, in recent years charter schools have become hot-button issues in education circles. Charter schools are publicly funded and while some follow the standard "school away from home" model, a growing movement has embraced home-based, virtual charter schools—these are public schools in the home. Public money is used and various other sources of public support are also available in varying degrees (teacher/consultants, textbooks, etc). The argument behind charter schools is that taking students and money out of the traditional public school setting will force the public schools to innovate, and presumably improve to the point that people and money would return. In the meantime, it is suspected that, at least in some cases, parents may have used charter school money to offset homeschooling, which may then be guided by religious conviction and curricula. This has drawn the ire of critics who claim that public money is being siphoned off from local schools for the purpose of advancing religious education. But leaders in the Christian homeschooling movement have specifically disavowed this practice, and come out against charter schools in general. Home School Legal Defense Association attorney and author Chris Klicka, in the January/February 2002 issue of the *Home*

School Court Reporter called on Christian homeschoolers to stop looking for "freebies" from the government. He urged them to not take public money, arguing for both philosophical and practical reasons that private schooling should not be publicly funded.[5]

As Chapter 3 made clear, the resource drain argument in not just about money. Critics have also argued that private schooling robs public education of necessary human capital by refocusing the energies of a number of parents away from public institutions.[6] But advocates of religious schooling argue that they are still very much invested in education, and that they embody the best practices in American schooling. The justification for this was provided by Michael Farris, but his observations are in line with what earlier advocates from different religious communities said as well. Answering the question as to why homeschoolers should care about issues in American public education, Farris acknowledged that the vast majority of American school children are in public schools, and encouraged Christian homeschoolers to concern themselves with their well-being too.[7]

When critics contend that withdrawal from public schools depletes the social capital necessary to make education more effective, they often point to everyday activities and support for the classroom experience. Advocates of faith-based schooling on the other hand focus their energies on somewhat larger issues, usually in the legislative arena. One of the primary efforts religious school advocates have undertaken aimed at improving the quality of education for all Americans is to decrease the federal government's role in schooling, including the permanent closing of the Education Department. This may sound counterproductive to some. After all, government oversight of the schools resonates with the recent talk about accountability in education. But religious school advocates routinely point out that the Constitution mentions nothing about a federal role in education, and is therefore the prerogative of the states. This, they argue, is consistent with the idea of local control and face-to-face accountability, long a hallmark of America's support for public education.

The constitutional point is an important one, but opposition to a federal role in education is based on more than legal reasoning. Federal support, advocates of private schooling warn, mandates federal oversight. This has never been the panacea some thought it would be. According to Farris, before 1965 the federal government's role in education, at least in terms of financial resources, was limited to lunch programs given to disadvantaged students or to districts deemed "federally impacted."[8] In 1965 the Johnson administration passed the Elementary and Secondary Education Act (reauthorized in 1994) that rapidly increased federal involvement in, and spending for, education. Farris pointed out that real spending is up more than 50 percent per child since the 1960s, the same period of time in which SAT (Scholastic Aptitude Test) scores have fallen and the moral climate of the schools has deteriorated. Indeed, the rhetoric of decline and denunciation is very prevalent among late twentieth-century advocates of Protestant schooling, as it was even in government-sponsored reports like *A Nation at Risk* published in 1983. Since 1980, when the federal Department of Health, Education, and Welfare was reorganized into the Education Department and the Department of Health and Human Services, costs have continued to go up while the quality of education has gone down. Summing up his indictment, Farris wrote: "Americans are reaping a harvest of educational failure which is not unlike the economic failure which led to the demise of the Soviet Union. Simply put, centralized planning does not work. It did not produce the necessary consumer goods and food needed in the Soviet Union, and it has not produced the necessary educational gains needed in the United States." So what is the answer? Farris proposes abolishing not only the Education Department, but also the entire idea of a federal role in education. "Education works when the teacher is free to make professional judgments about how to meet the needs of each individual child, provided that the parents have a real ability to hold that teacher accountable. That balance of teacher professionalism and parental authority will never return to American schools so long as there is any federal role in education."[9] Thus, for Farris, the academic failure of public education, which is much more pronounced in the debate surrounding the Protestant schooling than it was around either Catholic or Jewish schooling, is a direct result of their organizational status and government oversight.

Opposition to a federal role in education is a longstanding feature of religious schooling. Indeed, the Education Department may be relatively new, but the idea of a cabinet-level government agency focused on education has been around for a long time. Particularly in the opening decades of the twentieth century, bills were proposed in the House or Senate to establish a federal Department of Education. American Catholics often came out in opposition to such a measure on the grounds that it was unconstitutional and, beyond that, bad for education. The 1923 correspondence between Father Burke and A. Duncan Yocum, a professor in the School of Education at the University of Pennsylvania, details Catholic opposition to federal responsibility for education and reaffirms Catholic support for public schools administered at the state level as the surest way to protect freedom.[10] In a 1924 letter from Father James Ryan to Idaho Senator William Borah, chairman of the Senate Committee on Education and Labor, Ryan laid out the position of the American Catholic hierarchy on the federal role in education. Assuring the senators that the National Catholic War Council (NCWC) favored legislation for decreasing illiteracy and Americanizing the "foreign born," Ryan nevertheless argued that no federal action was necessary to promote these worthy goals. Federal control over education, he argued, would "weaken the education work of the different states, and at the same time, destroy the spirit of democracy, which never calls upon the government for money until it has exhausted every local possibility . . . " In a long list of reasons for opposing a federal role in education, Ryan closed with the following:

> Many other reasons might be advanced why we are opposed to the Sterling-Reed Bill. But one other point we wish to emphasize, namely, that our opposition is based solely on constitutional, economic, and educational grounds. We believe that this bill, if enacted into law, would do incalculable injury to education, and, in company with some of the most prominent statesmen and educators of the country, numerous teachers, the American Bankers' Association, and the United States Chamber of Commerce, to mention but some of the organizations opposed to federalized education, we respectfully ask that the Sterling-Reed Bill be judged incompatible with American ideals, constitutional and education, as well as a menace to the best and truest interests of our country . . . [11]

Acknowledging that the NCWC would favor a federal agency charged with research and dissemination of matters related to schooling, Ryan argued that authority and control over education must be under local influence.[12] Critics assert that advocates of faith-based schooling are not actually working to better public education by trying to abolish the federal role in schooling, but the advocates themselves believe that local control of the schools is not just constitutional, but superior.

Religious school advocates are active in other arenas too. Recent studies show that the privately schooled have higher levels of civic engagement than do their publicly schooled counterparts.[13] They are active in precisely the kind of networks that promote social capital and enhance democratic life, from meeting at museums and zoos to attending conferences and monitoring family and education-related legislation. In fact, action in the public sphere by advocates of religious schooling is a long-standing feature of American educational history.

For instance, the current generation of homeschool leadership, particularly in the Christian wing of the movement, spent the last two decades in legal and political battles securing their right to exist. Staving off criminal prosecution, signing petitions, and court appearances all required faithful and continued participation lest the right to homeschool be jeopardized. Farris and fellow homeschool advocate Scott Woodruff likened homeschoolers to any minority or reformer "who stands to lose the most precious things in his or her life at the stroke of a legislative pen."[14]

An example of this occurred in the Home School Legal Defense Association's (HSLDA) successful attempt to impact legislation they deemed harmful to their cause. Through their Congressional Action Program, their National Leadership Summit, and finally through the founding mission of Patrick Henry College, HSLDA encourages homeschoolers to participate in civic and political life. The Congressional Action Program (CAP), founded in 1993 in an attempt to safeguard homeschooling from the Clinton administration, serves as a Congressional watchdog association to lobby legislators on issues relating to homeschooling. Their main task is to publicize relevant legislation to the homeschooling community and to coordinate efforts at influencing that legislation favorably. Through letter-writing campaigns, phone calls, and even visits from Washington DC area home educating families, CAP coordinates most of the Christian homeschooling community's response to Congressional action. In 1994, House Resolution 6, a reappropriations bill for the Elementary and Secondary Education Act, was amended to require certification of all teachers in their field of study. HSLDA viewed the amendment as posing an unacceptable risk to homeschooling families and spearheaded an effort to communicate the disapproval of the homeschool community to Congress, with Congressman George Miller's office (the sponsor of the amendment) alone receiving more than 20,000 calls. In the end, the offending passages were amended, and the political abilities of the supposedly withdrawn homeschooling community could not be doubted.[15] A similar strategy was pursued when a California appeals court ruled that a 1953 California law mandates that parents send their children to full-time public or private schools, or provide a credentialed tutor in the home. This ruling, announced in late February 2008 as this book was in process, caused significant alarm in the homeschooling community, as it could affect more than 166,000 homeschooled children in California. Though it began as a child welfare investigation after a report of physical and emotional mistreatment, a juvenile court judge found that parents Philip and Mary Long were neglecting the education of their eight children. The Long children were enrolled in Sunland Christian School under the auspices of its independent study program, but were educated almost entirely by their mother, who does not have a teacher certification. HSLDA announced its support for the family's petition for review to the California Supreme Court, and plans to file an amicus brief should the case be accepted for review. In less than two weeks, they collected more than 250,000 signatures on a petition to depublish the decision, meaning that it could not be cited as precedent by other California courts.[16] Regardless of the outcome of this case, the political muscle and savvy of HSLDA and other pro-homeschooling advocacy organizations are once again on display.

Nor is this the only example of political involvement by Christian homeschoolers. For instance, with regard to securing parental rights in America, HSLDA took an active role in the battle against senate ratification of the United Nations Convention on the Rights of the Child. In February of 1995 then first lady Hillary Clinton announced that the United States would sign the treaty and submit it to the senate for ratification, setting the stage for what HSLDA attorneys called the "Parental Rights Battle of the Decade."[17]

According to HSLDA, there are numerous features of the treaty that make it objectionable, all of which are compounded by their contention that Article VI of the U.S. Constitution, which makes ratified treaties the law of the land in the United States, means that parents would be subject to the provisions of the treaty. The federal government would be obligated to ensure that every child born in America would be registered immediately after birth. Corporal punishment would be "outlawed" in schools, thus rendering spanking illegal in homeschool families. Children would have the legal right to express themselves as they see fit, and to indulge their own tastes with regard to entertainment, including pornography. Children would also be legally guaranteed the rights of freedom of conscience and religion, making it possible for children to reject the religious traditions of their parents. With regard to education, HSLDA saw the UN treaty as a move toward government control over curriculum, even in private Christian schools. The treaty, according to HSLDA, gave the state control over the moral formation of all the children within its boundaries, something homeschoolers specifically rejected: "It is clear from these few examples above that this Treaty would virtually undermine parents' rights as we know it in the United States. Parents no longer would have the basic right to control what their children watch on TV, whom they associate with, and what church they attend. Parents could be prosecuted and children be taken away simply because they spank their children or refuse to honor the various rights that the children are guaranteed [under the Treaty]."[18]

HSLDA's political activity on parental rights is not purely defensive. In 1995, Senator Charles Grassley and Congressman Steve Largent proposed the Parental Rights Act to the federal legislature with the outspoken support and political muscle of the Christian homeschooling community. Citing the opinion of the New York Court of Appeals in *Portnoy v. Strasser*, HSLDA's Michael Farris argued that this bill recognized that the "right of a parent, under natural law, to establish a home and bring up children is a fundamental one and beyond the reach of any court." Essentially, the bill elevated parental rights to the status of "fundamental rights" for American families. It protected the right to "lovingly administer reasonable physical discipline" and, most importantly, educational decisions would be placed more squarely under the realm of familial jurisdiction, making it harder for professional educators or state bureaucrats to interfere. Explaining why HSLDA lobbied Congress on behalf of this legislation (which Farris himself penned), Farris explained that "Congress has no authority to regulate family life, but has express authority to protect the liberty of parents. Congress should be in the business of protecting liberty, not regulating our lives."[19] When the bill was introduced to the legislature in June of 1995 under the new name "Parental Rights and Responsibilities Act," HSLDA's political lobbying arm, CAP organized congressional visits from homeschool families to capitalize on their earlier efforts. By the time the bill was introduced, it had seventy-four cosponsors in the House of Representatives and four in the Senate. That same month, and coupled with some of the lobbying on behalf of the parent's rights legislation, HSLDA announced that thirty-five senators had committed to opposing the UN Convention on the Rights of the Child, enough to keep it from passing.

While educational legislation was not the focus of either the UN Convention on the Rights of the Child or the Parental Rights Act, HSLDA saw the opportunity to advance the cause of home education by shoring up parental rights under the law in general. Knowing that in a precedent-oriented legal system like the United States, a victory in one area may benefit a subsequent, but seemingly unrelated, issue later on, HSLDA marshaled their resources for political action.

Religious freedom is the other issue that attracts HSLDA's attention. Knowing that many of the earlier legal decisions that legitimate parental rights in education were based in the concept of religious freedom, HSLDA was active in this arena as well. A June 2000 Special Report by the National Center for Home Education (a division of HSLDA) made the link between religious freedom and homeschooling explicit: "One of the goals of the Home School Legal Defense Association is to work in the Federal and State legislatures and the courts to protect our right to freely exercise our religious beliefs. Because most homeschoolers teach their children at home in order to train them up in the nurture and admonition of the Lord, our right to freely exercise our religious beliefs is paramount."[20]

All this is to say that homeschoolers are not abandoning the democratic process, but are instead quite involved in it. This is particularly true when education is up for discussion. In fact, in a paradoxical moment, HSLDA representatives attended, by invitation, the swearing in of Rod Paige, the first Secretary of Education under George W. Bush, even as they campaigned to eliminate his job. The presence of an HSLDA attorney at the swearing in of the new head of the Department of Education is both ironic and reminiscent of another period in American educational history. In January of 1921, P.P. Claxton, then the Commissioner of Education in the United States, attended the opening of the NCWC's Bureau of Education as an honored guest, this in spite of the fact that the Catholic schools were controversial and that Catholics were well-known for their opposition to expanding the federal role in education.

Since at least the middle of the nineteenth century and the efforts of Bishop John Hughes, the effort to pull out of public schools has led advocates into the public realm rather than away from it. In 1840 Governor William Seward, a Whig, recommended the establishment of more schools for immigrant children in which they could be instructed by members of their own faith. Although Seward did not offer public money, Catholic leaders recognized an opportunity when they saw it. Barely a month after Seward's proposal, the Catholic Church submitted a plea to the city's Board of Assistant Alderman requesting a share of the public money earmarked for the public schools. Identifying education as a "common benefit," the

Catholic petition lamented the fact that Catholics could not participate in this benefit without violating their conscience. Identifying the schools of the Public School Society as sectarian (Protestant) and anti-Catholic, the Catholics argued that their rights were being violated by their own city government.

Winding its way through New York City's political bureaucracy, and suffering several defeats along the way, the proposal finally arrived in the state senate in Albany and was in turn handed over to one of Seward's advisors, John Spencer, for study. Spencer's report changed the very nature of the debate. Instead of openly endorsing the Catholic appeal for common funds, he argued that it was unfair that the Public School Society should be allowed to maintain their monopoly on the education of New York City's poorest children. He cast the debate not as an argument about religion and public education, but as one over who controlled local schools. Essentially, Spencer held that the public schools should be under the control of the local public, not a self-perpetuating board of directors like that of the Public School Society. The local public would be free to determine the content of moral and religious training in their schools.

Hughes and the Catholics were, of course, pleased with Spencer's report. A bill was introduced to the state senate enacting Spencer's recommendations, but it was repeatedly tabled for future discussion by opponents of the effort and those who wanted to await the November elections before taking any action. When the assembly adjourned in May of 1841 the school issue had generated much heat, but no decision had been made. With the November elections so close on the horizon, Hughes and his opponents both took every opportunity to argue their case before different legislative committees and public gatherings. After much complicated political maneuvering, Hughes put forth an independent ticket in the November elections nominating five Catholic candidates for state office. In the end, the election was a huge victory for the Democrats, but also for Hughes and the Catholics. The only Democrats who lost were the ones who failed to gain Catholic endorsement, thus the power of the Catholic vote was on dramatic display for all to see.

Hughes' foray into so obviously a political matter prompted nativists to denounce him personally, and provided fodder for those who were already suspicious of a Catholic plot to gain control of America.[21] The anti-Catholic press warned that this was one more step in the Catholic plot to unite church and state. Hughes' independent ticket made tangible a fear that while widespread had up to then lacked embodiment, namely that Catholics were trying to take over America. Political cartoonists mocked Hughes by picturing him as the new dictator of New York. Thus, in the first round of the ongoing bout between religious and public school advocates, being politically active as citizens, supposedly something that faith-based school advocates would miss out on in their isolated institutions, in fact resulted in more trouble for them.

Beyond obvious examples of political activity and other measures of civic engagement, critics of religious schooling have argued that in pulling out of public institutions advocates have shortchanged the democratic dialogue the schools supposedly promote. The history of religious schooling, however, suggests just the opposite is true. Religious communities, as they embraced the idea of building their own schools, participated in precisely the kinds of debate their critics accuse them of squelching. We can see this especially clearly in the American Jewish community's debate over the day schools. First in Orthodox, then later in both Conservative and Reformed circles, Jewish Americans struggled to balance their religious and political identities. Since at least as far back as the debate between rabbi Isaac Leeser and civic activist Isidore Busch in the middle of the nineteenth century the language of citizenship, rights, liberty, and responsibility was very much part of their deliberation. Leeser worried that Jewish children would be subject to coercion in the public schools, but businessman and philanthropist Busch was more concerned with what he saw as the inevitable, if unintended, results of day-school education; namely, outbreaks of anti-Semitism and second-class citizenship for Jews. The Leeser/Busch debate foreshadowed the intercommunity conversations of Orthodox, Conservative, and finally Reform Jews of the twentieth century. While some members of these various communities have held that building their own schools was the best option for their communal well-being, others argued that support for public institutions was the better avenue. Though this matter is still, to some extent, unresolved, the dialogue about schooling and democratic living has clearly not been stifled. Both within their subcommunities and with external critics and observers, advocates of religious schooling have been very active in debates about education in America, and have, in their own ways, been active in trying to improve education for all Americans.

THE SOCIAL DIVISION CHARGE

Let us assume that faith-based schooling can produce active citizens capable and willing to discharge their duty. This still begs the question of whether or not what they are doing is good for America. In the present context, good for America has meant that it serves the goal of national unity. Involved in public affairs or not, after all, faith-based schooling is still *sectarian*. Surely, the critics warn, this bodes ill for how future generations of citizens will get along with one another. Before examining the way advocates of religious schooling have answered this criticism, there are several empirical points that are worth noting. First, public attitudes on this issue are somewhat complicated. The 1986 Gallup Poll of the Public Attitudes Toward the Public Schools noted earlier found that only 4 percent of Americans cited learning to get along with other people as one of the chief reasons for getting an education. Ten years later, when asked to consider possible purposes for America's public schools 13 percent said that promoting cultural unity among Americans was either not too important or not important at all. On the one hand, a full 86 percent thought that it was important for the schools to promote that unity is noteworthy, but it is perhaps telling that for this later survey the list of purposes for public schooling was provided by the questioner. Respondents were not asked to come up with the reasons for supporting public schools on their own. Cultural unity is important to Americans, yes, but it is not necessarily what they thought of first when asked about the public schools.

Second, the social division charge assumes that religious schools are substantially more homogenous than public schools. Religiously, of course, that is probably true. But as some advocates of private schooling have pointed out, on other measures of heterogeneity private and religious schools do not lag that far behind their public counterparts. Consider the following percentages, all taken from the National Center for Education Statistics 2002 report on the conditions of education in America. At first glance, public schools seem to be doing significantly better in terms of establishing the conditions in which students of different racial backgrounds may come together. Only 1 out of every 25 public schools in America have less than 1 percent minorities among their student population, while 14 percent of private schools do. Among non-Catholic religious schools, almost 1 out of 4 institutions have virtually no minority students. A more focused look at the evidence, though, suggests a different picture. About 36 percent of both public and private schools have a concentration of minority students ranging from 1 to 10 percent of their entire student body. Though there is considerable variation among private schools (almost 50 percent of Catholic schools have a 1 to 10 percent range) almost one-third (30 percent) have the same concentration. If we look at increased concentrations of minority students, religious schools once again do not fall too short of the public school accomplishment. While 20 percent of public schools have a minority concentration of 11–30 percent (a significant range, to be sure) 19 percent of Catholic and 21 percent of other religious schools also fall somewhere within this range. Only about 13 percent of public schools have minority concentration ranging from roughly a third to half. Among religious schools, those numbers are 5 percent for Catholic schools and 9 percent for other religious institutions.[22]

Finally, it is worth noting that numerous advanced societies around the world have a more pluralistic educational scene than America. Several European countries, for instance, use public money to support nongovernment and religious schooling, and these societies are not coming apart at the seams. Though practitioners from the various religious communities have not often appealed to the experience of these other countries, in their handling of the social division charge, sympathetic scholars have amassed considerable evidence against the idea that educational pluralism disrupts social order. For instance, Charles Glenn has noted that the concern over social unity, which has been sounded for more than 200 years, still lacks any solid historical support. Having examined the social, political, and legal arrangements of schooling in dozens of countries around the world, he notes that the vast majority of these countries allow for parents to send their children to various forms of non-public schools, including religious institutions, and do so without significant social harm. In fact, in some cases the quest to promote national unity through a common school system was a major cause of social tension and disorder. In his aptly titled *The Myth of the Common School*, Glenn showed how the very idea that a common school experience could be formative for national loyalty itself trampled on the views and preferences of various groups of citizens. The contention that common schools are by default the most democratic, and democracy building, institutions is more assertion than reality. Many advanced Western democracies have found ways to institutionalize educational pluralism and parental choice without tearing apart the social fabric of the nation. The key seems to be the careful designing of schooling system coupled with public accountability. Religious and denominational schools can still be subject to public regulation and support, material or otherwise, and can be linked to the acceptance by the school of democratic virtues such as tolerance or equality. For Glenn, educational pluralism is a necessary feature of respecting the rights of parents in a free society, and a reasonable measure of public accountability will prevent the anticipated negative effects such pluralism is supposed to have on social order.[23]

On a more theoretical level, the charge that religious schooling, or any religious behavior for that matter, is always socially divisive, and that because it is a source of division it is somehow inconsistent with democratic living is itself open to debate. Religiously motivated action in the public realm is not automatically more divisive than other courses of action. Nor does religiously based social division mean that society is doomed to repeat the religious wars of the past. Indeed, as government activity expands more into the lives of citizens, strong communities and institutions that stress independent action may be a helpful antidote to government intrusion.[24]

All that said, the criticism aimed at religious schooling over this issue has been both vocal and constant. Advocates, too, especially practitioners on the front line of this criticism, have responded in numerous ways. First, they have correctly perceived that this argument has multiple levels. While public schools have been heralded as temples of diversity where students from various subcommunities mingle with one another, religious school advocates have questioned whether or not they have actually accomplished that goal. Even in the proceedings over the Oregon school law, advocates for the Society of Sisters denied that the "common schools were much of a melting pot." Advocates of Jewish day schools, too, noted that most public schools in the 1940s and 1950s were neighborhood schools, and thus probably had only a limited sort of "pluralism" to begin with. Residential communities in this country tend to be segregated by race and class especially, and thus the assumption that public schools have always been intersections for intercommunity meetings may be more intention and wish than reality. Second, they have also denied that this separation is something they want. Ethnic or religious ghettoes have never, according to religious schooling advocates, been their goal. Here again the Jewish case is noteworthy because of its intra-community nature. Advocates of the Jewish day schools often pointed out that old-world ghettoes had not emerged as a product of Catholic, Lutheran, or Episcopal schools in America, and that American Jewry would surely follow a similar course. The general lack of structural prohibitions coupled with other mechanisms for contact between various communities, including sports leagues and commerce, would surely promote contact with those outside the subcommunity. Homeschoolers, too, have pointed to the myriad of ways they come into contact with their public school peers. The increasing cooperation between the homeschooling community and public institutions such as local high schools and community colleges has only amplified the intercommunity connections. Many homeschoolers take specific classes at public institutions, and in some places participate in extracurricular activities through the public schools.

Homeschoolers also pointed to the increasing diversity within their movement as a means stressing their opportunities for interaction with other racial and ethnic groups. The Homeschool Court Report for July/August of 2001 was dedicated to exploring cultural and racial diversity in Christian homeschooling. They point to increasing numbers of African-American homeschoolers (between 30,000 and 50,000 estimated in 1999) and the growth of networks and support groups dedicated to the minority homeschool experience. For their part, leaders in the African-American homeschooling community point out that they do not mean to discriminate against whites, but the occasional encounter with racism coupled with the strength that comes from the common experience and cultural heritage of African-Americans justifies their separate support groups. Of course, the existence of segregated networks may only reinforce the charge that homeschoolers are culturally isolated.[25] Nevertheless, Michael Smith, HSLDA's cofounder and second president, pointed to the increasing diversity at national and state conferences as evidence that homeschooling is not just a manifestation of "white flight" from public education.[26] He likened the relationship between the predominantly white movement and the "new pioneers" in minority homeschooling to a passage in the fourth chapter of Ecclesiastes promoting cooperation:

> Two are better than one, because they have a good reward for their labor. For if they fall, one will lift up his companion. But woe to him who is alone when he falls, for he has no one to help him up. Again, if two lie down together, they will keep warm; but how can one be warm alone? Though one may be overpowered by another, two can withstand him. And a threefold cord is not quickly broken.

RELIGIOUS SCHOOLS, DISSENT, AND AMERICAN LIFE

It is in their response to the charge that they promote social divisions that we begin to see the outline of the positive justification advocates of faith-based schooling have developed over the years. This is not so much a part of their motivation for religious schooling, but rather an affirmation of the role their schools play in American education and political life. On the educational level they argue that their schools have several advantages, some of which we have already mentioned. Most importantly, their institutions do not sideline religious and moral development, which, as we have seen, is of major importance to their worldview. Less subjectively, they also claim to save money for taxpayers while at the same time contributing to the financial support of public education. Additionally, they claim to model a more effective and responsive form of administration in that their institutions tend to be less bureaucratic. The teachers in religious schools, their advocates claim, have more time to concentrate on academics because they are not bogged down by government officialdom. In short, they just plain have better schools.

More recent advocates, especially in the homeschooling community, have argued that in providing competition to the government monopoly they contribute, perhaps somewhat indirectly, to improved education all around. Advocates of Jewish day schools pointed to their schools as evidence that all American school children could handle a heavier and more demanding course load than many public schools provided. They saw their institutions as leading the way in raising the academic bar for American schools more broadly. Though it is difficult to point to specifics without getting caught up in pedagogical debates about the best ways to teach reading or math, it is nevertheless true that even some public school advocates have praised private and religious schools for their innovation and commitment to a different model of education. During the Oregon school controversy, Commissioner of the Department of Education P.P. Claxton was quoted in favor of the place of nonpublic schools in keeping the public system from being too autocratic.[27] More recently Rod Paige, Secretary of Education from 2001–2005, also affirmed the track record of private and religious schools as an alternative delivery system for education that benefits all Americans.[28]

Politically, at the basis of much of the criticism of religious schooling is a suspicion that religious communities build their own schools because they do not want to encounter the "other." They are ideological and spiritual purists, afraid of contamination from those not like them. In the minds of religious schoolers, however, they *are* the other. They see themselves not as purists afraid of confrontation, but as beleaguered cultural (if not numerical) minorities practicing their right to dissent. Of course, dissent is not often associated with institutions bent on defending and promoting religious orthodoxy, but on a political level that is how advocates see their actions. It is, for them, about freedom of conscience and freedom of religion. They are acting in accord with the liberty guaranteed them by America's political heritage. In their view, it is the public school monopoly, with its insistence on standardization and uniformity, which threatens authenticity, pluralism, and freedom itself.

The basic logic to this argument was put forward by John Stuart Mill in *On Liberty* as early as 1859: "A general State education is a mere contrivance for molding people to be exactly like one another; and as the mould in which it casts them is that which pleases the predominant power in the government or the majority of the existing generations; in proportion as it is efficient and successful, it establishes a despotism over the mind . . ."[29] Homeschool advocate Chris Klicka appropriated Mill to argue that the use of America's public schools to instill a uniform set of political and religious values "poses a serious threat to the marketplace of ideas and the integrity of the democratic process."[30] At stake was the very diversity the public schools claimed to appreciate and promote. Whether it is Catholics claiming that the public schools were too Protestant, or conservative Protestants perceiving that the schools are too secular, advocates of religious schooling have repeatedly argued that the public schools simply do not make room for their worldview. Thus, any form of nonstate-sponsored education is not a flight from diversity but is actually a means of protecting and ensuring it.

Farris and Woodruff elaborated on this point by stressing the independent thinking that has always been a part of American national character. They argue that a centralized education creates a compliant population trained to be supportive of the government's agenda:

> . . . genuine education is potentially subversive in that it may lead a person to disagree with his or her government. This subversive tendency is, paradoxically, the only safeguard of our liberty this side of the Divine. We cherish our right to disagree with our government. We need it. It is, therefore, a potential or actual conflict of interest for the government to control education. The extent of the conflict increases in direct proportion to the degree of governmental, and especially federal, control. Precisely because it is not controlled by the government, homeschooling is uniquely situated to foster the continuation of our rich and honorable tradition of civil opposition, preserving the things we value most in a free society and eliminating the things that threaten the foundation of liberty.[31]

It is one thing for advocates of religious schooling themselves to make such arguments. They are, after all, members of religious communities and have a vested interest in safeguarding the transmission of their beliefs and practices to the next generation. But it is not just advocates and other interested parties that have defended the rights of parents and religious communities to build their own schools. The elements of the democratic case for religious education are all present in Justice

McReynolds' majority opinion for the Supreme Court in the *Pierce* decision. One of the most notable aspects of that case, however, is that it was at least partially decided on a somewhat more narrow legal issue. Representatives for the Society of Sisters and the Hill Military Academy, cooperating petitioners in challenging Oregon's compulsory attendance law, had argued that the material and business interests of their respective clients would suffer under the conditions created by the 1922 law. If all students are required by law to attend public schools, it follows that private schools will soon be out of business. The court agreed: " . . . without doubt enforcement of the statute would seriously impair, perhaps destroy, the profitable features of appellees' business and greatly diminish the value of their property."[32] McReynolds went on to identify the business the school was engaged in (education), the fact that it owned property, and that it was remunerative, with an annual income in excess of $30,000. He also argued that the material interests of the school, and therefore all those in business with it (teachers, families, etc.) had already been impacted by the law. Neither the Society of Sisters nor the proprietors of Hill Military Academy could be deprived of their property without due process. The business angle was a significant aspect of the legal case, with all sides making reference to the various factors involved.

The legal specifics of property deprivation aside, the petitions made by both sides show that everyone was aware that other issues were at stake. Willis Moore, Oregon's assistant attorney general, argued that the state stood "in the position of *parens patriae*," and therefore exercised "unlimited supervision and control" over the occupation and conduct of anyone dealing with minors. Representatives for Governor Pierce acknowledged that the underlying issue was the authority of the state and parents over minor children:

> Under all governments, even those which are the most free and democratic in their character, the citizen must always owe duties to the State; and it necessarily follows that the State has an interest in making it certain (which can only be done by appropriate legislation) that the citizen is fitted, both in mind and body, to perform these duties. The discretionary powers of a State are broad enough to permit it to decide that compulsory attendance at public schools is a proper "precautionary measure against the moral pestilence of paupers, vagabonds, and possibly convicts." (Parenthesis and quotations are in the original.)

They continued:

> The voters in Oregon might also have based their action in adopting this law upon the alarm which they felt at the rising tide of religious suspicions in this country, and upon their belief that the basic cause of such religious feelings was the separation of children along religious lines during the most susceptible years of their lives, with the inevitable awakening of a consciousness of separation and a distrust and suspicion of those from whom they were so carefully

guarded. The voters of Oregon might have felt that the mingling together, during a portion of their education of the children of all races and sects, might be the best safeguard against future internal dissentions and consequent weakening of the community against foreign dangers . . . It would therefore appear to be both unjust and unreasonable to prevent them from taking the steps which each may deem necessary and proper for Americanizing its new immigrants and developing them into patriotic and law-abiding citizens.[33]

Arguments put forth by the Society's legal advocate William Guthrie also acknowledged the business and commerce aspects of the case, but his more far-reaching analysis dealt with the freedom of advocates of private, including religious, schooling. Arguing that the teaching of disloyalty or subversion was already illegal, and that the Governor's claims to the contrary were "a mere chimera," Guthrie argued that private schools, religious or secular, could certainly instruct students "in any fundamental principles of freedom and democracy or in reverence and righteousness." The public schools had no advantage over faith-based or other private institutions when it came to Americanizing students, and, Guthrie pointed out, no evidence had shown otherwise. Furthermore, the rights of both parents and children to support private schools were under assault by Oregon's legislation. "Reflection should soon convince the court that those rights which the statute seriously abridges and impairs are of the very essence of personal liberty and freedom. In this day and under our civilization, the child of man is his parent's child and not the State's."[34]

Justice McReynolds, writing for the court, agreed with Guthrie. It was, to him,

entirely plain that the Act of 1922 unreasonably interferes with the liberty of parents and guardians to direct the upbringing and education of children under their control . . . The fundamental theory of liberty upon which all governments in this Union repose excludes any general power of the State to standardize its children by forcing them to accept instruction from public teachers only. The child is not the mere creature of the State; those who nurture him and direct his destiny have the right, coupled with the high duty, to recognize and prepare him for additional obligations.[35]

Guthrie and McReynolds both acknowledged that property rights and material interests aside, the rights of parents were at least as important, and perhaps more so, than any of the other considerations in this case. Even though the *Pierce* decision did not secure the existence of religious schooling until 1925, the sentiments and claims made by Guthrie and endorsed by the court had been made much earlier. Indeed, the language of a right to private schooling predates the legal squabbles and learned opinions of the early twentieth century. True, after 1925 advocates of religious schooling could rely on the protections inherited from the *Pierce* decision, but to assume that every time the concept of a "right" surfaced in their justifications they mean to claim a legal privilege is to miss the way post-*Pierce* sentiment coincides with pre-*Pierce* sentiments about private education and parental responsibility. When John Hughes set out to defend Catholic schools, he did so not with precise exegesis of the law, but by appealing to broader public sentiments such as freedom, fair-mindedness, and the importance of family. Hughes was not only an effective speaker and motivator, but also a fine strategist. He understood that the real issue was that the public perceived Catholics as less than 100 percent Americans, and that Catholic refusal to attend the public schools reinforced that perception. A committee report designed to explain to the general public the Catholic position made it clear that Catholics were not seeking special treatment, but only equal treatment as American citizens. "We are Americans and American citizens. If some of us are foreigners, it is only by the accident of birth. As citizens, our ambition is to be Americans; and if we cannot be so by birth, we are so by choice and preference . . . We hold, therefore, the same ideas of our rights that you hold of yours. We wish not to diminish yours, but only to secure and enjoy our own."[36] Catholics, he argued, were merely acting on the rights guaranteed by the constitution:

> . . . first of all I would direct your attention to the number of times in which he (public school advocate Hiram Ketchum) repeats that the petitioners are Catholics. He twists and turns that in a variety of ways, in order to convince the Senators, that though we applied in the character of citizens, that advantage was to be taken away from us, and we were to be clothed before that honorable body with our religious character . . . he has exerted himself in vain to fix on us the epithet of Roman Catholics, when we appeared in the character of citizens, and when our right to worship God according to the dictates of our conscience had been already, a priori, recognized by the constitution of the country. And I ask is there any crime in being a Roman Catholic?[37] (parenthesis mine)

Nearly a century later, in the events and rhetoric surrounding the *Pierce* case, John Lapp and Detroit Bishop Michael Gallagher argued that educational monopolies, almost by definition, violated the rights of any dissenting citizen. The state, they argued, was not to be understood as an end to itself, but merely as a means to an end, namely liberty. The state, then, could not act in such a way as to hinder the liberty of her citizens. Any attempt to monopolize education was interpreted as hindering the liberty of parents by suppressing their right to oversee their children's education.

> The most sophistical argument that was brought against us by the leaders of this movement was that the public school is an American institution, and that therefore it was good enough for all Americans, and that anyone who would not uphold and support this American institution was un-American. One answer that we gave to this argument was that any institution, or any movement, to deserve the name "American" should accord with the fundamental principles

upon which this government was founded. If it were antagonistic to the principle of liberty, then, not only could it not be called American, but it was clearly un-American, and this movement was designed to deprive Catholic parents of the right to give their children their religious education. We proceeded to show that this was depriving them of a liberty guaranteed to them by the principle of liberty on which our government is founded.[38]

Gallagher went on to argue that in exercising their rights, Catholics were acting within the best traditions of American education:

> ... when parents establish schools to educate their children according to the dictates of their consciences, they are acting as Americans. They are using the freedom that the God gave them; the freedom that the Declaration of Independence says they have. They are acting in accordance with the fundamental principle of liberty, and, therefore, as far as the principle is concerned, the founding of such schools is just as American as the founding of the public schools.[39]

Later practitioners of faith-based education agreed, and though they could rely on the protections of *Pierce*, made larger appeals as well. Christian schooling advocate John Whitehead appropriated both Aldous Huxley's *Brave New World* and Hitler's Germany to show how schools can inculcate values to staggering degrees. He further argued that while most Americans assume there is significant freedom for parents to direct their children's education such is not the case. His own summary of America's educational history focused on the gradual displacement of parental responsibility for and authority over the education of their children by the state. "The acceptance of these assumptions, that public schools are more competent in the area of education and are therefore responsible for the education of children, has increased the public schools' control over the upbringing and education of American children while diminishing that of the family."[40] The public schools, Whitehead concluded, have a "virtual monopoly" on education. The solution, as he sees it, is to broaden the inalienable rights guaranteed by the first amendment to include values and belief formation, thereby giving parents a legal protection for directing their children's education.

The democratic case for religious schooling does not rest exclusively on the claim that monopolies by the state schools violate the rights of parents to direct the upbringing of their children. Religious schools, their defenders claim, are capable of producing good and loyal citizens just as the public schools can. Nowhere is this contention that religious schools could and would produce good, loyal citizens more clear than in the records of the Catholic struggle for their schools. In an oft-quoted line, the Bureau of Education, a division of the NCWC identified earlier, cites as one of its guiding principles that it supported "the platform that it is the duty of every American citizen to contribute to the support of public schools, but it is his right to send his children to any type of school he may wish provided such school is truly American in its teachings."[41]

Being "American in its teaching" could take several forms. For instance, the *Bulletin* asserted that Catholics would agree that English should be the language of instruction in all elementary schools.[42] More often than not, though, they simply pointed to the citizenship education program administered by the NCWC as evidence that their schools could not be un-American since the whole point was to promote citizenship and loyalty. They pointed to the widely distributed Americanization textbooks *Fundamentals of Citizenship* and *Civics Catechism* as evidence of their loyalty.

Catholics also argued that public education neglected the religious component of human development and was therefore incapable of providing the moral basis necessary for good citizenship:

> An education that unites intellectual, moral, and religious elements is the best training for citizenship. It inculcates a sense of responsibility, a respect for authority, and a considerateness for the rights of others which are the necessary foundations of civic virtue—more necessary where, as in a democracy, the citizen enjoying a larger freedom has a greater obligation to govern himself. We are convinced that as religion and morality are essential to right living and to the public welfare, both belong to the work of education.[43]

They denied that educational segregation was inherently bad for democratic life. American history showed that institutions of private education predated public schools, and that the graduates of such private schools had made valuable contributions to American life. Arguing that the founders of America had all been educated in private schools and that no one questioned their patriotism, Dr. James Ryan, a leading Catholic educator, condemned what he called the "nationalist idea" in education. This referred to the notion that the state had ultimate authority over the child, which he claimed was a relatively recent invention. The private school, which embodied the exact opposite of the nationalist idea, had proven itself a backbone of democracy every bit as effective, if not more so, than the public schools when it came to promoting democratic life. In his *Civics Catechism* Ryan devoted several pages to this issue, arguing repeatedly for the importance of religious training as a means of cultivating civic virtue and encouraging national progress.[44]

The years after World War I witnessed the publication of numerous essays detailing for the essential compatibility between American patriotic life and Catholic teaching. The sentiments that make democracy possible, such as faith in your fellow man, hope, and forgiveness, were all found wanting in the public schools, but were stressed by Catholic educators. One author went so far as to suggest that Lenten observation and meatless Fridays, long a feature of Catholic life, had prepared American Catholics for the deprivation of the war years when resources were redirected to the Armed Forces.

Not only was religion necessary for good citizenship, but also on a purely pragmatic level Catholic schools produced better citizens because they simply spent more time on civic education. As early as 1919 the NCWC charged the American public schools with neglecting civics. The schools, said the NCWC, reserved civic instruction for later grades, while the great majority of students dropped out of formal schooling by grade eight. Considering their own superior system, the NCWC called attention to the two civics textbooks in widespread use in elementary schools. They estimated that in the early 1920s only about 10 percent of public school students received formal civic instruction. By 1928 that number was essentially unchanged, with 15 percent of all public school students receiving some form of civic instruction. All of this meant that Catholic schools were actually doing a better job at promoting citizenship because they were reaching children before the majority of them left school, thus assuring that they received at least some civic instruction. Evaluating their own programs, the NCWC said, "that in the great majority of the parochial schools of the United States there is today being presented an elementary knowledge of our American democracy and of the rights and responsibilities of citizens under it."[45]

Advocates held that religious schools were capable of promoting citizenship through the curriculum and that the schools themselves were uniquely American. At the 1889 meeting of the National Education Association, Rev. John Keane of Washington, DC, asked whether or not Americans should educate their children in denominational schools, and set out to defuse the argument that good Americans would choose public schools because they were the backbone of democracy. Acknowledging that the schools were democratic institutions, Keane held that America was essentially a Christian nation. Therefore, Christian education actually served American interest.

> The intelligent Christian parent knows well that what ought to be true of every nationality within the pale of Christian civilization is preeminently true of ours—that the best Christian is sure to be the best American, and that the school which aims at sending forth his child a model Christian, in equal degree tends to send him forth a model American; and he knows, besides, that if under every form of government a man needs to be a good Christian in order to be fully trustworthy and self-sacrificing and faithful as a citizen, much more is that true in our blessed land of popular institutions . . . The schools in America ought to be the most truly Christian schools in the world.[46]

Advocates of Jewish day schools advanced similar arguments, the specific focus on Christianity in Keane's statements not withstanding. Always careful to be less critical of the public schools than their Catholic predecessors had been, they did admit that some Jewish families found the state's education "insufficient" for the needs of their children.[47] Focusing on just this issue, day school advocate Jack Cohen argued that religious schooling was actually a means of ensuring religious freedom and diversity. A religious community reinforced by its own school is, in his view, more likely to make their necessary contribution to American life more broadly. Community leaders Jacob Fried and Philip Rubin made similar arguments. Each held that a vibrant Judaism, made possible by the intense Jewish education available in day schools, would help to renew American respect for scholarship and ethical living. Jewish day schools could aid the spiritual strengthening of America, and as such served a positive purpose in society that the public schools could not.[48] What the advocates of day-school education sought was "harmonious growth" between Judaism and American life. Because the day schools were the only real means of maintaining continuity with Jewish tradition, the various supplementary education programs being so depressingly ineffective, they were the only hope for truly blending a strong Judaism with American life. Day schools were a "Torah environment" where the implementation of the principle of synthesis (blending Jewish life with American values and practices) was most possible.

Herein we see the honest conviction behind the day-school advocate's position that day schools were not parochial institutions aimed at segregating children. Consistent with their argument that day schools would serve only a small minority of American Jews, but that those Jews would serve as the leaven for the entire Jewish community, proponents of the day school held that their schools were vital for Judaism, and that Judaism had a contribution to make to American development. In essence, being a good American required them to be good Jews, so that Judaism could make its contribution to American life. What they sought was not the ghettoized Jew of their opponent's nightmare, but a genuine harmonization of Jewish and American culture in which both "sides" benefited.

Defenders of Jewish day school education argued that the tendency toward uniformity in American life would undermine the very promise of America. Instead of subsuming Jewish identity within Americanism, they wanted to add the best part of Judaism to an already robust conception of what it means to be an American: "The cohesion of the American people will not be endangered by such separate schools which will, naturally, have the same general program of education and will be based on the same principles of Americanism as are to be found in today's public schools, plus the additional knowledge required as a result of the loyalty to the children to their own separate group . . . "[49]

Nahum Goldman portrayed the struggle for maintaining Jewish identity in America as one expression of a larger resistance to the tyranny of the modern state.

No state can claim the exclusive loyalty of its citizens. This is the classic concept of totalitarianism in its worst form. A state is one of the great instruments of civilization, one of the many expressions of human civilization. There are many other instruments, morally and spiritually not less legitimate than the state, such as religion, family, etc. Nothing is more essential for the development of humanity . . . than to do away with this deification of the state and oppose with all force any claim to our total and exclusive loyalty.[50]

He saw the need for a system of dual loyalties in which American Jews could thrive. Patriots yes, loyal to America, yes, but this did not require an abandonment of their religious identity.

Will Herberg, in his justly famous book *Protestant, Catholic, Jew* argued that membership in one of these three religious traditions was the means through which Americans expressed their identity as Americans.[51] Advocates of religious schooling have made a similar claim. Strong attachment to their religious community, which is both part of the motivation for, and the outcome of, their educational choices, is understood as acting upon the best traditions of American political and social heritage. Far from being socially disruptive, religious schools both reflect and promote freedom, making possible the very diversity and pluralism that their critics claim they want to avoid. They do not see themselves as being at odds with America. To the contrary, as the next chapter will show advocates of religious schooling seek to attach themselves to many of the very symbols Americans revere.

NOTES

1. See Brian D. Ray and Nick Weller, "Homeschooling: An Overview and Financial Implications for Public Schools," in *School Business Affairs* (May 2003): 22–26. See also John T. Wenders and Andrea D. Clements, "Homeschooling in Nevada: The Budgetary Impact," available from the Education Consumers Consultants Network at http://www.education-consumers.com. See also the Council for American Private Education's Web site at http://www.capenet.org/index.html.

2. John Hughes, "A Review and Refutation of the Remonstrance of the Public School Society and the Argument of Hiram Ketchum," *New York Freeman's Journal* (June 1841): 6.

3. See Milton Himmelfarb, "Reflections on the Jewish Day school," previously cited. Himmelfarb also puts forth the claim, somewhat modestly, that perhaps there is a class bias here. If the critics of the day school have their way, he suggests, then private education would become the exclusive privilege of the rich. Although he doesn't carry through with this, his logic would mean that day school education was a democratization of private schooling, since it was not as expensive as the elite prep schools most people think of when they think of private education.

4. Alexander Dushkin, "The Role of the Day School in American Jewish Education," previously cited, 13.

5. Chris Klicka, "Charter Schools," *Home School Court Report* (January/February 2002): 1–9. Klicka also explores vouchers in this essay. The religious schooling community is split over the issue, with some seeing vouchers as a fair way to increase

the quality of all education through the benefits of competition, and others seeing them as an invitation for public, meaning government, oversight.

6. While all are agreed that more parental support for public education would be beneficial, it is not clear why the charge of abandonment should fall on those that have chosen, for whatever reason, to pull their children out of public schools. Surely, those parents whose children are in the public institutions should be held just as accountable, perhaps more so, for whatever lack of volunteer support the public schools face.

7. Michael P. Farris, "Abolish the Department of Education? Why Should Home Schoolers Care?" *Home School Court Report* 11 (1) (1995): 28.

8. A federally impacted area was one in which federal projects (dams, power plants, military bases, etc.) accounted for a large part of the workforce.

9. Michael P. Farris, "More than the Department—It's Time to Abolish the Federal Role in Education," *Home School Court Report* 11 (1) (1995): 4.

10. Fr. John Burke, correspondence to A. Duncan Yocum from February, 1923, in NCWC archives Box J42, Catholic University, Washington, DC.

11. James H. Ryan, correspondence from January 23, 1924, in NCWC archives Box 122, File 159D, Catholic University, Washington, DC.

12. The correspondence of the NCWC from the early 1920s contain several letters from various members of the Catholic hierarchy detailing plans to defeat the measure, including a meeting with President Harding in which he stated his own opposition to the measure, but nevertheless told Father John Burke of the NCWC that Catholics "would have to fight." See Fr. John Burke correspondence to Bishop Muldoon from February 1922, in NCWC archives Box 122, File 159D, Catholic University, Washington, DC.

13. See Smith and Sikkink, "Is Private Schooling Privatizing," *First Things*, previously cited.

14. Michael P. Farris and Scott Woodruff, "The Future of Home Schooling," *Peabody Journal of Education* 75 (1 and 2), 2000: 252.

15. HSLDA archives contain several self-congratulatory editorials and essays by organizational representatives as well. They continue to see this as one of their major victories and it surfaces in more than one account of homeschooler's political activities. For a more extended discussion of this incident, see Mitchell Stevens, *A Kingdom of Children*, previously cited.

16. This decision was handed down after this book had been delivered to Praeger. It is too early to tell what the long-range effects of the ruling will be, though the California Superintendent of Public Instruction has already announced that he does not believe homeschooling will be made illegal.

17. See HSLDA's national newsletter, *The Home School Court Report* (March/April, 1993): 21.

18. Chris Klicka, "The UN Convention on the Rights of the Child: The Most Dangerous Attack on Parents' Rights in the History of the United States," available through HSLDA's Web site at http://www.hslda.org/docs/nche/000000/00000020.asp.

19. See Michael Farris, "The Parental Rights Act: Establishing a Standard of Liberty," *The Home School Court Report* 11(2) (1995).

20. Chris Klicka, "Religious Freedom is Endangered But States are Fighting Back," available on line at http://www.hslda.org/docs/nche/000000/00000029.asp.

21. For examples of this literature see Samuel Morse, *Imminent Dangers to the Free Institutions of the United States through Foreign Immigration* (New York: E. B. Clayton, 1835). For an excellent analysis of anti-Catholic thought in American history see Ray Billington *The Protestant Crusade 1800–1860: A Study of the Origins of American Nativism* (New York: Macmillan, 1938).

22. *Private Schools: A Brief Portrait* (Washington, DC: National Center for Education Statistics, 2002).

23. Glenn has marshaled considerable empirical support for the idea that a common school system is not inherently necessary to promote social order and loyalty in a pluralist democracy. See his *The Myth of the Common School,* previously cited, or *Educational Freedom in Eastern Europe* (Washington, DC: Cato Institute, 1995). See also Charles Glenn, "Protecting and Limiting School Distinctiveness: How Much of Each?" in *School Choice: The Moral Debate,* ed. Alan Wolfe (Princeton, NJ: Princeton University Press, 2003).

24. See Christopher Eberle, *Religious Conviction in Liberal Politics* (Cambridge, MA: Cambridge University Press, 2002).

25. Additionally, the claim that the public schools promote diversity must strike advocates of religious schools as somewhat ironic. The "voluntary unity" the Educational Policies Commission praised in the 1950s as part of America's understanding of itself has a complicated history. It is worth remembering that many of these groups built their own schools precisely because the contribution they wanted to make to America's melting pot was not, in their view, welcome. Having left the public schools because they experienced them as hostile to their way of life to then be criticized for not promoting diversity must seem like a no-win situation.

26. Michael J. Smith, "Encouraging the New Pioneers," *Home School Court Report* 17(4), (July 2001). The passage quoted is from Ecclesiastes 4: 9–12.

27. Tyack, *The Perils of Plurlalism,* previously cited, discusses the various sources of opposition to the Oregon law.

28. See his 2003 interview with Baptist Press available at http://www.bpnews.net/bpnews.asp?ID=15707.

29. John Stuart Mill, *On Liberty* (Indianapolis, IN: Hacket Publishing Company, 1978): 105.

30. Christ Klicka, *The Right to Home School: A Guide to the Law on Parents' Rights in Education* (Durham, NC: Carolina Academic Press, 1998): 46.

31. Farris and Woodruff, "The Future of Homeschooling," previously cited, 253.

32. *Pierce v. Society of Sisters,* United States Reports volume 268, Government Printing Office, Washington, DC (1926): 531.

33. Ibid., 524–526.

34. Ibid., 517–518.

35. Ibid., 535.

36. See Ravitch, *Great School Wars,* previously cited, 48.

37. Hughes, *New York Freeman's Journal,* 1841, 40.

38. NCWC, "Bishop Gallagher's Able Defense of Catholic Schools," *National Catholic Welfare Council Bulletin* 3 (October 1922): 16.

39. Ibid., 17.

40. John Whitehead and Alexis Crow, *Home Education: Rights and Reasons* (Wheaton, IL: Crossway Books, 1993): 63.

41. NCWC, "Opening of N.C.W.C. Bureau of Education," previously cited, 9.

42. C.N. Lischka, "State Laws Affecting Parochial Schools," *National Catholic Welfare Council Bulletin* 3 (June 1921): 21.

43. NCWC, "Agreement of American Ideals and Catholic Teaching," *National Catholic Welfare Council Bulletin* 2 (November 1921): 28–29. See also George Johnson, "Contribution of Catholic Education to American Life," *National Catholic Welfare Council Bulletin* (August 1929): 7–10.

44. James Ryan, *Catechism of Catholic Education,* previously cited.

45. Elizabeth Sweeney, "Discharging the Duties of Citizenship," *National Catholic Welfare Conference Bulletin* (June 1928): 28.

46. John Keane, "Should Americans Educate Their Children in Denominational Schools." in *Denominational Schools* (New York: Kansas Publishing House, 1889): 10. Keane was one of the speakers at the 1889 National Educational Association meeting addressing the role of denominational schools in American education.

47. JDS advocates often went to great pains to argue that for a variety of reasons, their schools were not properly understood as parochial institutions. On the surface, this claim can seem disingenuous, and indeed, many of the critics held that issues of ecclesiology and administration aside, day schools were essentially parochial. Berkson held that the Jewish day schools, for all their differences with Catholic schools, are still segregating institutions and are therefore accomplishing the same objectionable ends as parochial schools. But a more careful reading of the advocate's position gives evidence of a more sophisticated argument. The lack of a centralized authority meant that Jewish day schools were largely under the direction of local bodies. Groups of parents, educational boards, and less frequently specific synagogues, were the driving force behind the day schools. Even Torah Umesorah did not own or even control the day schools they founded and sponsored. The ultimate authority and locus of decision-making rested with local individuals and school boards. Indeed, Dushkin and Engelman's national survey, conducted in the latter half of the 1950s, showed that 77 percent of the day schools were not under the control of a synagogue and represented the "parent-society" type of school. While this may appear to be a minor point, day school advocates were responding to what they perceived had been a point of contention between American society and Catholic parochial schools, namely, control by a hierarchical, and perhaps even foreign, body. Day schools, it was argued, were under no such influence. See Isaac Berkson, *Theories of Americanization,* previously cited. See also Gershon Gelbart, *Jewish Education in America: A Manual for Parents and School Board Members* (New York: Jewish Education Committee of New York), 1963.

48. Jack Cohen, *Jewish Education in Democratic Society* (New York: Reconstructionist Press, 1964); Jacob Fried, "Public School or Jewish Day school," *Congress Weekly* (May 25, 1953): 11–12; Philip Rubin, "Why Jewish Day Schools," *Congress Weekly* (September 8, 1958): 12–14.

49. Nahum Goldman, "Jewish Education and the Future of Jewish Life in the Diaspora," *Jewish Education* 33 (Winter 1963): 76.

50. Ibid., 80.

51. Will Herberg, *Protestant, Catholic, Jew* (Garden City, NY: Doubleday and Company), 1955.

5 Joining America's Civil Religion

Educational activists were busy in the early 1980s. The institutional mobilization required to get the newly opened Education Department moving occasioned a debate about the direction of American education in general. Then in 1983 the National Commission on Excellence in Education released their report entitled *A Nation at Risk*, likening America's public schools to an act of war by a foreign power. The provocative language of this report guaranteed it media coverage, and thus education, always a contentious topic in America, was once again on everyone's mind. More than just starting conversation, *A Nation at Risk* also embraced and promoted a sense of crisis. The language of indictment and decline dominated the public educational lexicon, and numerous prescriptions for improving America's schools were discussed. One of the major efforts to shore up America's schools revolved around the establishment of national standards that would guide teachers in classrooms all across the country. Lynn Cheney, then the director of the National Endowment for the Humanities (NEH), charged a number of academics and educators with developing these standards for different fields of study. For American history, the NEH and the Education Department turned to the National Center for History in the Schools (NCHS) under the direction of Professor Gary Nash at the University of California, Los Angeles.

In 1994, just before the standards were released, Cheney, who had by then moved on from her tenure at the NEH, savaged the very product she had commissioned. The standards, she argued, exalted political correctness and multiculturalism at the expense of "traditional" history. Her essay, published in the *Wall Street Journal*, brought public attention to what might have otherwise passed without much comment. Senator Bob Dole of Kansas attacked the Standards in a speech to the American Legion, and the entire senate voted 99–1 to condemn them. The Standards themselves were revised and rereleased, but are now known for the controversy they caused more than anything else.[1]

The conflagration over the National History Standards generated more heat than light. Though the conflict presented an opportunity for talking about the purposes of learning history, the debate instead focused on who should be included in the bullet points of a given lecture. It reinforced the idea that history is a list of names, dates, and locations to be memorized and stored away: Columbus sailed in 1492; George Washington was the first president. These statements are true enough, but surely they are not the whole story. Columbus did indeed sail in 1492, but does saying he "discovered" America do a disservice to the native people groups who were already here? Does American history begin with Columbus' voyage, or thousands of years before with the first people to inhabit the "New" World? This is the sort of question that separates traditional history from what is often characterized as "revisionist" history. Though usually discussed in oppositional terms, traditional and revisionist history share many tools and methodologies. Both require careful documentation and sifting through data in a search for patterns. Both seek some illumination from the past for the quandaries of the present. To say that it is a matter of perspective sounds minimizing, as if the distinction was ultimately unimportant. Nothing could be further from the truth. It is a matter of perspective, yes, but that is no small consideration. When approaching America's past, advocates of traditional history see a sometimes sputtering but still coherent narrative moving in the direction of liberty. That movement has stalled, at times, but the overall trajectory is clear. America is the land of the free, and our history is the gradual unfolding of that basic premise. The heroes of this story are those individuals, usually men, who risked their own well-being in pursuit of a polity that could reflect and promote that ideal. Names like Washington, Jefferson, and Adams loom large in traditional history. Revisionist historians do not doubt the importance of these men, but they do widen the historical lens to include the experiences and contributions of women, minorities, and other disenfranchised groups. The revisionist project can be understood as the attempt to recover not only the history of marginalized groups, but also the role of marginalization itself in America's past. The grand narrative, they point out, focuses on a select few, and interprets history from their vantage point.

On the surface, the revisionist project appears to be one part of multiculturalism in American society, but in fact contemporary revisionists are not the first group to bring attention to the neglected aspects of traditional history. Advocates from virtually every system of religious schooling have argued that their own group's contributions have been overlooked or omitted from the general story promoted in the public schools. This is not to say that they are revisionists. For the most part they are not. Their goal is not to undermine or even to challenge the traditional narrative. Rather, they seek to secure their place *inside* America's traditional narrative by highlighting for their students the contributions made by members of their own religious community. In this way, their communal history joins rather than upends traditional history. This phenomenon has been noted before. Jonathan Zimmerman examined two streams of conflict in American education, one related to issues of science and one focused on inclusion and marginalization in American history. Taking up the latter, he notes, correctly in my view, that many of the marginalized groups in American society have been supportive of the grand narrative approach to America's past. This is true even when the revisionist historians who were bringing some of their contributions to light have been more critical of the traditional approach. To some marginalized groups, being part of the grand narrative is preferable to seeing it disintegrate.[2]

Becoming part of the grand narrative, however, is not so easy, particularly for those who have left (or been forced out of) the primary institutional setting in which that narrative is told. In most cases, members of these marginalized communities have produced their own resources, including textbooks or other supplementary materials, for use in their schools. Textbooks from Catholic schools have been the subject of several studies. In his work on periods of conflict over the content and production of history texts, Joseph Moreau argued that American Catholics set out to produce their own history texts, stressing their unique role in America's past.[3] Timothy Walch noted both similarities and differences between Catholic and public school textbooks.[4] As this chapter will show, Catholics were not the only religious community to embrace this strategy. Both Jews and conservative Protestants employed similar methods in an attempt to prove the essential compatibility between their specific religio-communal identity and America itself, a particularly worthy goal when that compatibility is under attack.[5]

CATHOLIC TEXTBOOKS AND AMERICAN HISTORY

Although American Catholics often made use of the textbooks produced for non-Catholic schools, the idea to develop their own materials was always present as well. Both the First and Second Provincial Councils of Baltimore in 1829 and 1833 respectively drew attention to the problem of anti-Catholic bias in public texts, and at the 1833 meeting plans were put in place for a committee composed of various members of the Church hierarchy to supervise the production of more suitable materials. Increased immigration to America on the part of European Catholics brought with it increased attention to Catholic materials for both home and school, with several

Catholic publishers opening in major cities. Catholic textbooks appeared for everything from spelling and math to history and astronomy.

Comparing nineteenth century Catholic and secular texts, Timothy Walch found many similarities. Nature, for instance, was consistently upheld as a source of educational value. The bee is upheld as an example of hard work while the grasshopper is the epitome of sloth and laziness. Other themes included American exceptionalism and the superiority of conservative social and economic values in the pursuit of economic mobility. The standard implication was that if one worked hard, at least middle-class rewards were available, a clear improvement over the lot many in America endured, especially those among poor and immigrant classes. But the Catholic and secular texts have significant differences as well. Even while endorsing the idea that America was the greatest nation in the world Walch found the Catholic presentation of American history to be "clearly partisan."[6] The Catholic texts stress the importance of Catholicism in making America the great nation it is. Whether that was accomplished through the exploits of specific Catholics, or a more summary argument of Catholicism's resonance with American life, the Catholic texts make clear that America's greatness has not come in spite of its Catholic population, but, at least in part, because of it.

One series of Catholic school books, the Excelsior series, published by W.H. Sadlier, Inc., issued several American history texts as part of its curriculum. The "Points to be Specially Noted" section of their 1894[7] text, *Sadlier's History of the United States* makes clear that in this "brief outline" special attention was paid to American Catholics, so that they are given their "proper place in the annals of our land." The first section of the book deals with the discovery of America, concentrating on Columbus but not unmindful of earlier voyages, and already notes the contributions of Catholics to American history.

Relating the frustrating rejections of Columbus' proposal by Venice, France, England, and Portugal, the Sadlier text suggests that while his immediate reception in Spain was favorable, many years passed before anyone acted on Columbus' ideas about a western route to India. According to the Sadlier text, an accidental meeting between Columbus and Father Juan Perez, a monk at the monastery of Santa Maria de la Rabida, set in motion events that culminated in America's discovery. At their meeting a conversation ensued, and Perez became convinced of the soundness of Columbus' proposal to the Spanish crown. Some years later when Columbus thought of leaving Spain because of inaction on his request, it was Perez that "restored him to confidence and hope." Perez made a midnight journey to Queen Isabella, who bid the priest to summon Columbus at once. What follows is well-known. Columbus received the necessary funds for his journey, and in 1492 sailed West across the Atlantic landing in what he thought was the West Indies but was, in reality, the coastal islands of the Americas.

In the Catholic school books, the search for and discovery of the New World was a thoroughly religious undertaking. Students were assured that Columbus and his crew "devoutly prepared themselves for the dangers of the deep by the reception of the Sacraments of Penance and Holy Eucharist." Columbus, sensing the guiding hand of God, sailed through the Atlantic, and over the discord of his crew, until on the shores of the island he christened San Salvador (Holy Savior) he fell to his knees chanting the "Te Deum." Erecting a cross on the island, Columbus took possession of the New World. Summing up the discovery of America, the Sadlier text taught that

> The discovery of America was pre-eminently a Catholic enterprise. In fact, Protestantism did not as yet exist. The voyage was made under the protection of the Blessed Virgin, and for truly Catholic motives, namely: first, to carry the light of Christianity to pagan lands; secondly, to raise funds sufficient to defray the expense of equipping a large army to rescue the Holy Sepulchre from the hands of the Turks. Such were the motives of Columbus . . . To make it, if possible, still more Catholic, the reigning Pontiff, Alexander VI, issued a Bull (May 9th, 1493) in which he laid it as an obligation on the Spanish sovereigns, to send to the newly found islands and continent "tried men who fear God, learned, and skilful, and expert, to instruct the inhabitants in the Catholic faith, and teach them good morals.[8]

The Sadlier text was not alone in its Catholic-laden history of America. Charles McCarthy's 1919 text assures readers that the "conspicuous facts" relevant to Catholics will be front and center in his narrative. Summing up his own approach in the preface, McCarthy wrote "[t]hus it is made clear that Catholics discovered, and, in a large way, explored these continents, that Catholics transferred civilization hither, that they opened to the commerce of Europe the trade of the Pacific, and that they undertook the conversion of multitudes of dusky natives, of whom few had risen to the upper stages of barbarism." Like earlier Catholic texts, he detailed the efforts of Father Perez, and adds several other members of the Catholic hierarchy to the list of Columbus' supporters, including the Dominican friar Diego de Deza and Cardinal Pero Gonzales, who first advocated Columbus' cause before the Spanish sovereigns. Spanish priests, bishops, and archbishops were, according to McCarthy, Columbus' best and most influential friends. This text also teaches that the discovery of America and the triumph of European civilization in the New World was a thoroughly Catholic effort stretching all the way back to the discovery and first settlements at Vineland around the year 1000. According to McCarthy, even that accidental discovery was the result of Norway's King Olaf's desire to have the Christian religion proclaimed in Greenland.[9]

Of course, at the time of Columbus' voyage, any religious motives would have been Catholic in origin because, as the texts point out, Protestantism did not yet exist. Though the Catholic texts acknowledge that America became a largely a Protestant nation, they also continue to stress the contributions made by Catholics to America's unfolding narrative. McCarthy stressed the intense patriotism of American Catholics, and this in spite of the fact that Catholics had been unjustly discriminated against in the years before war with England. The "patriotic conduct" of Catholics during the Revolution and the assistance of Catholic nations from Europe were credited with the beginnings of religious toleration. After the war and the election of Washington as the new nation's first president, Roman Catholics sent a collective letter of congratulations, to which Washington made the following reply:

> I hope ever to see among the foremost nations in examples of justice and liberality; and I presume that your fellow-citizens will not forget the patriotic part which you took in the accomplishment of their Revolution, and the establishment of their government, or the important assistance they received from a nation, in which the Roman Catholic Faith is professed . . . May the members of your Society in America, animated alone by the pure spirit of Christianity, and still conducting themselves as the faithful subjects of our free Government, enjoy every temporal and spiritual felicity.[10]

The general strategy, made plain by their treatment of men like Columbus and Washington, revolved around injecting Catholicism into critical or influential moments of American history. In a similar vein, these texts highlight the role of Catholics in the westward expansion of America in the nineteenth century. This strategy would be quite self-consciously identified in the tumultuous years following World War I. While Catholic schools were under frontal assault from legislation like that in Oregon, they continued to focus on the positive contribution Catholicism in general and parochial education in particular could make to American democracy. The National Catholic War Council (NCWC) *Bulletin,* for instance, makes much of Catholic support for the annual American Education Week sponsored by the United States Bureau of Education, the American Legion, and the National Education Association. This program, aimed at promoting citizenship and patriotism, called on all schools to devote more time than usual on the greatness of America, and was endorsed by the NCWC's Department of Education.

The Catholic program varied from year to year, but a recurring theme was the value of religious education, celebrated on "For God and Country Day." Patriotism and constitutional studies were also popular. Each day of American Education Week had a slogan aimed at promoting the place of Catholic education in America. For instance, Patriotism Day, which was celebrated almost every year through the 1920s, held to slogans such as "The tide of patriotism runs high in the Catholic school," or "Every Catholic school is a nursery of patriotism." Constitution Day, also a popular theme, promoted slogans like "The Catholic School stands for authority—the foundation of all government," and "Let us guard this priceless heritage of our age." Even the days set aside for celebrating the place of Catholic colleges in the United States focused on their place in American society, with slogans like "Catholic parish schools inculcate whole-hearted loyalty to America," and "The Catholic college is a bulwark against socialism and anarchy." While we cannot know what happened in individual schools, A.C. Monohan, director of the Bureau of Education for the NCWC, encouraged all Catholic schools to observe American Education Week and further encouraged Catholic support and participation in "any general programs" that may be held in their community.[11]

In short, Catholic texts stress the importance of individual Catholics as well as those of Catholics as a whole to argue that the historical record is on their side. In these books and programs, Catholics have always been good Americans, as non-Catholic notables like George Washington and Benjamin Franklin observed. The point here is not to dissect their use of evidence, or even to evaluate their general claims about history. It is to show one mechanism through which a religious community, at precisely the point in time when their place in America was under fire, asserted the value and worth of their community to America's history and identity. Catholics were not the only ones to feel this tension, nor were they alone in their remedy.

JEWS IN AMERICAN HISTORY

Like their counterparts in the Catholic community, advocates of all-day Jewish schooling also sought to use American history as one means of securing their place in society. The Jewish experience on this point is in some respects unique. During the Era of Great Expansion, most of the day schools were in one geographical area, namely New York City, which had stringent educational requirements mandating that the normal U.S. history curriculum be standard fare in all schools. This, of course, limited the time available to cover material related to Judaism in America. Perhaps because of this requirement, some observers have suggested that the Jewish day schools did less than they might have with regard to including Jewish material into their presentation of American history.[12] Further complicating the story is the fact that Jewish day schools served only a small fraction of Jewish children, the vast majority of which learned whatever they did about the Jewish experience in America in after-school programs or other supplementary education programs.

Nevertheless, the American Jewish community, or rather communities, did produce their own resources stressing their contributions to American life, and even made some efforts to incorporate them into the prescribed U.S. history curriculum. Rabbi Lee Levinger, in 1930, authored the first textbook on Jews in American history for use in Jewish schools, only to see it go through three revisions and more than a dozen printings over the next fourteen years. Levinger's text is somewhat narrower than his Catholic predecessors, but the overall purpose of the book is similar. Rather than telling American history with a special emphasis on the role of a particular group, Levinger produced a history of American Judaism, though, of course, the chronology and major events map onto American history more broadly. For example, Judah Touro, a name unknown to most American history books, is recognized as a business leader and philanthropist who "share[d] in America's struggle for liberty" (he was wounded in the Battle of New Orleans in 1815, and served under Andrew Jackson). Like the Catholic books, Levinger also elaborates on how Judaism's influence can be seen in American history, for instance in the political ideals of both the Deists and the Puritans, both of whom, in Levinger's telling, were particularly influenced by the Hebrew Bible.[13]

During Schiff's era of great expansion in the post-World War II era, educator and day school advocate Samuel Goodside, later the editor of *Yeshiva* magazine, extended Levinger's efforts and prepared a supplementary syllabus for teachers of social studies in Jewish day schools. Using as his basis the New York City Board of Education syllabus for public schools, Goodside set out to "provide teachers of secular subjects in Jewish all-day schools, in particular, and those in general education, in general, with a teaching aid that demonstrates the nature of the Jewish group and its contributions to our American heritage."[14] Seeking to integrate religious and secular instruction in one setting, Goodside's syllabus closely followed the program of instruction in public schools, supplementing it with material of particular interests to Jewish students. Citing both lack of information on Jews in the regular course of study, and misinformation in what material did exist, Goodside argued that the schools could not eradicate the bias and prejudice in society unless they took account of the many positive contributions Jews made to American society and culture. His stated goal, a "more harmonious American culture," was possible only if children learned to value difference and diversity. Jewish education should "teach children to have pride in their background and cultural inheritance" and yet also to develop a uniquely Jewish culture that could "fit" into American democratic society.[15] Goodside recognized that just producing good Jews was only the bare minimum requirement for Jewish schooling. It must also be evaluated on how well it satisfied the requirements of education in a democracy made up of numerous groups, each with their own particular characteristics and yet of part of the same general culture.

In his attempt to define American Jewish history, Goodside argued that "Jewish history in America is not that of a separatist group. It is the history of one component essential part of the whole American community in the development of land, life, and democratic ideology which makes the America we know today."[16] He then proceeded to point out the role of specific

Jewish groups in shaping American society and specific social institutions. His method here was simple enough. Goodside identified various admirable features of American life and stressed, sometimes with evidence and sometimes with conjecture, the influence of either the Jewish people as a whole, or more often, specific Jews. For instance, in a one-sentence reference to economic mobility, German Jewish peddlers are credited with decreasing the relevance of observable class distinction by producing and selling quality garments. Similar arguments are made for real estate, organized labor, and philanthropy, among others. More grandly, Goodside held that:

> Colonial Jews were the cogs in the wheels of the democratic process when the experiment of American democracy was demonstrated. These Jewish settlers proved that a minority can adhere faithfully to a religion abhorrent to the majority and yet be able to discharge all obligations of good citizenship. Truly, they helped test the value of a new enlarged policy of religious life for the first time in a modern state. They proved the practicability of freedom of worship as a right inherent to all mankind. It proved also that a majority group may work successfully with a minority group.[17]

Beyond the conjectures of the contributions made by Jews, Goodside argued that the very nature of political democracy rested on the concept of equality, a concept which he held was embodied in the Jewish principle of the brotherhood of man. Making a commitment to brotherhood and equality the basis of cherished American freedoms such as speech, association, and the press, Goodside was in fact crediting Judaism with part of the intellectual and social groundwork that made American democracy possible. Equality, as articulated in the brotherhood of man, also resulted in a commitment to reason over force and even the system of checks and balances between the three branches of government established by the Constitution! Far from being foreign to America then, in this program of study Judaism is actually the basis of much of what American's hold dear.

The method of the proposed syllabus was to follow the New York City Board of Education's course of study, adding in age appropriate lessons that point to the contributions of American Jews. For instance, second graders in New York City schools observe the birthdays of Presidents Lincoln and Washington, using those days to study the accomplishments of both men and also the cultural and political matrix in which they served. In Jewish day schools second graders study those same issues, but add elements of both presidential administrations that resonate with Jewish children. On Lincoln's birthday, social studies teachers in Jewish day schools are encouraged to draw parallels between the Emancipation Proclamation aimed at freeing African slaves and the exodus of Hebrew slaves from Egyptian bondage. This then permits further stories about the legendary leadership of Moses over the people of ancient Israel. An American hero is thus likened to a

Jewish hero, and significant events in America's past are likened to Israel's own ancient history.

Similarly, Washington's birthday occasioned lessons about Haym Solomon, a Jewish broker who, of his own financial means, supported the Continental Congress and the American Revolution.[18] Solomon loaned money to various Revolutionary leaders, provided supplies for American troops, and was even imprisoned by the British for a time as a spy against the crown. Solomon's contributions to the patriot cause were eventually honored with a statue of Washington, Solomon, and Robert Morris (another financier of the Revolution) paid for by the Patriotic Foundation of Chicago to be located in that city. A postage stamp with Solomon's likeness and the inscription "financial hero of the patriot cause" was also issued to commemorate his work.

Beyond presenting the stories of previously unsung heroes such as Haym Solomon, Jewish social studies also looked at the relationship between venerated American heroes and Jews. In the third grade, New York City school students were supposed to examine Columbus' voyage. In American public schools, such studies often take place around October 12, Columbus Day. The same is true in the Jewish day school syllabus. Students learn of the three-ship voyage across the Atlantic, but they also study numerous issues of interest to Jews. For Jewish students, the year 1492 is significant not just because of Columbus' voyage. It is also the year of the Spanish Inquisition in which the same King Ferdinand and Queen Isabella that financed Columbus expelled thousands of Jews who refused Christian baptism. Those Jews that accepted baptism were known as Morranos, and were suspected of secretly keeping their Jewish faith alive. Thickening the historical connections, other authors pointed out that Queen Isabella signed the expulsion papers the same day she signed Columbus' orders for the voyage, and that the majority of the direct financial support for the voyage came from Luis de Santangel and Gabriel Sanchez, two Morranos. Their contribution has been summed up in an oft-cited line, to the effect that "not jewels but Jews unlocked the gates of a hemisphere."[19] Further Jewish support for Columbus' voyage came in the form of astronomical tables and maps compiled by Jews and made available to Columbus before he left Spain. Golden and Rywell suggested that Columbus himself may have had a familial connection to Judaism, an issue to which the proposed New York City syllabus drew the attention of students several times. Columbus' background is uncertain, they admit, but they point to several passages of his personal correspondence that, in their view, raise the possibility of a Jewish family line on his father's side.

Similar motifs appear in the Jewish day-school syllabus material on George Washington, though no one makes the claim that Washington himself might have been Jewish. As early as second grade, school children in Jewish day schools learn of the relationship between Washington and the Jews of his day. For instance, at least two of the officers on his staff were Jews (Major Benjamin Nones and Colonol Isaac Franks). One of Washington's surgeons in Valley Forge, Phillip Moses Russel, later recommended by Washington himself, was Jewish. Great attention was also paid to three letters Washington himself wrote to various Jewish congregations that congratulated him on his election to the presidency. Congregations from Philadelphia, Richmond, Charleston, and New York joined together to send one letter, while Jewish congregations from Savannah and Newport also wrote letters to Washington. In his responses, Washington thanked each congregation for its adulation, and also affirmed the liberality of America's citizens with regard to making room for all groups of people. Other Jewish educators and leaders have also drawn attention to the role of Jews in American history, and praised these contributions as sources of authority and security in American political life. For instance, Lee Friedman argued that Washington's letters should rank with the Constitutional interpretations of Chief Justice John Marshall or Alexander Hamilton's *The Federalist*.[20] Goodside also encouraged social studies teachers in the day schools to once again, as they did with Lincoln, compare Washington to famous figures from Israel's past. Thus the first president is likened to Hebrew notables Moses, Joshua, Nehemiah, and Judas Maccabeus.

One of the most interesting factors of the Jewish day school program of study compared early American political organization to the Hebrew Commonwealth of old. The executive officer of American government, the President, was likened to the elective magistrate of the so-called Old Testament era known as the Judge. The Supreme Court, the final authority on legal interpretation was compared to the Sanhedrin, a council of seventy elders whose interpretation of the law was unimpeachable. Finally, the general assembly of the people was compared to the Congress. In short, the structure of America's government, while not taken directly from the history of Israel, mirrored the political structure of the Hebrew people, thus making democratic governance in America resonate with Hebrew history.

Beyond the specifics of the course of study in Jewish day schools, the larger strategy that guides the syllabus and many of their texts endorsed for use in day school classrooms, was to make plain the contributions of Jews to the western world. Advocates of Jewish day schooling, like their Catholic predecessors, used the history curriculum to do more than relate names and dates to students. They also tried to establish historical precedents for just how American they were.

BIBLICAL CHRISTIANITY AND AMERICAN HISTORY

Resources for those conservative Protestants that opt for religious schooling, either in the form of Christian day schools or homeschooling, are readily available. Besides the many Internet resale shops and home-study programs, there are correspondence courses, unit study programs, satellite schools, managed work texts, and, of course, "Complete Christian Curriculums." Two of the most prominent complete curriculums are A Beka Book and Bob Jones University Press' series for Christian schools.[21] It is worth noting that both curricula are associated with well-known Christian colleges. A Beka Book is a ministry of Pensacola Christian College, a Christian liberal arts college in Florida, and claims to be the largest publisher of Christian textbooks in the world. The college promises potential students that:

> Our instructors will never harm your faith; rather, they are dedicated to imparting a Biblical philosophy that will stay with you throughout your life, no matter what your vocation or calling. The spiritual and academic emphasis of PCC [Pensacola Christian College] is and will continue to be determined by the Word of God. You can count on this, and so can your parents. It is this philosophy that makes the difference and assures a high-quality Christian education.[22]

Bob Jones University in Greenville, South Carolina, is a well-known and often controversial college founded in 1927 as the vision of evangelist Dr. Bob Jones. According to the university's Web site, Jones meant to counteract the tendency he witnessed for students from Christian homes to begin doubting the Bible and losing their faith in colleges across the nation, Christian and secular alike. Both Bob Jones University and Pensacola Christian College stress their high academic standards, but both also make a point of identifying Christian maturity as the primary goal of their enterprise. This same philosophy of education influences the textbooks they produce that are embraced by Christian schools and many homeschooling families, as the inside cover of every A Beka Book textbook makes clear.

> A Beka Book, a Christian textbook ministry of Pensacola Christian College, is designed to meet the need for Christian textbooks and teaching aids. The purpose of this publishing ministry is to help Christian schools reach children and young people for the Lord and train them in the Christian way of life.[23]

Examining their U.S. history textbooks, along with civic and government texts, reveals further similarities between these two curriculums. In fact, several thematic lines emerge in these texts that bear directly on the way these books locate their audience in the American story. Both series employ a providential view of history. That is, they see a directed purpose in world events that, to the eyes of the faithful, supplies evidence for the hand of God in world history in general, and in American history in particular. Second, both series make much of the public influence of Christianity on America's early political and cultural elites. Finally, both series highlight the role of faith in the lives of notable American heroes, even if these men are not held up as exemplary Christian witnesses.

With regard to a providential view of history promoted by both series, both Bob Jones University's *United States History for Christian Schools,* and A Beka Book's *United States History in Christian Perspective: Heritage of Freedom* point out that the discovery of America came only when God deemed it appropriate. *Heritage of Freedom* declares that

> God, in His wisdom, allowed America to remain hidden until the Modern Age had dawned in Europe, bringing with it a number of important changes that would profoundly affect the course of American history. In the words of Alexis de Tocqueville, a French intellectual of the Modern Age, North America was discovered at just the right time, "as if it had been kept in reserve by the Deity and had just risen from beneath the waters of the Deluge."[24]

As for why the end of the fifteenth century was the right time for Columbus' voyage, the books explain that the age of world exploration coincided with Martin Luther's perhaps unwitting commencement of the Protestant Reformation. Many U.S. history texts discuss the social upheaval in Europe as part of America's own past, but these books identify the New World as a God-ordained refuge for "His people," usually understood to mean "Biblical Christians." Both texts make reference to the Roman Catholic persecution of early Protestants and portray the Reformation as the restoration of a more Biblically legitimate church. *Heritage of Freedom,* for instance, argues that Swiss Reformer John Calvin's ideological heirs made up a large portion of American's early immigrants and therefore exerted much influence on early American life. Protestantism is linked to freedom and liberty while Catholicism is routinely linked to coercion and "crushing" wars designed to thwart the spread of Biblical Christianity. The implication here is that Protestantism is a religion of freedom while Catholicism is the prerogative of kings and monarchies.

This implication is concretized in *Heritage of Freedom's* suggestion that the religious freedom pursued by these early Protestants preempted the political freedom guaranteed some years later in the American Revolution. The revivals of Biblical Christianity in the Great Awakenings are credited with reinvigorating the moral purity of the colonies and preparing the way for a kindred spirit that transcended denominational boundaries. "As never before, colonial Americans felt a sense of unity and responsibility, characteristics they would need to rule themselves wisely and well."[25] In this way, Biblical Christianity takes center stage at precisely the historical moment in which America's political fortune changes from colony to independent nation.[26]

The second theme, which is Biblical Christianity's influence on America's development as a free society, is better seen in the books on the Revolutionary War and its aftermath. These books suggest that key documents and events cannot be separated from the influence of Biblical Christianity. Regarding the Declaration of Independence, unanimously adopted by the

Continental Congress on July 4, 1776, A Beka Book's civics primer, *American Government in Christian Perspective*, sees several Christian elements shaping the famous document. God is acknowledged as the creator and ruler of the universe, which the authors interpret as consistent with the theological view of creation that signifies respect for the dignity of the individual, a key requirement for political freedom. Without this conviction, the book warns, humans exist only for the benefit of the state. The Declaration also identifies God as the judge of men and nations, a view consistent with Biblical Christianity. Summarizing the influence of Christianity on the Declaration, the authors cite approvingly John Quincy Adam's remark that the Declaration of Independence "laid the cornerstone of human government upon the first precepts of Christianity."[27]

Or consider Bob Jones University Press' discussion of the American Constitution. Identifying James Madison as the primary architect of America's most enduring political document, *United States History for Christian Schools* argues that Madison's own political thought took shape during his years at Princeton as he sat under the tutelage of "parson and patriot" John Witherspoon. Without discussing Witherspoon's views in great detail, the textbook suggests that his views on the sovereignty of God and the moral depravity of humanity influenced Madison and other framers of American government. In *United States History for Christian Schools* Madison designed the system of checks and balances that limit any one branch of government power because he took seriously the "degree . . . of distrust" made necessary by the fallen nature of humanity.[28] The influence of Christianity on the Constitution and the deliberations out of which it grew are summed up by James Madison in a passage the Bob Jones University textbook cites with approval:

> We have staked the whole future of American civilization, not upon the power of government, far from it. We have staked the future of all of our political institutions upon the capacity of each and all of us to govern ourselves, to control ourselves, to sustain ourselves according to the Ten Commandments of God.[29]

This section concludes with a presentation of three "major contributions" Christianity made to American government. First, Biblical Christianity promoted the idea of personal liberty, which the Bob Jones authors trace to Martin Luther and the Protestant Reformation that broke the spiritual and political monopoly of the Roman church. One sentence later this personal liberty is equated with Thomas Jefferson's "unalienable rights" with which the Creator endows men in the Declaration of Independence. Of course, most students of American history can cite Jefferson's passage by heart, but in *United States History for Christian Schools* this is understood as more than a general statement in favor of a deity. It is theological and political fact. Second, Protestant Christianity provided a tradition of dissent that manifests as "opposition to ecclesiastical and political authoritarianism."[30] Freedom from Rome is likened to freedom from England, and thus once again Biblical Christianity is at the center of American political life. Finally, the influence of the Bible upon society was so pervasive that even non-Christians could not escape its reach. Fully aware that many of the founders were less than orthodox with regard to Christian theology, these books argue that the culture as a whole was thoroughly Christianized, if not actually Christian. The Bob Jones University Press textbook closes by reminding students that the Christian legacy in America is not just history, but an inheritance that sorely needs to be owned in present-day America.

With regard to notable personalities, the books point to the lives of specific individuals that they can claim as their own that played an important part in shaping America. Instances of Christian piety in the lives of famous Americans serve to connect all members of the Christian faith with these American heroes. A Beka Book, for instance, displays a picture of George Washington in prayer during the winter at Valley Forge. The Home School Legal Defense Association's Generation Joshua initiative claims to teach civics and history, and it, too, draws attention to Washington's supposed piety and Christian character.[31] HSLDA does not produce its own textbooks, but it does invest heavily in civic education and political activism through programs like Generation Joshua or the Congressional Action Program, and, of course, Patrick Henry College near Washington, DC. Though these are generally more aimed at civics and activism, they do incorporate America's history, as their material on Washington makes clear. Part of their overall objective is to reinforce the idea that this nation was founded on Christian principles and that reading the primary sources, from the Constitution to various speeches, provides, in their view, irrefutable evidence that their particular religious convictions were, and should be, at the center of American life.

Of course, Washington is not the only founder worthy of exploration by homeschoolers studying America's past. Perhaps paradoxically, even more attention is paid to Benjamin Franklin's call for prayer during the heated exchange of the Constitutional Convention. Franklin, citing disagreements that threatened to derail the whole convention, urged his fellow attendees to "appl[y] to the Father of Light." He went on to cite the prayers, graciously answered, during the Revolution that protected the interests of the fledgling nation. Great attention is also paid to Patrick Henry, the "Voice of the Revolution." A hero to many Christian homeschoolers, Henry is credited with moving, by means of oratory, many of his listeners into the revolutionary camp. The Bob Jones University textbooks also make clear that Henry's oratorical ability, while partly inherited, was honed by hours of listening to famous preachers like George Whitefield and Samuel Davies. Biblical allusions as well as the tenor and rhythm of scriptures shaped Henry's speeches. The text even calls him the "American Joshua" and cites his famous speech in St. Johns Episcopal Church in which Henry preferred death to life without liberty.

The specific examples aside, the pattern that emerges in the Christian textbooks is one of highlighting the Christian, by which they mean Protestant, influences on early American life and character. Not only were some notable persons Christian (similar to claims made by both Catholics and Jews) but even the irreligious among the founders were surrounded by Biblical imagery and language. The same is true for America's founding documents. Christian or not, they were forged in a time and place in which the truths Biblical Christians adhere to shaped public life. In short, these texts imply that you cannot tell the story of America's past without recognizing the prominence of Protestant Christianity. And as the Bob Jones texts remind us, this is more than history; it is inheritance. This history belongs to modern-day Christians who are the keepers of the flame with regard to both Biblical Christianity and American character.

American history is always contentious. Names and dates might be readily agreed upon, but the context and implications of the events, personalities, and ideas that shaped this country can and have been seen from several different perspectives. The textbook, usually considered a work of summation rather than new analysis, is itself controversial precisely because it legitimates the material it presents. The mere act of deciding what to include, an editorial decision made necessary by space and time constraints, means that some people or events will not receive the attention they or others think warranted. But why should the teaching of American history be so important? Surely there are other topics on which religious epistemology might influence the content of a textbook, not least of all in the sciences, a field in which frequent and public clashes between religious adherents and secular school systems are almost expected. American history is important because it is more than a list of names and dates. It is the reservoir for national identity. The examples of celebrated historical figures are intoned to praise desirable attributes of character such as honesty or perseverance.[32] Political movements seeking action often call attention to specific events or characters from the past to legitimate their plans. Establishing continuity with history is particularly relevant for those social groups, like modern nations, whose collective identity encompasses people who may have little in common other than their ties to what Benedict Anderson famously called the "imagined community."[33]

"Imagined" is an especially appropriate word. In classrooms all across America, students are asked to imagine themselves into different parts of America's history. Especially in the primary years, students may act out great events from American history such as the first Thanksgiving or the Continental Congress. They memorize portions of documents or speeches such as Lincoln's Gettysburg Address or the preamble to the Declaration of Independence. To see how these are more than just clever pedagogical innovations, we can turn to Robert Bellah's influential statement on civil religion in America. He argued that participating in patriotic celebrations, or observing the birthdays of men like Washington or Lincoln was part of the promotion and cultivation of loyalty and patriotism in a society that needed the social glue not provided by more obvious sources such as religion or language. Seen in this light, the efforts of religious schoolers to link their histories to America's own history is an attempt to participate in the civil religion while simultaneously celebrating their community's distinctiveness. In fact, their whole effort is to show how that distinctiveness is, and always has been, a part of American life.

What makes the efforts of advocates of religious schooling unique on this score is that, by definition, they have removed their children from the primary institutional means used to retell our collective history and thus forge a collective identity. That is, they have by their own initiative opted out of the primary institutional means that confers upon citizens their legitimate place in American public life, built competing institutions, and then used those institutions to make the case that they were, separated locations aside, an integral part of American life all along. Debates about the place of their schools aside, advocates of church schooling have set out to convince their students that they are every bit as American as the public school counterparts.

NOTES

1. For an account of the whole affair from the perspective of those on the panel, see Gary Nash, Charlotte Crabtree, and Ross Dunn, *History on Trial: Culture Wars and the Teaching of the Past* (New York: Alfred A. Knopf, 1998). See also the symposium in *Society* 34(2), (January/February 1997); Lynn Cheney, "The End of History," *Wall Street Journal*, (October 20, 1994). For a summary and analysis of these events, see Mark Noll "Some Recent Battles," *Books and Culture* 5(3), (May/June 1999): 30–34.

2. Jonathan Zimmerman, *Whose America? Culture Wars in the Public Schools* (Cambridge, MA: Harvard University Press, 2002).

3. Joseph Moreau, *School Book Nation: Conflicts over American History Textbooks from the Civil War to the Present* (Ann Arbor, MI: University of Michigan Press, 2003). He examines, for instance, post-Civil War sectionalism, race, and class issues as they erupted in textbook production and use. Studies of textbooks, especially those used in Catholic schools, are not uncommon. See Diane Ravitch, *The Language Police* (New York: Alfred A. Knopf, 2003).

4. Timothy Walch, "Catholic School Books and American Values," *Religious Education* 73(5), (September/October 1978): 582–591. Though I have benefited from both Walch's and Moreau's work, my own foray into this particular field was somewhat accidental. I purchased a box of old books at a yard sale near the University of Virginia only to find Charles McCarthy's Catholic history textbook in the bottom of

the pile. Commenting on this to my graduate advisor led me to pursue the repetition of this effort in subsequent movements for religious schooling.

5. For each of the communities identified so far, Catholics, Jews, and conservative Protestants, I have selected popular or otherwise influential textbooks produced for their schools. Exact numbers are not easily ascertained, but each of the books or lines examined in this chapter was recommended to me by advocates of religious schooling within each community. I have made an effort to examine those texts that were produced or were already available during each specific community's most contentious period with regard to their schools. Thus, for Catholics I examined books from the late nineteenth and early twentieth century, while for Judaism I examined resources available during the middle of the twentieth century, the period identified by Schiff as the Era of Great Expansion. Finally, for Christian day and homeschooling, I examined books that were popular in the 1990s when the debate over homeschooling's political implications was just getting underway. The logic behind this approach was suggested by Mark Noll, George Marsden, and Nathan Hatch in their book, *The Search for Christian America*. Focusing on American evangelicals and their concerns for American history, the authors point out that in moments of crisis, it is natural to seek for comfort and direction from the past. It seemed productive, then, to examine resources from each community's experience of crisis as the political consequences of their educational institutions were under the most direct criticism. See Mark Noll, George Marsden, and Nathan Hatch, *The Search for Christian America* (Colorado Springs, CO: Helmers and Howard, 1989).

6. Of course, the grand narrative promoted in the secular texts can be viewed as partisan as well. Catholic school leaders and advocates accused the public schools themselves of being religious and partisan, and it is not unreasonable to assume that they would have viewed public school textbooks as such. Revisionists, too, have seen the supposedly neutral grand narrative as particularistic and agenda-driven.

7. The Excelsior series comprised history books for various levels of education, though most were similar if not identical in content. Only the amount of detail and the complexity of causal factors for events like the American Revolution changed.

8. *Sadlier's History of the United States* (New York: William H. Sadlier, 1894): 13, 21. Moreau also quotes part of this dramatic passage. It perfectly captures the spirit of the Catholic school-book effort.

9. Charles McCarthy, *History of the United States for Catholic Schools* (New York: American Book Publishing Company, 1919).

10. Ibid., 232.

11. A.C. Monohan correspondence, NCWC, Archives, Box 542, Washington, DC., 1921.

12. Jonathan Sarna, personal correspondence, July 27, 2006.

13. See Lee Levinger, *A History of the Jews in the United States*, third edition (Cincinnati, OH: Union of American Hebrew Congregations, 1944): 158–161.

14. Samuel Goodside, "A Social Studies Syllabus for Secular Teachers in Jewish All-Day Schools: A Companion Bulletin to the Social Studies Curriculum Bulletins of the Board of Education of the City of New York," 1951, Ph.D. diss., New York University: 3. A teacher in both public and Jewish schools, Goodside was well-versed in the needs and history of Jewish education. Long active in the day school movement,

Goodside's primary contribution in this proposal is to outline a curriculum for the larger effort aimed at highlighting the role of American Jews in the nation's history.

15. Ibid., 9–11.

16. Ibid., 13.

17. Ibid., 14.

18. In subsequent grades students were exposed to more and more of Solomon's efforts on behalf of the Revolution, similar to the way studies of the same topic increase in depth as education progresses. Goodside's syllabus includes only short references to various figures and a list of sources for teachers to actually find material suitable for the classroom. What follows here draws on the lessons children in Jewish day schools would have learned up through the sixth grade.

19. Harry Golden and Martin Rywell, *Jews in American History: Their Contribution to the United States of America* (Charlotte, NC: H.A. Stalls Printing, 1950): 6.

20. Lee M. Friedman, *Jewish Pioneers and Patriots* (Philadelphia, PA: Jewish Publication Society of America, 1942).

21. A Beka Book and Bob Jones University Press are the most well-known curriculum lines. Neither company would reveal sales figures or income to me, but they are both prominently advertised in homeschool media and, at least in my experience, are usually the two largest vendors at homeschool conventions. Informal inquiries made to various homeschool advocacy groups, including HSLDA and *The Teaching Home* support the contention that A Beka Book and Bob Jones University Press are very popular with their constituencies. Both lines are available to Christian schools and Christian homeschool families, the latter of which may also purchase home-study guides for parent-teachers and workbooks for students.

22. See http://www.pcci.edu/WhyPCC.html, 2002.

23. *United States History: A Christian Perspective* (Pensacola, FL: A Beka Book, 1996): ii.

24. Ibid., 5.

25. Ibid., 78.

26. A similar motif in these texts is the way in which biblical Christianity is credited with success stories from America's past. After a discussion of the early fortunes of various attempts at colonizing America, A Beka Book's *Heritage of Freedom* suggests that the Pilgrims succeeded where other colonizers failed because they followed biblical principles for civic affairs.

27. *American Government in Christian Perspective* (Pensacola, FL: A Beka Book, 1997), 51.

28. Timothy Keesee, *American Government for Christian Schools* (Greenville, NC: Bob Jones University Press, 1993), 21.

29. Ibid., 21.

30. Ibid., 24.

31. Generation Joshua is a training program put together by HSLDA. It comprises various units in American history and civic life, and much attention is drawn to notable American heroes, particularly those whose Christian faith is well-established. The Generation Joshua Web site (the whole course is Web based) contains original writings or speeches from various figures in American history, especially the Founding Fathers, and then, for Washington, it provides links to another essay to affirm Washington's own Christian faith. See the HSLDA Web site at http://hslda.org.

32. On the relationship between history and communal identity, see Keith Barton and Linda Levstik, *Teaching History for the Common Good* (Mahweh: Lawrence Erlbaum Associates, 2004). See also the Organization of American Historian's 2004 report *The Debate over History's Role in Teaching Citizenship and Patriotism,* available online at http://www.oah.org/reports/tradhist.html.

33. Benedict Anderson, *The Imagined Community* (London: Verso Press, 1991).

6   Islamic Schooling in America

T hus far we have seen that over the course of the twentieth century multiple religious communities embraced the strategy of faith-based schooling, including some whose energies, in earlier generations, had been spent in the service of public education. Catholic, Jewish, and conservative Protestant schooling, while still criticized by some, is fairly well embedded in American legal and social policy. Even homeschooling is now widely recognized as a legitimate, if still unfamiliar, option. Though polls suggest most Americans think we would be better off if all children attended public schools, the institutions associated with religious communities that are well integrated in the social order have attained a level of credibility in the eyes of much of the public. But I suspect that many Americans who pass Catholic, Jewish, and Christian schools everyday might cast a somewhat more suspicious eye toward a Muslim school constructed in their neighborhood. The expansion of religious pluralism in the United States to include more significant numbers of Muslims, and especially the emergence of Islamic institutions and voices in public dialogue and civil society, mandate an examination of Islamic schooling in America. It is worth noting here at the outset that several of the features evident in the experience of other religious communities, including epistemological and familial concerns, public suspicion, and even the attempt to write themselves into the grand narrative of American history are already present in the collective biography of Islamic schooling.

The first frustration one encounters when trying to write about Islamic schooling in America is the lack of precise figures for estimating the total Muslim population in the United States. It is difficult to gage the community support for religious schooling or its potential for future growth if one has little idea how large the community itself is. The U.S. Census, the most comprehensive counting of Americans available, does not, as a matter of policy, ask questions about religious affiliation or adherence. The absence of an actual count means that we must rely on extrapolations and estimates from surveys, which, though sophisticated, are seldom without controversy. For instance, political clout is partly a function of numbers since more members can mean more voters, thus Muslim organizations themselves may be seen to have a stake in inflating their population. On the other hand, one of the most recent attempts to estimate the American Muslim population was commissioned by the American Jewish Committee, a group that some American Muslims claim has their own agenda.

Commonly cited estimates on the number of Muslims in America range from just over 1 million all the way up to 7 million. The 2001 Religious Identification Survey carried out by the Graduate Center of the City University of New York found that there were some 1.1 million Muslims in America, up from 527,000 in 1990.[1] The Council on American-Islamic Relations, also in 2001, affirmed the 6 to 7 million estimate.[2] In 2002 Tom W. Smith, director of the influential General Social Survey at the National Opinion Research Center at the University of Chicago penned a wide-ranging review of the various estimates in the journal *Public Opinion Quarterly*. Covering the American Religious Identification Survey, and the Mosque in America studies, as well as several others, he estimated the number of Muslims in America to be approximately 2.8 million, or just about 1 percent of the population. Of the 23 estimates he reviewed, 16 placed the number of American Muslims between 5 and 7 million, thus accounting for the media's common citation of the 6-million figure, an estimate Smith rejects as much too high. Smith, it should be noted, had been hired by the American Jewish Committee to conduct his own study, a point that casts some doubt on his estimates in the minds of some American Muslim leaders.[3] Most recently, the Pew Research Center estimated in May of 2007 that there were some 1.4 million adult Muslims in the United States, though their report makes a point of identifying reasons their estimate might be too low. Using data from the Census Bureau and a birthrate/nationality model developed by demographers at the Pew Hispanic Center, the Research Center estimates that there are approximately 850,000 Muslims in America under the age of 18, bringing the total number of Muslims in America to 2.35 million, less than 1 percent of the population.[4]

The number of Muslims in the United States, then, is controversial, but no more so than their history in North America more generally. There is some speculation that, after being forced to leave by Spain's Catholic monarchs Ferdinand and Isabella in the fifteenth century, some Muslims may have made it all the way to the Caribbean Islands, perhaps even to the present-day United States. Though this cannot be proven as of yet, it is a claim that will occupy our attention later in this chapter. The more well-documented history of Muslims in America can be traced to a series of migrations from different parts of the Muslim world, though this too is problematic. Not everyone who comes from a "Muslim" area is actually Muslim. Muslim regions often have sizable religious minorities, the members of which might have very specific motivations to emigrate. Still, it is not uncommon for the history of Muslim immigration to America to be described as coming in waves originating from Muslim regions. Jane Smith, in her book *Islam in America*, argues that there have been five periods of Muslim migration to America. The first, beginning some ten years after the American Civil War, brought a relatively small number of Muslims from Syria as part of a larger migration from that region. Political changes at the end of World War I prompted another migration from the Middle East, which lasted into the early 1920s. According to Smith, minor migrations occurred throughout the following decades until 1965 when President Lyndon Johnson did away with the quota system for determining the number of migrants from different communities around the world. That action, coupled with the political turmoil associated with events such as Israel's victory in the 1967 war and the Iranian Revolution of 1979 led to an increase in the number of Muslim immigrants.[5]

Of course, Islam in America can also be traced back to before the Civil War through slavery and the trans-Atlantic slave trade. Though specific numbers are hard to determine, there is no doubt that some of the slaves taken from Africa were Muslims, but it appears that their religion did not survive the institution of slavery itself.[6] Then, too, the Nation of Islam and the various groups of African-American Muslims must be considered as well, though both their numbers and their relationship to Islamic groups with Middle Eastern origins are problematic, a reality that further confounds counting Muslims in America more generally. For instance, the relationship between Noble Drew Ali's Moorish temples and Islam in America is not easy to discern, though it is worth noting in the present context that education has long been a part of the African-American Muslim community. The Nation of Islam (NOI) promoted schools for the children of community members, many of which are still in operation today, though their affiliation with the NOI is not always clear.

When it comes to questions of fitting in, the Muslim community does not speak with one voice.[7] Nearly half (44 percent) think that newly arrived immigrants should adopt American customs, while just over a quarter (26 percent) think that isolation from mainstream America is the better option. Interestingly, native-born Muslims are less likely to be pro-assimilation than are foreign-born Muslims. A full 16 percent volunteered that Muslim immigrants should both assimilate and remain distinct, suggestive, perhaps, of the same tension most minority communities experience.[8] Political involvement, too, is a difficult topic for American Muslims. While almost half say that mosques should keep out of political matters, 43 percent favor involvement. As independent citizens, Muslims are somewhat less active than most citizens. It is worth noting that more than 77 percent of Muslims in America are citizens of this country and that educational opportunities was the most commonly cited factor in terms of reasons for immigration (economic opportunity and family connections were also commonly cited). Although the growth of Islamic philanthropic organizations, parachurch associations, schools, and a host of other advocacy groups suggest that Muslims in America are well on their way to building a healthy civil society concerned with issues of importance to their community, it is also true that many of these organizations remain somewhat marginalized, even suspect. The financial and ideological connections between these organizations and the Muslim world, especially Saudi Arabia, are a frequent source of speculation in the media and certain very vocal portions of the population.

Those favoring participation and involvement argue that Islamic faith and practice have always stressed the effort to build up the good in a society while avoiding the bad. In their view the lack of specific injunctions in the Koran or the Sunnah against involvement in society mean that prohibitions against participation are inconsistent with Islam. In the absence of specific prohibitions, the concept of *maslaha* (benefit), should guide action. According to this principle, whatever is in the best collective interests of Muslims should prevail. Given the growing American Muslim community, and America's place in the world, surely, they reason, Muslims should avail themselves of whatever opportunities are available to them for pursuing their personal and collective goals. Additionally, the idea of withdrawal is illusory given realities like mandatory taxes which go to support domestic and foreign initiatives that Muslims may wish to impact. Importantly, some Muslim scholars have argued that if Islam is to gain political influence in the United States, the role of mosques and schools in community building cannot be overlooked.[9]

Some Muslims, on the other hand, are skeptical of too much participation in American society. Participation itself can be seen as corrupt given that most Americans are not Muslims and do not conform to Muslim practices. Participation on any level lends credibility, they fear, to institutions and practices that may not be hospitable to Islam. Assimilating into the institutions of unbelievers is simply not permissible.[10] The empirical data suggests that the majority of the leadership of mosques in America believes participation in American social and civic life is in the best interest of the American Muslim community. A survey of mosque leadership showed that more than 90 percent of African-Americans, South Asians, and Arabs all supported participation and were eager to discuss their own institutional programs.[11] Support for participation remains high even among those leaders who think that America is largely immoral and ultimately hostile to Islam. Citizenship has always been an important consideration in Islam, and given the growing numbers and affluence of American Muslims their participation in community and even national affairs is not surprising. Like other groups before them, Muslims know that part of forging their place in American life depends on their being seen as engaged in issues like community renewal, crime control, and education.

MUSLIMS AND EDUCATION

As with other religious communities, learning and the acquisition of knowledge are an integral part of Islam. Muhammad himself is often cited as stressing the importance and value of learning, exhorting his followers to learn "from the cradle to the grave."[12] Learning is an act of worship in Islam, and is central to keeping Muslim identity alive. The first word of the revelation to Muhammad was the order to recite, that is, to read and memorize. History has bequeathed to modern Islam an impressive intellectual legacy. Particularly during the glorious days of the ninth through the fourteenth centuries, Muslim accomplishments in astronomy and mathematics (especially algebra), as well as technical and mechanical sciences, were second to none. Nor were their successes set apart from their religious practices. Arabic, as a common language for Muslims, promoted interdisciplinary discourse and was conducive to building a body of shared knowledge coming, as it did, from separate intellectual trajectories. In philosophy, too, there was a firm commitment to Islamic principles undergirding some of the most impressive scholarship of the era.[13]

This history, however, stands in stark contrast to what Muslim educational leaders themselves saw in the twentieth century. Over the last thirty years Muslims all over the world have renewed their attention to schooling, at least part of which has been in response to their encounter with western society. In the eyes of some Muslim thinkers, colonialism and the broader cultural hegemony of the West had introduced a foreign, ultimately hostile, understanding of education into the Muslim world. In an effort to combat this trend, beginning in March of 1977 Muslim educators hosted a series of world conferences to address such questions as the purpose and philosophy of Muslim education, the challenges of curricular and textbook development, and teaching methodology in Islamic schools. The recommendations from the First World Conference on Muslim Education also allude to the importance of these events to Islamic education in the West. Conference participants called for the preparation of educational policies and materials that addressed the peculiar situation of Muslims living as minorities in non-Muslim societies. They even called for the establishment of a special fund, contributed to by Muslim countries, for the building up of Islamic schools around the world, and called for Muslim countries to use their political clout to further the aims of Islamic education in non-Muslim countries. Though far removed from America's shores, the ideas emanating out of these conferences are a good place to begin our analysis of Islamic education in America because they provide a condensed overview of the connections between Islamic views of the person, knowledge, and education with particular attention to how these concepts mesh with modern western ideas and institutions. Additionally, conference participants highlighted some of the major inconsistencies between Islamic and Western education (as Muslim educators saw it), and thus some of the reasoning that might lead American Muslims to reject public schools.[14] One must be careful not to overstate the place of these conferences. It is not the case that they led directly to the founding of Islamic schools in the United States. They did, however, give voice to some of the same concerns and agendas that other Muslims in the West were struggling with, most notably Islamization, or the attempt to connect modern insights and advances to Muslim principles. In America, this effort was institutionalized in the (among others) International Institute for Islamic Thought (IIIT), established in 1981 in Pennsylvania and now headquartered in Herndon, Virginia. The IIIT is dedicated to developing Islamic scholarship in the humanities and social sciences. Its ultimate goal is to reinvigorate the Ummah, or Islamic Nation, as a dynamic force in modern civilization. Methodologically, the IIIT and its affiliated scholars seek to integrate revealed and human knowledge, a paradigm they call the Islamization of knowledge. Aside from the normal institutional burdens such as funding and administration, Islamization has been the most significant challenge facing advocates of Islamic schooling in America, and perhaps the Muslim community more broadly, though in recent years noteworthy progress has been made on just this front by those most involved in the intellectual and spiritual formation of the next generation.

The basic narrative of Islamic education laid out by the more than three hundred first world conference attendees locates the challenges of Muslim education within the social crises occasioned by the rapid development and modernization of the Muslim world in the middle decades of the twentieth century. Muslim nations, still mired in "want and poverty, disease and epidemic, colonialism and economic humiliation"[15] envied the perceived cultural superiority and hegemony of the West. That superiority was rooted, supposedly, in the West's mastery over technology and science, both of which were stressed in western education. Muslim societies, then, embraced western-style education as the key to their advancement.

That embrace has presented two challenges to Muslim society. First, Western education was seen as secular education. It presented no center, no shared, trusted body of knowledge to provide a foundation for society. This was not surprising given that Western society itself was also seen as lacking a center. The implications of this lack of cohesion could be seen on both the social and individual level. Socially there was no glue to hold society

together and more importantly there was no moral framework that everyone in the society agreed to recognize, much less honor. A society without
a center risked moral bankruptcy, then, and was in a constant if slow dis-
integration. On the individual level, graduates of an education that lacked
this center were seen as themselves cut adrift from any sure anchor. Such
a man (or woman) would be in a constant search for something that their
education had not, indeed, could not have, provided. No secular education
could meet the full needs of humankind because, in keeping with Islam's
understanding of the person, one's spiritual needs inevitably go unmet. Education, of course, is not limited to the schools. Numerous agencies from
the family to the social community are charged in Islam with promoting the
development of the individual. Especially in secular societies, though, the
need for formalized instruction in Islamic faith and practice as well as other
bodies of learning suggests the need for specifically Muslim schools.[16]

This is not to say that there are no connections between western and
Muslim educational thought and practice. With their western counterparts,
Muslim educational theorists recognize that all education must begin with
the end already in sight. Muslim schools are supposed to produce good
Muslims, just as Catholic schools seek to produce good Catholics and Jewish
schools seek to produce observant Jews. The end of Islamic schooling is the
full development of the individual in an effort to become *Khalifatullah*, the
vicegerent, or deputy, of God on earth. Rejecting the notion of original
sin, Muslims believe humans are basically good and that their potential
is essentially unlimited. What they actually achieve is the product of their
education. With this understanding in mind, those gathered at the First
World Conference on Muslim Education put forth the following concept of
education:

> Education should aim at the balanced growth of the total personality of Man
> through the training of Man's spirit, intellect, his rational self, feelings and
> bodily senses. Education should cater therefore for the growth of Man in all its
> aspects: spiritual, intellectual, imaginative, physical, scientific, linguistic, both
> individually and collectively and motivate all aspects towards goodness and
> the attainment of perfection. The ultimate aim of Muslim education lies in the
> realization of complete submission to Allah on the level of the individual, the
> community and humanity at large.[17]

From this several ideas flow that shape Islamic education. First, though
education should aim at "balanced growth," there is a hierarchy of knowledge, with spiritual knowledge at both the base and pinnacle of human
development. Second, the acquisition of knowledge is the means of this
development. Thus, in Islamic education there is no bar on the types of
knowledge gained, provided the right balance is maintained and that a
priority is given to the spiritual realm. This is possible because all knowledge has its origin in God (a conviction they share with other advocates of

religious schooling), and therefore the search for knowledge will, almost inevitably, lead the inquisitor toward an encounter with the divine. Even completely modern fields of study are perfectly appropriate, perhaps even beneficial, provided that they are built upon an Islamic, as opposed to a secular or other religious, foundation.

The second major problem with Muslim societies' embrace of Western education, at least as identified by those affiliated with the world conferences, has to do with the speed with which the West's concepts were picked up. There was not enough time to integrate the various concepts.[18] The educational practices of the West brought with them philosophical assumptions antagonistic to Islam. With sufficient time, concepts could have been developed by Muslim scholars and practitioners that would have been more consistent with Islamic life.

The general perception of this crisis was well captured by Abdulla Omar Naseef, the Vice Rector of King Abdulaziz University, in his forward to the 1979 book *The Crisis in Muslim Education*, an outgrowth of the first world conference:

> The Muslim World is passing through a transition period of tremendously fast geo-political transformation and rapid social change. God-given wealth has brought both worldly prestige and unforeseen worries. In order to cope with these problems and at the same time save the Muslim world from being over-run or controlled by alien ideas and forces, the authorities had to learn and teach modern knowledge in all its forms. Along with this came modern W[w]estern methodology and W[w]estern secular concepts dominating all branches of knowledge. The rapidity with which expansion of education was considered necessary made it extremely difficult for authorities to wait till Islamic concepts were evolved by Muslim scholars.[19]

Naseef went on to write of the "brainwashing" western methodology and education inflicted upon Muslim students. The educational crisis resulted from the lack of time available for Muslim scholars to formulate an adequate Muslim counterpart to those Western ideas that were part and parcel of modernization itself. This is no mere matter of a few footnotes and creative interpretations of revealed knowledge. At stake here is the very possibility of human fulfillment because humans, by nature, seek stability and a connection with the absolute. To the extent that Western education recognized no absolute, it could not ultimately solve the problems it created. This crisis was exacerbated by the rapidity of social change in the modern world brought on both by modernization itself but also the concomitant encounter with other cultures and societies. The very cosmopolitanism that is promoted by western, liberal education was anathema to those in attendance at the world conferences and continues to be a problem to those who think education should root students into a particular community, Muslims included.

While modern, Western education is too trapped in its own milieu to offer much hope, Islamic education, with its commitment to a firm destiny for mankind and its substitutes for the purely scientific ways of knowing, can turn the tide:

> [The] Islamic concept of education, therefore, as enunciated in the earlier section of this paper, needs to be interpreted and implemented in the context of modern life . . . let us reassert the hierarchy of values, let us reformulate the concepts of social and natural sciences and humanities, let us reorganize and rearrange the curriculum, let us produce textbooks written on the basis of concepts and let us train our teachers so that they are able to instill in children those values through their character and their methods of teaching. Only then will education become truly Islamic and can we hope for the betterment and safety and security of mankind.[20]

Providing for the betterment, safety, and security of mankind is a tall order, but Islamic educators fleshed out this very goal in subsequent world conferences. They saw the need for something new in Islamic education. The then current educational landscape was composed of two systems of schooling. The first was a very traditional system, largely confined to classical Islamic knowledge. While valuable in its own right, world conference supporters did not see that this system would equip rising generations of Muslims with the ability to engage the modern world. The second system was essentially imported to the Muslim world from the West, and was therefore already too secular to be of much value. An integrated system was called for that would promote an Islamic point of view across all the modern disciplines, and to that end the world conference set out to produce the curricular and pedagogical tools necessary for the task.

The first step in the production of an Islamicized curriculum was to reject European and American concepts of knowledge. Basing their characterization on the Harvard Committee Report *General Education in a Free Society*, Muslim educators argued that Western education had omitted anything that would lead man beyond his senses. Western knowledge, they held, could be broken down into three fields: the natural sciences, the humanities, and the social sciences. Theology and divinity had been purposefully left out. Islamic educators, on the other hand, recognized a two-fold classification of knowledge. Perennial knowledge is based on divine revelation, in this case the Koran and the Sunnah, while "acquired" knowledge referred to the more human branches of inquiry. Perennial knowledge included the mastery of various sacred documents or bodies of tradition. Arabic, too, along with broad subjects such as Islamic metaphysics, comparative religion, and Islamic culture, were part of the body of perennial knowledge. Acquired knowledge, which could be borrowed cross culturally, nevertheless had to be consistent with perennial knowledge. Islamic epistemology rejects the compartmentalization of religious and moral ideas it sees as required by a public committed to secular education. This anti-compartmentalization motif is particularly pressing when the socialization of children is at stake because any agent of socialization, for instance a school, which is by definition neutral or cut off from the goal of socialization, in this case the production of a good Muslim, is doomed to failure: the more successful the compartmentalization, the more deleterious the consequences. Acquired knowledge encompassed everything from the arts to the natural and social sciences, along with the applied fields of medicine, engineering, and even practical fields such as commerce. In the West, these topics are sometimes presented as neutral with regard to religious truth, but Islamic educators reject that neutrality as incomplete at best. The unity of knowledge is paramount.

Recognizing that there were still political and philosophical hurdles to producing the requisite texts, world conference leaders did identify a number of short-term projects that would at least create a momentum toward the ultimate goal of an Islamicized curriculum. These included the production of syllabi drawn up by Islamic experts from various fields that would guide textbook writers themselves (parts of the second world conference were devoted to this project), the introduction of a new series of courses into the secondary schools (again proposed at the second world conference), and the development of grade appropriate philosophy and literature/grammar courses "infused with the essence of Muslim life and culture."[21]

Administration and teaching, too, are different in Islamic education. The kind of leadership exercised in school administration has a specific foundation in Islam. Efficiency, for instance, which they held to be a western criterion, is secondary to social responsibility and human dignity. Administrators in Muslim schools have responsibilities for the moral and spiritual development of their charges (the same is true in all religious schooling), a fact that impacts everything from the length of the school day to curriculum. Strategic and long-term planning, too, would be different in Islamic schooling. Long-term goals are not sacrificed for immediate successes, a trend some Islamic educators think indicative of Western, public schooling.[22] Similarly, in Islam the teacher is to be valued and ultimately judged for more than their academic abilities. Their morality and piety are also expected to be worthy of emulation, and thus teachers are held in reverence in the traditional model of Islamic education. This emphasis on the whole person of the teacher rather than just their efficacy as instructors is not just pious window-dressing. It is related to the concepts of education and humanity more broadly. If the destiny of man is to be the vicegerent of God on earth, and if education is to promote the development of the full person, then a strict divorce between academic ability or credential and personal faithfulness is impossible. The whole point of the teacher/student relationship in Islamic education is based on the premise than a teacher must be imitable by the student. To restrict this to only technical or acquired knowledge is to deny the most important part of the person. On the one hand, these expectations for the teacher in an Islamic school might be understood as a sort of standard for a performance review, but they are also part of the tension between Islamic education and Western, largely secular, schooling.[23] Where, in the American public schools, will Islamic students find role models of the sort described by the world conferences? It is to this matter that our attention must turn.

ISLAMIC SCHOOLING IN AMERICA

Islamic schooling is an increasingly important topic to American Muslims. As with other religious communities, Muslim parents know that at stake are the very survival of their community and the religious lives of their children.[24] As early as 1928 there were Muslim learning institutions in America, though relatively little is known about them, and almost nothing is left of them on the institutional level.[25] In the early 1930s a University of Islam, which was actually an elementary and secondary school, was founded in Detroit in connection with the labors of Fard Muhammad, the enigmatic inspiration behind the original Nation of Islam. Elijah Poole, later Elijah Muhammad, was an early convert whose home served as the site of an early Nation of Islam school. Muhammad's wife, Clara, served as a teacher and it is for her that the schools usually associated with the Nation of Islam were eventually named. Over the next three decades, there were several schools in cities where the Nation of Islam was active. Elijah Muhammad's death in 1975 was a watershed year for African-American Muslims, and for the African-American community more broadly, including the schools associated with the Black Nationalist Nation of Islam. Muhammad's son, Wallace D. Muhammad took leadership of the movement, and over several years moved the group toward Sunni Muslim orthodoxy and to some extent away from Black Nationalism, even changing the name of his group to the American Muslim Mission. He called on the schools associated with the movement, many of which were named for his mother, to embrace a more traditional understanding of Islamic identity. Unhappy with Wallace D. Muhammad's efforts, Louis Farrakhan then reconstituted the Nation of Islam in 1978. These events had significant ramifications for Islamic schooling in America, as the organizational schism in the larger African-American Muslim community made finding support and institutional affiliation more difficult. In the early 1990s there were some forty Sister Clara Muhammad schools in America, and a movement was underway to professionalize the institutions and to begin to rebuild support networks and an institutional identity.[26]

The Sister Clara Muhammad schools are not the only Islamic schools in America. A number of mosques have schools affiliated with them, and there are independent institutions as well. Though the estimates vary, there is good reason to suspect that, at this time, the number of Islamic schools in America is fairly small. The Pew Research Center's 2007 survey, which bills itself as the "first ever nationwide survey to attempt to measure rigorously the demographics, attitudes, and experience of Muslim Americans" did not even mention schooling. In 2001, the Council on American-Islamic

Relations produced their major report entitled "The Mosque in America: A National Portrait." Of the 1209 mosques identified by this study, 21 percent, or 253, claimed to have full-time schools associated with them.[27] The 2003–2004 Private School Survey, a biannual initiative of the National Center for Education Statistics, found that there were only 182 Islamic schools in America. Most recently, Karen Keyworth, of the Islamic Schools League of America, estimated that in 2006 there were 235 Islamic schools in America. This figure represents the culmination of eight years of effort to identify, locate, and contact every Islamic school in the United States. Using the Internet as their primary research tool, Keyworth and her colleagues rejected estimates of more than 300 as unreasonable, though they do admit to probably having missed a few institutions.[28] Regardless of which number one chooses to recognize, Islamic schooling is still a relatively small phenomenon, representing only a fraction of the total religious schooling enterprise in the United States.

That is not to say that it is irrelevant. Nor is it reducible to the efforts of a few isolated Muslims or Muslim organizations. In the last several years, Islamic schooling has shown the potential for longevity and growth, and there are numerous efforts to secure its place in American education more broadly, typified by the founding of Islamic education groups and associations all of which seek to advance the cause of Islamic schooling. And, of course, there are other options as well. As with Judaism, there are supplementary programs for Islamic education based on weekend, evening, or even Internet prepackaged programs. Though these options have been criticized for reasons similar to their Jewish predecessors, they do suggest an interest in Islamic education on the part of this growing minority.[29]

Outside the Sister Clara Muhammad schools, the history of Islamic schooling in America is comparatively short. There is no single organization that oversees Islamic schooling in America the way the National Catholic War Council or to a lesser extent Home School Legal Defense Association did for their respective constituencies, though there are several Muslim organizations in the United States concerned with education. These include the Muslim Student Association, the Council on American-Islamic Relations, the Islamic Society of North America (ISNA), the Council of Islamic Schools in North America, the Muslim American Society (MAS), and the Islamic Schools League of America. There are also regional associations and networks of Muslim schools that dot the Islamic educational landscape. There are even Muslim homeschool organizations. There is significant overlap in the goals and programs of these various organizations, and there are also institutional linkages between them. The Muslim Student Association, founded in 1963 at the University of Illinois' Urbana campus to coordinate and pool efforts on behalf of Muslim college and university students, played a significant role in the founding of the broader Islamic Society of North America in 1983. ISNA, whose annual conference draws thousands of participants, is the largest Muslim organization in North America. Like many national organizations, there is an education component to its work, including an annual forum, special issues of its journal *Islamic Horizons* devoted to schooling, and other initiatives aimed at supporting Muslim families in America.[30] Also tracing its institutional origins to the Muslim Student Association, the Muslim American Society was launched in 1992. Among its goals, the MAS seeks to "promote understanding between Muslims and non-Muslims . . . to build a virtuous and moral society . . . and to promote the human values that Islam emphasizes: brotherhood, equality, justice, mercy, compassion, and peace."[31] One of their chief strategies for promoting these, and other goals, is to provide technical and support services and professional training to those working in Islamic schools. The Muslim American Society Council of Islamic Schools (MASCIS) seeks enhanced cooperation between what are now largely independent schools as a means of strengthening Islamic education, and to this end it also seeks to develop a unified curriculum for use in Islamic schools.

Also noteworthy is the Islamic Schools League of America. Founded by four parents convinced that their own children benefited from Islamic schooling, the League aims to connect schools one to another and, beyond that, to connect schools with other agencies that provide ancillary services. The League also hosts the Islamic Education Research Archive, which contains papers and essays about Islamic education, many of which come from the League's own national conferences. Two organizations focus more on public education. The Council on American-Islamic Relations (CAIR) is a civil rights organization that has focused on the rights of Muslim students in America's public schools, including matters of accommodation for religious observance of prayers and dietary laws, religious garb, and in some cases release time or excused absences for religious holidays. The Council of Islamic Education, founded in 1990, is active in reviewing national and state standards for world history and geography to ensure that Islam is accurately portrayed. Committed to American democratic principles and the First Amendment, the Council promotes the study of religion as part of a well-rounded education. All these organizations, and many more, are also involved in the more general effort to project a positive image of Islam in America, a challenge made more difficult and more pressing after September 11, 2001.

It is too early to tell which of these organizations, if any, will come to represent Islamic schooling in America. The movement itself is still in its infancy. Only the schools associated with the Nation of Islam banner go back more than a few years. Still, National Center for Education Statistics (NCES) data does suggest a trajectory of growth.

Obviously, these numbers are still fairly low. Muslim schooling accounts for less than 1 percent of the total private school enrollment in America.

Table 6.1. The Growth of Muslim Schooling[32]

Report year	Number of schools	Number of students
1995–1996	97	9,707
1997–1998	96	11,412
1999–2000	152	18,262
2001–2002	188	22,951
2003–2004	182	22,958
2005–2006	202	26,209

But these small numbers can be misleading. The American Muslim community has poured significant resources into their schools, and is both serious and optimistic regarding their future outlook. While the number of schools might seem insignificant, American Muslim educational leaders have been developing various plans and programs so that as new schools are established they will have easy access to educational and institutional resources, including informational networks, professional organizations, and, of course, educational materials. That is not to say the Islamic schools will not face many of the same issues their peer institutions faced. Aside from the obvious budgetary and infrastructural issues, the Muslim community itself will have to ask the same hard questions about the place of religious schooling. Some of this debate is already present. Twenty years ago Yvonne Haddad and Adair T. Lummis, in their study of immigrant Muslim communities in America, found that 40 percent of those surveyed did not think having a full-time Islamic schooling was important in their mosque, while a quarter thought it was "very important." Among those who say they would not send their children to Islamic schools the lack of integration was the most common motivation for keeping their children in public schools.[33] Contemporary advocates for safeguarding appropriate values for Muslim children in North America have promoted Islamic schooling as a means of countering the materialism and secularism they see as indicative of public education. Explaining the rationale of a full-time Islamic school, they claim "[t]hey (the school children) develop a strong sense of belonging to the Muslim Ummah. They not only preserve rich Islamic heritage, but contribute toward the development of and progress of the Muslim Ummah in general."[34] They also defend the educational and intellectual mission of Islamic schools and to assure parents that their children will not be overly isolated or grow up in a shell: "Besides, Muslim children who attend Islamic school are never totally out of touch with American society. Their exposure to the larger American culture is still considerable. Television, news media, neighborhoods, and non-Muslim staff in their own institutions keep the windows to the larger world wide open."

This is exactly the sort of dialogue that occurred in the American Jewish community regarding the place of day school education. Indeed, to some extent this debate can be found in every religious community that establishes its own schools, just as it can be found in the home of every parent who had to decide where to educate his or her children. There is always a tension between assimilation and maintaining group boundaries, a tension exacerbated in the Muslim case by the fact that the schools, as agents of assimilation, are not always welcoming the Muslim lifestyle. Daily prayer requirements, dress codes, and dietary restrictions can all reinforce the "otherness" Muslim students already experience. Thus, an institution that reinforces a Muslim lifestyle can be a more attractive option, especially to parents concerned with the fidelity of the next generation.[35]

The intercommunity debate is not the only one advocates of Islamic schooling face. Islamic schools were almost completely ignored before 9/11, but immediately after the towers fell all Islamic institutions were subjected to suspicion and investigation. Even other religious schools have been skeptical of Islamic institutions and their place in America. In 2004, the Dar-Ul-Arqam school applied for membership in the Texas Association of Private and Parochial Schools. The Association, whose membership is largely Christian, requested more information as to why the Dar-Ul-Arqam school was seeking membership, questions that, according to national media, included whether or not they supported war on Christians, and further asking why a Muslim school would want to join a group in which they might not be welcome. Numerous national advocacy groups weighed in on the issue, including the Anti-Defamation League, the American Civil Liberties Union, and the Council on American-Islamic Relations.[36] Two years before the events in Texas, but reflecting similar concerns, a February 25, 2002 article in the *Washington Post* made an issue with what students in some Islamic schools may be learning. Aside from lessons in physics and math, the Islamic studies curriculum at one school encouraged Muslim students to attack Jews as part of the Day of Judgment. Other schools featured maps of the world with "Israel" crossed out and Palestine written in, for many a charge that bespeaks more than just a name preference. The *Post* reporters also found that some Islamic schools are funded by the Saudi government, an arrangement that may bring with it a rigid strain of Islam that some American Muslims find particularly out of step with life in the West. Indeed, ties between Saudi Arabia and Islamic schools in America are among the most potentially explosive aspects of this issue.

Critics charge Saudi Arabia's rulers with aligning themselves with Wahhabism, a particularly narrow strain of Islam dating back to the eighteenth-century Arabian peninsula. The house of Sa'ud, suspected of less than zealous commitment to Islam, agreed to promote Wahhabi teaching in exchange for religious respectability and the social legitimacy it offered. Wahhabism, however, is highly controversial even within the Muslim world for its derogatory teaching on competing schools of Islamic thought, to say

nothing of its attitude toward other religions such as Judaism and Christianity. As the house of Sa'ud consolidated power, Wahhabism emerged
as the official religion of Saudi Arabia and as such its clerics were in a position to influence policy, both domestic and foreign. Inside Saudi Arabia,
the ministry of education controls some 25,000 schools, educating approximately 5,000,000 children. Outside Saudi Arabia, there are thousands of
madrassah schools across the Middle East, all, according to critics, promoting Wahabbist Islam. Indeed, promoting Wahabbist teaching is a mainstay
of Saudi foreign policy, an arrangement New York Senator Charles Schumer
has called a "deal with the devil."[37]

Raising the possibility of a much more widespread effort, numerous journalists and authors have "uncovered" the financial connections between
Saudi Arabia and a number of Islamic organizations in the United States.[38]
These connections are usually presented as sufficient to taint the organization as at least sympathetic to, if not run by, Wahhabi influence. Stephen
Schwartz, among others, in his June 26, 2003 testimony before the Senate Subcommittee on Terrorism, Technology, and Homeland Security estimated that up to 80 percent of American mosques are under Wahhabi control, though he was quick to point out this does not mean that 80 percent
of American Muslims are Wahhabists. The Wahhabist influence in military
chaplaincy, prisons, and university-based Middle Eastern studies programs,
many of which have received significant grants from Saudi Arabia, is also
a source of concern. For that matter, numerous organizations in America,
including the Islamic Society of North America, the Council on American
Islamic Relations, and the Graduate School of Islamic and Social Sciences
are also part of the problem.[39]

While it is estimated that Saudi Arabia has spent perhaps hundreds of
millions of dollars promoting Wahhabism around the world, it is their support for Islamic schools in America that is of most interest here. Aside from
various construction grants to Islamic centers and schools across the country, the ministry of education funds and controls the Islamic Saudi Academy
(ISA) outside Washington, DC. Graduates of the ISA have been suspected
of ties to terrorism. Ahmed Omar Abu Ali, a former class valedictorian, was
indicted for plotting to assassinate President Bush, and three others were
jailed after a letter was found in one of their possessions that appeared to
indicate a plan for a suicide bombing in Israel. The criminal complaint
against Mohammed Osman Idris, filed in the U.S. District Court for the
Eastern District of Virginia specifically mentions the ISA as the place where
all three suspects received part of their education. Former employees, too,
have been suspected of ties to Hamas and other radical Islamic organizations. School officials have denied that the school itself teaches extremism,
proclaiming instead that they do their best to teach tolerance and pluralism.
There has also been a more widespread concern of the use of Saudi-funded

textbooks in Islamic schools all over the United States, as well as other Wahhabist literature that is prevalent in mosques and Islamic centers around the country.[40]

Nationally syndicated columnist Cal Thomas, in an essay entitled "Where are the Sleeper Cells," identified Islamic schools as "training grounds of hate currently on American soil."[41] Schools that promote ideas "antithetical to the American way of life and are a threat to the very existence of our country" are guilty, in Thomas' words, of sedition and should be shut down. Though Thomas, relying on the *Post* article specifically focused on the Saudi-funded schools, no attempt is made to distinguish these from other Islamic schools. Noted and controversial Middle East expert Daniel Pipes has also written about Islamic schools and their "troubling" presence in America, making specific mention of their ability to alienate students from their own country and going so far as to call Islamic schools in America a cancer.[42] Similarly, the *New York Daily News* reported that textbooks used in Islamic schools in New York City were anti-Christian, anti-Semitic, and full of "triumphalist declarations of Islam's supremacy."[43]

Aside from journalists, certain sectors of the American public are alarmed about Islamic schooling as well. One group in particular, the Society of Americans for National Existence (SANE) has set its sights on mapping the location, ideology, and funding sources of every mosque and Islamic day school in America, a project they call "Mapping Sharia: Knowing the Enemy." SANE bills itself as a an organization of those who recognize the "evil design of Islam (that is, to destroy America and to create a worldwide Islamic Caliphate).[44] While hardly mainstream, SANE's suspicion of Islamic schools is a modern manifestation of the same fear an earlier generation of Americans raised about Catholics, namely that their institutions, schools especially, were hotbeds of subversive activity under the direct control of a foreign religious/political presence bent on conquering America.

In-between the headlines about new Islamic threats to America, advocates of Islamic schooling continue to work at improving both the image and the performance of their schools. Some of the most noteworthy achievements concern curriculum development. Participants at the world conferences lamented the Muslim world's embrace of Western education. Aside from being one more indicator of Western imperialism, this one, perhaps, welcomed if not initiated by their own people, these scholars drew attention to the fact that little effort had gone into the Islamization of Western knowledge. That is, no effort had been made to break down the assumptions and implications of Western knowledge in an effort to undergird the whole system with Islamic-friendly ideas. The epistemological problem has a very practical side effect. It forces a certain compartmentalization on the school day. Learning math, history, and science is largely divorced from Islamic truth not because Islam has nothing to say on these matters, but because these subjects have not been properly analyzed and rebuilt by Muslim intellectuals. This is a common problem for religious schools. How does one keep secular and religious subjects separate without automatically subjugating one (usually religion) to the other? Time constraints alone prompt some subjects to get short shrift, to say nothing of social and political pressures for the schools to equip students for the workforce or for further study. While voices from several religious communities have decried the entire idea of separation, the practical reality has been that until religious concepts have been integrated and synthesized with modern branches of knowledge, the school day can have a sort of schizophrenic feel to it.

The promises of an integrated curriculum are many. Without additional classes during the school day individual class periods can be lengthened, promoting better coverage of salient points. Integration also avoids excessive repetition since the context is different in each classroom. Most importantly, integration can help make learning more meaningful by modeling vocational inquiry and application of religious ideals, practices that students can draw on for the rest of their lives. Religion, in an integrated curriculum, is not something one does for a portion of everyday. It infuses the entire learning process, reaffirming the idea that all truth is Divine truth and that religion is central to every other aspect of life.[45]

This integration occurs on more than the philosophical or epistemological level. On a somewhat more practical level, subjects like math and science can serve as entry points for a discussion about the history and outlook of Islam. Science classes can hear about the past accomplishments of the Muslim empire in astronomy and engineering; math classes can learn about the advances in virtually every field of mathematical inquiry, from geometry to algebra. History, too, presents opportunities for learning about Islam. World history courses can no longer omit the importance and achievements of Muslim societies, past and present. Indeed, the Council on Islamic Education has spent the last two decades improving the coverage of Muslim civilization and Islam more generally in public school classrooms across America.

As with their counterparts in the Catholic, Jewish, and Christian homeschooling community, American history classes in Islamic schools draw attention to the role Muslims in America's past. This practice is not as pronounced in Islamic schooling as it is in some other communities. This is partly due to the fact that, in the absence of a full curriculum for Islamic education most Islamic schools have adopted the same general course of study as their local public institutions. Several leaders of Islamic schooling that I spoke with confirmed that they use the same textbooks as their nearby public schools, partly out of convenience and partly out of accreditation demands. Then too, given the relative youth of most Muslim schools, it is likely that many students will at some point also be enrolled in public institutions. Thus, it is important that students from Islamic schools have as much of the same knowledge as their public school peers as possible to ensure a successful transition. And, of course, Islamic school students take the same standardized tests everyone else does as part of their preparation for college, further necessitating common content between Islamic and public schools since they compete against one another for access to higher education.[46]

And yet there are glimpses of how American history classes acknowledge links to Islamic influence that most public school children will never hear about.[47] Though it does not develop specific lessons, the IQRA International Educational Foundation, a curriculum for use in Islamic schools, in its fifth-grade social studies program recommends the study of Muslim history in America. Susan Douglass, one of the leading Islamic educators in America and a long-time advocate of more complete and accurate coverage of Islam in school classrooms, authored a supplementary unit for fifth graders as part of the Islamic School Book project of the International Institute of Islamic Thought. *Traders and Explorers in Wooden Ships: Muslims and the Age of Exploration* begins with Columbus' voyages to the New World, but also claims that much of the astronomical and geographical knowledge in fifteenth- century Europe came from Muslim lands. Genoa, as Columbus' home, is pointed out as an important part of the trade routes used by Muslim traders in Columbus' time, thus allowing for contact and exchange not just of goods, but, as the book points out, of knowledge and information as well. The Crusades, too, are pointed out as instances of Europeans coming into contact with "a better way of life in Muslim lands than they knew at home."[48] This new knowledge, fifth graders learn, was part of the motivation for Columbus and other explorers to find new trade routes to the East, the search for which led to the discovery of the Americas. Not only motivation, but maps and tools for navigation as well as ideas for constructing faster, more reliable ships originally produced by Muslims was put to use on European voyages of discovery. Finally, in the "People to Remember" summary section of this workbook, it is instructive to note that there are six European names identified with the exploration and discovery of the New World, and seven Muslims.

Aside from formal workbooks and in-school resources, pro-Islamic day school groups promote books such as Amir Muhammad's *Muslims in America: Severn Centuries of History (1312–1998)* for their value in bringing to light the presence and contributions of individual Muslims in American history. Muhammad's work, which is basically a list of names with short descriptions attached, draws attention to the bravery of two Muslim slaves in the 1775 Battle of Bunker Hill, one of whom killed an officer of the British troops while declaring, prematurely, victory.[49]

These attempts to locate Islam in America's history are noteworthy in themselves, but they also put into practice one of Islam's core ideas, namely *tawhid*, or oneness. This is the very foundation of Islamic epistemology.

God has no equals, no partners, and is himself undivided. Everything that exists, therefore, originates in him. This means that all fields of knowledge, however varied their subject matter and methods of inquiry, will ultimately lead back to God, because there is no truth outside of him. Sociologically, *tawhid* implies that all people groups have their origins in God as well. Thus, Islam's representation of itself as a universal religion reflects not just a desire to dominate the world as some might claim, but a sociological/political corollary to this theological reality.

Tawhid has educational aspects to it as well. It is the driving force behind the idea of an integrated curriculum, and the foundation of one of the most ambitious and potentially influential efforts undertaken by Islamic educational leaders in America. The Tarbiyah Project is the brainchild of Dawud Tauhidi, one of the founding members of the Council of Islamic Schools in North America as well as Michigan Islamic Academy in Ann Arbor and the Crescent Academy International, a college-preparatory Islamic school in Canton. It began with an award from the *Dar al-Islam* Foundation as part of a competition revolving around the development of Islamic character education. Convinced that the survival of the Islamic community in America is threatened by sending Muslim children to public schools, the Tarbiyah Project puts forth a rationale and framework for Muslim children and youth, with particular attention paid to the needs of those growing up under the influence of western culture. *Tarbiyah* is usually translated as education, but the concept is somewhat richer than that literal translation allows. The word *tarbiyah* means "to cause something to develop from stage to stage until reaching its completion [full potential]."[50] The program makes a distinction between learning about Islam, and being Muslim, with the latter the preferred objective of Islamic education. The goals of the project are nothing short of a revolution in North American Islamic education, and Tarbiyah presents itself as a vision of what Islamic education should be if the goal is to "restore a sense of wholeness, wellbeing and holiness back into education, our children, and Muslim society as a whole."[51] Not content with just setting the agenda, the project also provides a framework of content and methodology for Islamic education, a series of programs field tested at project-affiliated schools, and finally a strategic plan for developing the necessary communal, institutional, and familial resources to reform Islamic education.

The Tarbiyah Project reflects the same basic crisis laid out by the world conferences. Modernity has been largely disintegrative of Muslim society, but offers enough distractions and temporal rewards to seduce those that get too close. Secularism and materialism, in particular, have wreaked havoc on the patterns and values of Islamic life. Secular education, especially, neglects the spirit and character of man. Recognizing that the position of Islamic families and the *ummah* (community) itself is not unprecedented, Tauhidi writes:

Muslim parents, educators and clergy, along with those of other faith-based communities, are in a dire struggle for the spiritual survival of their children and are faced with major challenges about how best to raise their children and prepare them for the challenges of the future...Only with the proper spiritual education can we stem the tide of secular materialism in Muslim society, restrengthen our community's connection to spiritual and moral values, and save our children from a life of enslavement to the ideology of materialism and other ills of modern living.

He continues:

...spiritual education cannot simply be an appendage to an otherwise secular and fragmented curriculum. Nor can it be merely a prescriptive or parochial litany of moral do's and don'ts. Instead, it must be woven skillfully and articulately throughout the curriculum and into the daily educational experiences of our children. [52]

The Tarbiyah Project is no call for a return to the past. It embraces much of the technology and pedagogy of modernity, but does so through an integrated approach that rests upon and reasserts the principle of *tawhid*. The curriculum is built around seven "big ideas," or "strands," with each strand producing a particular kind of literacy. These include spiritual and moral literacy, as well as intellectual, physical, interpersonal, cultural, and social literacy, meaning public service. Only by promoting the full development of each individual in each of these aspects can *tarbiyah* be achieved. The Tarbiyah Project is, by itself, a remarkable accomplishment and a milestone within American Islamic education. Since at least the 1970s, Muslim educators have tried to produce a coherent educational framework built on Islamic principles that would be of particular benefit for those Muslim students in non-Muslim lands. Though the curriculum will, no doubt, continue to evolve, it already has a small, but active constituency ready to put it to the test.

As Islamic schooling continues to grow in America, these institutions will be the subject of more study. There are legitimate questions to be asked about infrastructure and curricula, as there are of all schools in America. My purpose here is not to uncover some hidden conspiracy concerning Islamic schools, but rather to show that many of the issues they may face in the future have confronted other religious communities in the past. Given the current state of affairs in the world and the all too recent memories of terrorist violence in America, Islamic schools will face these issues under conditions of heightened scrutiny. Indeed, more may be at stake now than ever before. Leaders of the Islamic school movement in this country may find it incumbent upon them (and politically wise) to more fully document what goes on in their schools than some of their predecessors. Already, many of the same questions and challenges posed to their counterparts in other religious communities are being asked of advocates of Islamic schooling.

The answers given and embodied by this generation of American Muslims may very well determine the future of Islamic schooling in America.

NOTES

1. See Barry Kosmin, Egon Mayer, and Ariela Keysar, "American Religious Identification Survey," 2001, available online at http://www.gc.cuny.edu/faculty/research_briefs/aris/aris_index.htm. This survey also shows that just under two-thirds, 62 percent, of self-identified American Muslims claim affiliation with a mosque.

2. This study has been criticized for its methodology by both demographers and the media. Essentially, Bagby, Perl, and Froehle counted the number of mosques in America, and then multiplied that number by the estimate of how many adherents were associated with the various mosques in any way. This gave them an estimate of some two million Muslims, which they then tripled to confirm the six million figure. See Ihsan Bagby, Paul Perl, and Bryan Froehle, "The Mosque in America: A National Portrait," 2001, available online through the Council on America-Islamic Relations Web site, at http://www.cair.com. On the controversy, see Bill Broadway, "Number of U.S. Muslims Depends on 'Who's Counting,'" *Washington Post*, November 24, 2001.

3. See Tom W. Smith, "The Muslim Population of the United States: The Methodology of Estimates," *Public Opinion Quarterly*, 66 (2002): 404–417. See also the *Washington Post* article by Bill Broadway, "Number of U.S. Muslims Depends on 'Who's Counting,'" previously cited, for the reaction to Smith's estimate and the American Jewish Committee's support for his work.

4. The entire survey report, entitled *Muslim Americans: Middle Class and Mostly Mainstream*, is available online from the Pew Research Center at http://pewresearch.org/.

5. Jane Smith, *Islam in America* (New York: Columbia University Press, 1999).

6. See Karen Leonard, *Muslims in the United States: The State of Research* (New York: Russell Sage Foundation, 2003).

7. For an excellent overview of the tension between integration and maintaining a separate identity, see Yvonne Haddad, "The Challenge of Muslim Minorityness: The American Experience," in *The Integration of Islam and Hinduism in Western Europe*, ed. by W. A. R. Shadid and P. S. van Koningsveld (Kampen, the Netherland: Kok Pharos Publishing House, 1991).

8. All statistics in this section come from *Muslim Americans: Middle Class and Mostly Mainstream*, Pew Research Center, previously cited, 29.

9. See Muqtedar Khan, "Collective Identity and Collective Action: The Case of Muslim Politics in America," *Muslims and Islamization in North America: Problems and Prospects*, ed. Amber Haque (Beltsville, MD: Amana Publications, 1999). For a longer treatment of the prointegration, proparticipation perspective, see Khan's *American Muslims: Bridging Faith and Freedom* (Beltsville, MD: Amana Publications, 2002).

10. This is largely an intercommunity debate and the vast majority of Muslims believe in participation. For an insider's view of the issues involved, see Mohamed Nimer, "Muslims in American Public Life," in *Muslims in the West: From Sojourners to*

Citizens, ed. Yvonne Yasbeck Haddad (New York: Oxford University Press, 2002). See also Murad Wilfried Hofmann, "Muslims as Co-Citizens in the West—Rights, Duties, Limits and Prospects," *The American Journal of Islamic Social Sciences* 14(4) (Winter 1997): 87–95.

11. Conducted as part of the Faith Communities Today project under the auspices of Hartford Seminary, researchers conducted 416 telephone interviews with randomly selected leaders from more than 1200 mosques in America. See Ihsan Bagby, "The Mosque and the American Public Square," in *Muslims' Place in the American Public Square*, ed. Zahid H. Bukhari et al. (Walnut Creek, CA: Rowman Altamira, 2004).

12. See, for example, Susan Douglass and Munir Shaikh, "Defining Islamic Education: Differentiation and Applications," *Current Issues in Comparative Education*, (7)/1 (December 2004). See also Matthew Moes, "Creating Islamic Culture in Muslim Schools," available online at http://www.4islamicschools.org.

13. On the scientific and philosophical accomplishments of Islam, see Ahmad Dallal, "Science, Medicine, and Technology," in *The Oxford History of Islam*, ed. John Esposito (New York: Oxford, 1999). See also Majid Fakhry's chapter on philosophy and theology in the same volume.

14. On the world conferences, see Moneer M. al-Otaibi and Hakim M. Rashid, "The Role of Schools in Islamic Society: Historical and Contemporary Perspectives," *The American Journal of Islamic Social Sciences*, 14(4) (Winter 1997): 1–18.

15. Syed Saijad Husain and Syed Ali Ashraf, *The Crisis in Muslim Education* (Jeddah Saudi Arabia: Hodder and Staughton, 1979): 39.

16. See Mawdudar Rahman, "A Holistic and Institutional Analysis of Islamic Education," *The American Journal of Islamic Social Sciences* 11(4) (Spring 1994): 520–531.

17. See Syed Ali Ashraf, *New Horizons in Muslim Education* (Cambridge, MA: Hodder and Stoughton, 1985): 4.

18. On Islamization as a concept, see Shujaat A. Khan, "A Critical Review of Islamization of Knowledge in the American Perspective," in *Muslims and Islamization in North America: Problems and Prospects*, ed. Amber Haque (Beltsville, MD: Amana Publications, 1999).

19. See Naseef's forward in Husain and Ashraf, *The Crisis in Muslim Education*, previously cited, vii.

20. Ashraf, New Horizons, 21.

21. *New Horizons*, 66. For examples of Islamization, see M.M.M. Mahroof, "Toward the Islamization of History: A Historical Survey," *American Journal of Islamic Social Science*, 17(1) (2000): 65–83; Rosnani Hashim, "Islamization of the Curriculum," *American Journal of Islamic Social Sciences*, 16(2) (1999): 27–43.

22. On administration in Islamic schooling, see Aref T. M. Atari, "Prolegomena for an Islamic Perspective of Educational Management," *The American Journal of Islamic Social Sciences*, 16(1) (Spring 1999): 41–72.

23. On teaching in Islamic schools, see especially Syed Sajjad Husain and Syed Ali Ashraf, *Crisis in Muslim Education* previously cited.

24. Diana Eck, "Muslim in America," *The Christian Century* (June 6–13, 2001): 20–25.

25. See Matthew Moes, "Islamic Schools as Change Agents," available through the Islamic School League's Web site at http://www.4islamicschools.org.

26. For an overview of the Sister Clara schools, see Hakim M Rashid and Zakiyyah Muhammad, "The Sister Clara Muhammad Schools: Pioneers in the Development of Islamic Education in America," *The Journal of Negro Education*, v61(2) (Spring, 1992): 178–185.

27. See Ihsan Bagby, Paul Perl, and Bryan Froehle, *The Mosque in America: A National Portrait*, previously cited. For other estimates, see the summary of the 2003–2004 Private School Universe Survey, "Characteristics of Private Schools in the United States" from the National Center for Education Statistics, available online at http:// www.nces.ed.gov.

28. Keyworth's methodology is laid out in her 2006 conference paper, but she reviewed part of it in phone conversations with me in October of 2006 as well. Essentially, she gathered together all the lists she could find, eliminated duplicates, and then began searching for contact information on the schools she had left. She also communicated with the Islamic Educators Communication Network, numerous mosques, and other organizations to arrive at her figure. Given that she has, to some extent, a vested interest in a higher number, the fact that she rejects estimates of more than three hundred is worth noting. See Karen Keyworth, *Support Networks for Islamic Schools and Data Based Profiles*, unpublished paper, available online at http://www.4islamicschools.org.

29. For an overview of Islamic education, including a criticism of supplementary programs and an early call for more full-time Islamic schools, see Kamal Ali, "Islamic Education in the United States: An Overview of Issues, Problems and Possible Approaches," *American Journal of Islamic Studies*, 1/2 (1984): 127–132.

30. ISNA is not uncontroversial. It has been linked to Saudi funding sources and charged with promoting Wahabbism. Senators Charles Grassley and Max Baucus identified ISNA as one of the organizations that funds terrorism through its links to other, less publicly scrutinized, groups. Many of the groups with a national following, including ISNA, the Muslim Student Association, and the Muslim American Society (MAS) have been linked to the Muslim Brotherhood and other extremist organizations. This link will be explored more later in this chapter.

31. See the MAS Web site at http://www.masnet.org.

32. All figures come from the NCES' Private School Universe statistical profiles, released every other year by the NCES. All reports are available online at http://www.nces.ed.gov.

33. Yvonne Yazbeck, Haddad, and Adair T. Lummis, *Islamic Values in the United States: A Comparative Study* (New York: Oxford University Press, 1987).

34. See http://www.soundvision.com, "Why Islamic Schools? Some Questions and Answers."

35. For an ethnographic account of the issues in this debate, albeit focused on schools in Canada, see Jasmine Zine, "Safe Havens or Religious Ghettos? Narratives of Islamic Schooling in Canada," *Race, Ethnicity, and Education*, 10(1) (March 2007): 71–92. See also Asma Hasan's *American Muslims: The New Generation* (New York: Continuum, 2002).

36. In other places, however, Islamic schools became resources for public institutions, starting partnerships in which students at public or other private schools could visit Islamic schools to learn about Islam more broadly. Islamic schools in other western countries, particularly in Britain, faced similar challenges.

37. Schumer has been among the most vocal critics of the connection between Saudi Arabia's foreign policy and the promotion of Wahhabism, issuing several press releases and testifying at congressional hearings to that effect. See "Saudis Playing Role in Spreading Main Terror Influence in United States," press release from Senator Charles Schumer, May 10, 2003.

38. It is difficult to measure just how widespread Saudi Arabian support actually is. The Islamic Development Bank, for instance, does not publicly list every grant it gives, and institutions in America are not always eager to discuss their ties to foreign governments. Indeed, the one issue people I spoke with were not forthcoming on was school finance. Journalistic, think tank, and even government reports often cite one another more than any independently arrived at conclusions. Nevertheless, Saudi money and influence are an important part of the organizational infrastructure of the Muslim community in America. Both the Council on Foreign Relations and the U.S. Commission on International Religious Freedom have been critical of Saudi Arabia's record in religious freedom and promoting intolerance, a fact that reinforces much of the suspicion Saudi influenced institutions face.

39. Schwartz's testimony is available at National Review Online, at http://www.nationalreview.com. See also his book, *The Two Faces of Islam: The House of Sa'ud From Tradition to Terror* (New York: Doubleday, 2002).

40. See reports from the Center for Religious Freedom of Freedom House and the Institute for Gulf Affairs, both available at the Hudson Institute's Web site, http://crf.hudson.org/.

41. Cal Thomas. "Where are the Sleeper Cells?" March 7, 2002.

42. Daniel Pipes. "What Are Islamic Schools Teaching?" *New York Sun*, March 29, 2005.

43. Larry Cohler-Esses. "Sowing the Seeds of Hatred: Islamic Textbooks Scapegoat Jews, Christians," *New York Daily News*, March 30, 2003.

44. See their Web site at http://www.saneworks.us/.

45. Susan Douglass, Ann El-Moslimany, and Sommieh Uddin, "Modeling Methods for Integrated Curriculum—Three Teaching Units," ISNA Education Forum, 2005. Available from the authors. See also Valerie Strauss and Emily Wax, "Where Two Worlds Collide: Muslim Schools Face Tension of Islamic, U.S. Views," *The Washington Post*, February 25, 2002: A1.

46. I am indebted to Susan Douglass for pointing out the motivations Islamic schools have for using or closely following the public school curriculum.

47. The ISNA Education Forum Web site contains a wealth of papers and presentations made at their annual meetings, most from Islamic educators around the country. See Amirah Desai and Rabia Sonday, "Integrating Islam into Regular American School Curricula of Social Studies and Language Arts," from the 2005 forum, or Fawad Yacoob, "Strengthening the Islamic Identity through the History/Social Studies Curriculum" from the 2006 forum, both available at http://www.isna.com/conferences/educationforum/.

48. Douglass, Susan. *Traders and Explorers in Wooden Ships: Muslims and the Age of Exploration* (Herndon, VA: International Institute of Islamic Thought, 1995).

49. Amir Nashid Ali Muhammad. *Muslims in America: Seven Centuries of History (1312-1998)* (Beltsville, MD: Amana Publications, 1998). In a similar vein, tracing back the Muslim presence in the America's to the pre-Columbian era is almost a

cottage industry of publication. See, for example Dr. Abdullah Quick's book *Deeper Roots: Muslims in the Americas and the Caribbean from Before Columbus to the Present* (London: Ta-Ha Publishers Ltd., 1998). This and similar works are also recommended by some pro-Islamic school groups such as the IQRA Foundation and SoundVision.

50. On the Tarbiyah Project, see Dawud Tauhidi, "The Tarbiyah Project: A Holistic Vision of Islamic Education," Tarbiyah Institute, 2007. Available online at http://www.Tarbiyah.org. Mr. Tauhidi graciously granted me permission to quote from this document before it was published in a modified form.

51. Ibid., 1.

52. Ibid., 5.

7 Conclusion: Moving the Debate Forward

Let us return for a moment to an earlier insight. Schools are political institutions. For all the attempts to keep partisanship out of the curriculum and the laments when political maneuvering seems to guide educational policy, education is a political process. It must be so because at stake is the production of a certain type of person, one suited for life in their society. This insight is part and parcel of the very purpose of American public education, an enterprise that consumes billions of dollars and countless hours on the part of students, their families, educational professionals, and indeed the citizenry at large. The challenge is that in modern mass societies like the United States *the citizenry* is not uniform. Believers from every religious community act on the same insight about education and the production of a certain type of person when they try to use their schools to produce good Catholics, good Jews, good Muslims, and so on. They too are hoping that by promoting certain values and beliefs in their schools their children will be faithful and productive members of their community. Participants in this debate, on all sides, are competing for the right and opportunity to cultivate, within students, a certain set of values and attachments that will take precedence over others.

These values and attachments do not have to compete with one another. But when they do pull in different directions, when for instance religious claims about the origins of life come into conflict with political claims about self-determination and the rights of women, the question is which group's claims will be recognized as more binding by the individual. Critics of religious schooling believe that the convictions instilled and cultivated in such institutions may pose significant risk to social and political order. They fear that graduates will not have developed the attitudes and skills to get along in mainstream America. Advocates of religious schooling downplay the likelihood of conflict between membership in their religious community and their rights and responsibilities as citizens of a pluralist republic, and further argue that a free society must allow for educational pluralism and the cultivation of dissent.

Though this issue has ramifications beyond education, the issue of schooling is especially problematic because of the way schools socialize children into group life. Religious schooling is controversial not just because of specific religious claims promoted by various institutions, but because religious schools promote adherence to a set of particular values and ideals instead of a more general and neutral set to which, supposedly, all Americans can subscribe. To be sure, not all critics of religious schooling are cut from the same cloth, but they do share an assumption that the public schools promote mainstream American values necessary for social order and that religious schools are a means of resisting at least some aspects of American life.

There are different ways of framing this issue and thus of linking together critics of religious schooling, or advocates for that matter, across historical cases. Some see it as a matter of adjudicating between private choices and public obligations. Others see it as a contest between the liberal emphasis on the autonomous individual unconstrained by anything other than reason and communitarians seeking to reassert the importance of group attachments to both individual formation and social order.[1] These are important matters for any free society, and there is a considerable amount of scholarly literature generated every year on just these topics. While much of this literature is intellectually provocative and worthy of consideration, it often gives primacy of place to the development and modification of various terms such as "tolerance" or "civic education." The consequences of these terms for schooling are then elaborated. The problem with this approach is that the terms themselves are often so finely revised from theorist to theorist that the conversation about education, a conversation that virtually everyone acknowledges should be widely shared, is too insulated to be of help to all but specialists in dialogue with one another. Consider, for instance, the word "multicultural" in its various forms. Some advocates of multicultural education argue that American society has long benefited from the presence of a number of different groups, each of which has made specific contributions to the whole. A multicultural education is one that exposes all students to the vibrancy of these different strands of American society. Of course, different groups might stress their own contributions over those of other groups, as we saw in Chapter 5. They might even specifically challenge the version of events put forth by "competing" cultural traditions. Acknowledging that lots of groups have made contributions to American society, a worthwhile and overdue observation in my view, is not the same as agreeing that everyone's contribution is equally worthy.

Another group of educators, also claiming the banner of multiculturalism, could argue that recognizing the pluralism of American society requires separate schools for each group. Instead of surveying a broad swath of groups, these institutions could focus on the contributions of one segment of the society, perhaps to the exclusion of all others. The first group of educators seeks, in the name of multiculturalism, a wider story. The second group, also in the name of multiculturalism, promotes a much more restrictive course of study as a means of ensuring that their particular cultural tradition is not lost. Thus, advocating multicultural education can lead us in opposite directions, depending on what we mean by "multicultural."[2] Noted political and educational theorist Amy Gutmann, in drawing our attention to just this problem, advanced a concept of "democratic education," yet here too there are a number of specific terms put forth that invite the same sort of insular dialogue. The word "tolerance," was not so long ago a favorite concept among civic educators. Though it is by no means clear that we have achieved tolerance, the term itself is no longer satisfactory, "mutual respect" and "reciprocity" having supplanted it.

Even as academics have debated the finer points of the relationship between democracy, religious conviction, and education, generations of parents and religious community leaders have forged ahead, leaving in their wake a long list of institutions and ideas worthy of both examination and respect. Their own explanations of what they were doing, taken with the criticisms and accusations of successive generations of religious school opponents, provide contemporary researchers with opportunities for comparisons across groups, a strategy that yields new insights for how to move this debate forward. One of the things that critics of faith-based schooling have in common is that they speak from the perspective, if not the actual position, of the cultural majority. They believe that their values are central to the American experience and social order, and are therefore an appropriate part of public education. In their view, religious schools, either explicitly in their curriculum or implicitly through their very existence, undermine key aspects of the society's core values. Thus, anti-Catholic school forces claimed that Catholic schooling threatened the religious and political freedom, as they understood those terms, at the foundation of American society. Catholicism's emphasis on obedience and respect for authority, especially a foreign authority, was seen as inconsistent with American democratic ideals. Likewise, the Protestant tone of the supposedly nonsectarian public institutions rendered those schools unacceptable to American Catholics. Critics of the Jewish day schools (most of whom were themselves members of the Jewish community) held that American culture was benignly assimilative and thus offered new possibilities for Jews to fully integrate into a truly democratic

society. Separate educational institutions would only reinforce the very isolation that had been so much a part of their experience in other lands,
and could lead to the same sort of ethnic or religious ghettos that many
Jewish Americans had tried to escape. Many families in the Jewish community (better, communities) however wanted to retain a strong connection
to their own cultural and religious legacy. Attending public schools made
this too difficult, and thus they turned to their own institutions. Modern-day
critics of conservative Protestant schooling, especially of the homeschooling variety, worry that the narrow religious identity they believe it promotes
will be injurious to tolerance for the other, an idea they hold to be of particular importance to modern American life. More broadly, they question
whether faith-based schooling can sustain a commitment to a secular public square, an important element of America's promise to all citizens. But
their equation of secularism with neutrality has proven unacceptable in the
eyes of many devout Christians who, as a result, fled the public schools.
The Supreme Court's decision in *Engle v. Vitale* prohibiting even nonsectarian prayers from public schools was, in their view, a sign of lost ground.
It should come as no surprise, then, that they too constructed alternative
institutions. Finally, advocates of Islamic schooling have faced versions of
all three of these criticisms (as has each group to some extent), as they are
questioned about Islam's compatibility with democracy, religious pluralism,
and assimilation. Their defenders argue that Islamic schools are the best
way to maintain the faithfulness of their children, and seek to assure their
critics that Americans need not fear Islamic institutions, including schools.

    The underlying issue between critics and advocates of faith-based school-
ing is not one religious group against another, or even religious groups
against secularists. It is certainly not Americans against foreigners, though
specific contests over the place of religious schooling have taken all of these
forms. The history of faith-based education is better understood not as
two consistent groups squaring off, but as manifestations of a debate about
American national character and the place of strong sub-national identities
within it. Advocates of the public schools, though they come from radi-
cally divergent perspectives, have long held that schools should function
to integrate different segments of American society into a cohesive whole.
Public schools should promote the values and ideals that will be consistent
with what they perceived to be the core of American identity. Furthermore,
they believe that this core, which is usually presented as being nonsectarian
and therefore more appropriate for public life, should be acceptable to
all Americans regardless of their more particular, some might say private,
religious convictions.[3] They see themselves on the side of national unity,
and their schools as agents of America's democratic spirit.

    A comparative perspective also provides other insights. We noted ear-
lier some of the ironies in religious school history. Catholics built their
own schools to get away from what they perceived as Protestant-controlled

schools, winning the right to do so in the 1925 *Pierce* decision. Protestants have now fled the public schools to escape secularists, benefiting from the Catholic struggles they themselves helped set in motion.[4] Now we can see the full implication of that irony. The key elements of American identity have changed as a new group has taken over the institutional center of American education. The rise of conservative Protestant schooling is, in important ways, a reaction to what they see as the marginalization of their views in public institutions. This transition, as part of the larger secularization of American public life, was not just the result of massive and impersonal social trends. It was also part of a conscious effort to loosen the grip of organized religion on various aspects of society. The normative question of whether or not this transition was a good turn in American history will not be taken up here. The result, however, is unmistakable. Protestantism, at least in the public schools, has lost its place. Thus some Protestants, though certainly not all, have joined segments of the Catholic, Jewish, and Muslim communities on the institutional sidelines of American education. Representatives from some of these communities have even cooperated across theological and confessional boundaries to further their cause, and, as in the *Pierce* years, have even worked with non-religious advocates of private schooling in some cases. It is too early to tell where this sort of cooperation will go, and certainly some of the early signs are not encouraging (recall the Texas Association of Private and Parochial School's hesitancy to embrace an Islamic institution in Chapter 5), but it could represent new possibilities for interfaith dialogue and public action.

Generations of religious school advocates, though they may have significant disagreements with one another over matters of theology or politics, share certain characteristics as well. Chapter 2 has explored some of these common grounds already. There is some common attempt to construct a social space in which the truths of the religious community can be validated, and in turn validate, various fields of knowledge. There is also a widespread affirmation of the family's responsibility to direct the intellectual, moral, and spiritual formation of the child. Though religious organizations often carry out that program on behalf of the parents, many religious communities agree that it is the family more than the state that is ultimately accountable for education, and therefore the family should be empowered along these lines as well.[5]

Additionally, advocates of religious schooling believe that strong religious identities are not only their right, but actually enhance American life. While it is important not to downplay their defensiveness, some might say their stubbornness, their faith in American society to allow them to maintain their position, contrarian though it might be, is worth noting as well. Indeed, there is a recurring optimism about, even gratitude for, the right to practice this form of institutional dissent. With Will Herberg, they see the cultivation of a strong attachment to their religious community as an expression of their

American identity rather than a repudiation of same. To be sure, they put these two aspects of their identity together in different ways. Religion and politics are too complicated fields to be summarized with statements like "all religious groups want to be left alone," or "all religious schoolers want to take over the government." It is also not the case that all the advocates of religious schooling, even within one religious community, want the same things in terms of cultural influence. They can and do have different stances on political issues as well as different party affiliations. But they do share the idea that a strong religious identity should not be seen as disruptive of American life.

MOVING THE DEBATE FORWARD

It is not the case that all critics of private and religious schools think the public schools are thriving. The opposite is more often the case. Critics of faith-based education may also put forth programs to overhaul public education. What they defend, at least implicitly, is the potential of public education to promote national unity, and to contribute to a more democratic social order. But truly democratic social orders purposefully respect the rights of cultural minorities. While the political and educational theorists so active in the contemporary manifestation of this debate are well attuned to this requirement, the more public dialogue often lacks sufficient attention in this regard. Accusing the advocates of faith-based schooling of being aligned with a foreign power bent on overthrowing America, or of seeking to undermine the government the same way domestic terrorists do is hardly evidence of cultural majority's democratic superiority. Nor is it likely to result in the closing of religious schools. Indeed, just the opposite is true. External conflict often acts as a vise in that in condenses and tightens the membership of the group under pressure, thereby increasing whatever potential for social disorder that may be present. Those who would use the public schools to dissolve subgroup loyalties would do well to remember the advice of James Madison that in destroying liberty in an effort to curb factionalism we embrace a cure that is worse than the disease!

Those in power would also do well to consider their own self-interests in light of the fickleness of history. As we have seen, values and social position change over time. Those who think public schools should reflect and advance their own values should be reminded that their position may be no more permanent than was the Protestant's hegemony at the beginning of the twentieth century. Familiarity with American history should promote humility rather than the assumption that one's own values are the most advanced, the most likely to result in the good society. A similar point has been made by noted Yale Law professor, Stephen L. Carter. Familiarity with the history of education in America, Carter writes, might prompt one to ask why public schools are so readily identified as the norm and religious schools as the interloper. It is, after all, the religious dimension of life that is most specifically protected from public and government interference in the Constitution, thus surely religious schools are more than permissible in American life. Too, given the history of the public schools being used to harass religious minorities perhaps it is these institutions that are un-American.[6]

Critics of religious schools should also recognize that these schools are an example of a long-recognized aspect of American character. Tocqueville himself, in his masterful *Democracy in America*, drew attention to the independence and do-it-yourself attitude he considered part of the genius of America as far back as the 1830s. His well-known observations on political associations in America begin with the recognition that Americans are distrustful of social authority, having been "taught from infancy to rely upon [their] own exertions" to accomplish the tasks before them.[7] The work that goes into building and maintaining systems of religious schooling requires exactly the sort of collaborative effort, planning, and collection and allocation of resources that most observers consider part of the value of civil society in American life. Beyond just capitalizing on the right to direct the education of their children, families, often through the mediating institution of their church, have shouldered the corresponding responsibilities of educating their children. To varying degrees they have worked with public education officials to meet accreditation guidelines, they have pioneered curriculum innovations (with mixed results to be sure), and they have provided options for some families who, by virtue of their address, would have otherwise had to attend failing public institutions. In these and other ways, faith-based schools, and private schools more broadly, have empowered citizens to direct their own affairs.

Those who favor an education that imparts a more particular set of values and loyalties should do their utmost to find common ground with the broader currents of American life. The right for a community to exist on its own terms carries with it the responsibility to be supportive of the central value system as much as possible. Amitai Etzioni voiced a similar arrangement when he advanced his New Golden Rule. Individuals should support and uphold society's moral order just as they would expect society to uphold their autonomy. The same is true on the communal level. Specific communities, in the present case religious in nature, should recognize the numerous ways they are connected to the larger whole.[8] The roads that take children to their respective schools were built and maintained by the society at large, not individual communities. Fire and police protection, too, are public goods that even the most intensely private religious institutions depend on. Social order, respect for persons, and educational excellence should be promoted in all schools. Characterizing advocates of public education as agents of Satan bent on destroying all religion or brainwashing children should be unacceptable. It feeds, rather than denies, the criticism that graduates of faith-based schools will not be able, or even willing, to meaningfully participate with those outside their own religious community. Indeed, it suggests that those outside the community are not worth interacting with except as subjects of proselytization. This is hardly the best means of showcasing the democratic potential of religious schooling, and it ignores legitimate concerns about a common moral framework and the ability to interact with others as equal participants in American life. History curricula that stress the contributions of particular groups should not imply that all others are less than full recipients of America's political heritage. Surely the criticisms made by Arthur Schlesinger and others of the dangers of this kind of compensatory history apply to religious reconstructions of the past as well.[9]

Most optimistically, both sides would also do well to think about the debate itself as a constructive enterprise. We may not be able to reach a consensus on what constitutes a good education, but we need not let the elusiveness of the goal mean that we abandon constructive discourse. It may well be that our differences are incommensurate; religious families, for instance, will probably never be satisfied with an education that sidelines their most precious truths. Likewise, advocates of public education will in all likelihood continue to see religious schools as a threat to social order. But all of the points they both make to support their case are themselves relevant topics to discuss. What are the limits of parental authority? Should we disestablish schooling from the state altogether? What is the place of religious conviction in liberal polity? All of these are at play in the debate over the legitimacy of religious schooling, and all are absolutely appropriate, even necessary points for democratic dialogue. Indeed, thinking about the debate itself as part of the issue requires both sides to more thoroughly construct their various positions and thus may discover previously unrecognized points of common ground. Even if no such points are found, the debate itself encourages democratic discourse and rational deliberation as opposed to name-calling and demonization of the enemy, both of which characterize the status quo. The acceptance of the debate itself apart from all-out attempts to win (which too often take the form of power politics or courtroom litigation) may also invite voices from the middle positions rather than the extremes that tend to dominate public and media discourse.[10] Something like this can already be seen in the negotiations between homeschoolers and various local public school districts across the country. Students who receive the majority of their education at home often participate in team or club sports with local schools, or attend the school for certain classes. While national voices on both sides sound the alarm over the other, parents and local advocates for public education often find that they can work together more effectively than one might suspect.

Additionally, both sides would do well to think in less stark terms about group memberships. Strong religious identity need not mean that there is no sense of connection to the whole. Likewise, support for social order and common good does not require one to abandon all sub-national communal ties. Multiple loyalties are not only possible, but are arguably a much more realistic understanding of how people live. We are simultaneously members of multiple communities, and while these various obligations can conflict with one another, it is not the case that these conflicts always represent a mortal threat to the whole. Individuals, and communities too, have evidenced a remarkable ability to thrive in spite of the tension between familial, religious, and political obligations.

Finally, all parties in the debate should consider the richness of the individual traditions that have nourished the opposing viewpoints. Advocates of public education have a long history to draw on about the benefits of widespread literacy and most especially the nobility of empowering citizens to direct their own affairs. The public school, for all its problems, did indeed help forge a common identity for Americans, no small accomplishment in a land made up largely of immigrants. It also promoted competent citizenship on the part of disempowered segments of American society, helping American democracy live up to its promise. Proponents of religious schools, too, have much to commend their position. It was, after all, religious institutions that often promoted education and social order before the advent of public schools, and their institutions too have been active in the promotion of civic literacy. There is much to appreciate in their legacy as well.

Religious schools are a vital and vibrant part of American education. Like it or not, they are here to stay. The debate over their legitimacy is nearly two centuries old and shows no signs of abating anytime soon. Let us hope that the debate itself can move forward in such a way as to reflect and promote the best aspects of America's educational and political heritage.

NOTES

1. For a thorough examination of how this debate can be constructed, see Elmer J. Thiessen, *In Defense of Religious Schools and Colleges*, previously cited. Theissen defends the place of religious schooling in democratic societies on philosophical grounds, offering a sustained critique of Gutmann in particular.

2. On the challenges of multiculturalism in education, see Amy Gutmann, "Challenges of Multiculturalism in Democratic Education," available online from the Philosphy of Education society at http://www.ed.uiuc.edu/eps/PES-Yearbook/95_docs/gutmann.html.

3. The use of the public/private distinction is not without problems in this regard. For an analysis on the different kinds of thinking at play here see Jeffrey Henig, "Understanding the Political Conflict over School Choice," in *Getting Choice Right: Ensuring Equity and Efficiency in Education Policy*, eds. Julian R. Betts and Tom Leveless (Washington, DC: Brookings Institutions Press, 2005).

4. In presenting the Protestant exodus this way, I do not mean to imply agreement with the charge that "secular humanists" have taken over the schools that is at

the basis of their complaint. Rather, I mean to say that public education has moved away from the promotion of a common, generally progressive Protestantism toward the idea that public education should not advocate any religious tradition. On this transition, see Kraig Beyerlein, "Educational Elites and the Movement to Secularize Public Education: The Case of the National Education Association," in *The Secular Revolution: Power, Interests, and Conflict in the Secularization of American Public Life*, ed. Christian Smith (Berkeley, CA: University of California Press, 2003).

5. It is worth noting that the specific role of parents changes across religious communities, and even within the same community across time. Nineteenth-century Catholic pronouncements focused more on the church's role than the family's, and in some ways used as much coercion as the public schools, albeit of a different kind.

6. Stephen L. Carter, *The Dissent of the Governed: A Meditation on Law, Religion, and Loyalty* (Cambridge, MA: Harvard University Press, 1998).

7. Alexis de Tocqueville, *Democracy in America, vol 1* (New York: Vintage Books, 1945).

8. Amitai Etzioni, *The New Golden Rule: Community and Morality in a Democratic Society* (New York: Basic Books, 1996).

9. Arthur Schlesinger, *The Disuniting of America: Reflections on a Multicultural Society* (New York: Norton, 1991).

10. James Hunter has written extensively on the ways in which public dialogue is dominated by elites from the various factions, many of whom attain their positions precisely because of the stridency with which they campaign for their cause. See his *Culture Wars: The Struggle to Define America* (New York: Basic Books, 1991).

Bibliography

"A Case for Moral Absolutes," *Time Magazine*, June 8, 1981: 54–56.

Adams, Louise, Judith Frankel, and Nancy Newbauer. 1972. "Parental Attitudes toward the Jewish All-Day School." *Jewish Education* 42 (Winter): 26–30.

Ali, Kamal. 1984. "Islamic Education in the United States: An Overview of Issues, Problems and Possible Approaches." *American Journal of Islamic Studies* 1(2): 127–132.

al-Otaibi, Moneer M., and Hakim M. Rashid. 1997. "The Role of Schools in Islamic Society: Historical and Contemporary Perspectives." *The American Journal of Islamic Social Sciences* 14(4) (Winter): 1–18.

American Catholic Hierarchy. 1950. "The Child: Citizen of Two Worlds." In *Catholic Education in America: A Documentary History*, edited by Neil McCLuskey. New York: Teachers College.

Anderson, Benedict. 1991. *The Imagined Community*. London: Verso Press.

Apple, Michael. 1995. "Is Social Transformation Always Progressive? Rightist Reconstructions of Schooling Today." In *Social Reconstruction through Education*, edited by Michael James. Norwood, OH: Ablex Publishing.

———. 1996. *Cultural Politics and Education*. Buckingham: Open University Press.

———. 2000. "The Cultural Politics of Home Schooling." *Peabody Journal of Education* 75 (1 and 2): 256ff.

Ashraf, Syed Ali. 1985. *New Horizons in Muslim Education*. Cambridge, MA: Hodder and Stoughton.

Atari, Aref T.M. 1999. "Prolegomena for an Islamic Perspective of Educational Management." *The American Journal of Islamic Social Sciences* 16(1) (Spring): 41–72.

Bagby, Ihsan. 2004. "The Mosque and the American Public Square." In *Muslims' Place in the American Public Square*, edited by Zahid H. Bukhari et al. Walnut Creek, CA: Rowman Altamira.

————, Paul Perl, and Bryan Froehle. 2001. *The Mosque in America: A National Portrait.* Washington, DC: Council on American-Islamic Relations. http://www.cair-net. org.

Baron, Salo. 1948. "Communal Responsibility for Jewish Education." *Jewish Education* 19: Spring, 7ff..

Barton, Keith, and Linda Levstik. 2004. *Teaching History for the Common Good.* Mahwah, NJ: Lawrence Erlbaum Associates.

Bates, Stephen. 1993. *Battleground.* New York: Poseidon Press.

Ben-Horin, Meir. 1969. "From the Turn of the Century to the Late Thirties." In *A History of Jewish Education in America,* edited by Judah Pilch. New York: American Association for Jewish Education.

Berger, Brigitte. 2002. *The Family in the Modern Age: More Than a Lifestyle Choice.* New Brunswick, NJ: Transaction Press.

Berger, Peter. 1967. *The Sacred Canopy.* New York: Doubleday.

————. 1992. *A Far Glory: The Quest for Faith in an Age of Credulity.* New York: Random House.

Berkson, Isaac. 1920. *Theories of Americanization: A Critical Study.* New York: Arno Press.

Beyerlein, Kraig. 2003. "Educational Elites and the Movement to Secularize Public Education: The Case of the National Education Association." *The Secular Revolution: Power, Interests, and Conflict in the Secularization of American Public Life,* edited by Christian Smith. Berkeley, CA: University of California Press.

Billington, Ray. 1938. *The Protestant Crusade 1800–1860: A Study of the Origins of American Nativism.* New York: Macmillan.

Bishops 1919 Pastoral Letter. http://www.osjspm.org/majordoc_us_bishop_statement_pastoral_letter_1919.aspx.

Blau, Joseph. 1958 (November) 14. "The Jewish Day School." *The Reconstructionist.* 29–32.

Bowen, William R. et al. 1997. *American Government in Christian Perspective,* edited by Brian Ashbaugh. Pensacola, FL: A Beka Book.

Broadway, Bill (November) 24 2001. "Number of U.S. Muslims Depends on Who's Counting," *Washington Post.*

Browning, Don S., M. Christian Green, and John Witte Jr., 2006. *Sex, Marriage, and Family in World Religions.* New York: Columbia University Press.

Bruce, Steve. 1988. *The Rise and Fall of the New Christian Right: Conservative Protestant Politics in America, 1978–1988.* Oxford: Clarendon Press.

Buetow, Harold A. 1970. *Of Singular Benefit: The Story of Catholic Education in the United States.* New York: Macmillan.

Burgess, Charles. 1976. "The Goddess, the School Book, and Compulsion." *Harvard Educational Review,* 46, 199–216.

Burns, James A. 1969. *The Principles, Origin and Establishment of the Catholic School System in the United States.* New York: Arno Press; and the *New York Times.*

Burke, John. Correspondence to Bishop Muldoon from February 1922. In NCWC Archives, Box 122, File 159D, Catholic University, Washington, DC.

————. Correspondence to A. Duncan Yocum in February 1923. In NCWC Archives, Box J42, Catholic University, Washington, DC.

Butts, R. Freeman. 1973 (April 30). "Assaults on a Great Idea." *The Nation,* 553–556.

————. 1974 (Summer): "Public Education and Political Community." *History of Education Quarterly* 14, 165–183.

Carper, James, and Thomas Hunt. 1984. *Religious Schooling in America.* Birmingham: Religious Education Press.

————. 2007. *The Dissenting Tradition in American Education.* New York: Peter Lang Publishers.

Carter, Stephen L. 1998. *The Dissent of the Governed: A Meditation on Law, Religion, and Loyalty.* Cambridge, MA: Harvard University Press.

Center for Religious Freedom. 2005. *Saudi Publications on Hate Ideology Invade American Mosques.* Washington, DC: Center for Religious Freedom.

————. 2006. *Saudi Arabia's Curriculum of Intolerance.* Washington, DC: Center for Religious Freedom.

Cheney, Lynn. October 20, 1994. "The End of History," *Wall Street Journal.*

Cloud, John and Jodie Morse. 2001 (August 27). "Home Sweet School," *Time* 158, 47ff.

Cohen, Jack. 1964. *Jewish Education in Democratic Society.* New York: Reconstructionist Press.

Cohen, Naomi. 1992. *Jews in Christian America: The Pursuit of Religious Equality.* New York: Oxford University Press.

Cohler-Esses, Larry. 2003 (March 30). "Sowing the Seeds of Hatred: Islamic Textbooks Scapegoat Jews, Christians," *New York Daily News.*

Coleman, James, and Thomas Hoffer. 1987. *Public and Private High Schools: The Impact of Communities.* New York: Basic Books.

Coleman, James S. 1965. "Introduction: Education and Political Development." In *Educational and Political Development*, edited by James S Coleman. Princeton, NJ: Princeton University Press.

Coulter, Michael. 2008. "School Vouchers in America." *Church and State Issues in America Today 2*, edited by Ann W. Duncan and Steven L. Jones. Westport, CT: Praeger Press.

Crawford, John, and Sharon Freeman. 1996. "Why Parents Choose Private Schooling: Implications for Public School Programs and Information Campaigns." *ERS Spectrum.* (Summer): 9–16.

Cremin, Lawrence. 1957. *The Republic and the School: Horace Mann on the Education of Free Men*, edited by Lawrence Cremin. New York: Teachers College Press.

———— 1980. *American Education: the National Experience, 1783–1876.* New York: Harper and Row.

————. 1990. *Popular Education and its Discontents.* New York: Harper and Row.

Dallal, Ahmad. 1999. "Science, Medicine, and Technology." In *The Oxford History of Islam*, edited by John Esposito. New York: Oxford.

Desai, Amirah, and Rabia Sonday. (2005). "Integrating Islam into Regular American School Curricula of Social Studies and Language Arts." Plainfield, IN: Islamic Society of North America Educational Forum.

Dewey, John. 1916. *Democracy and Education.* New York: Free Press.

Dinin, Samuel. 1945 (October 5). "The All-Day Jewish School." *The Reconstructionist*, 11ff.

Douglass, Susan. 1995. *Traders and Explorers in Wooden Ships: Muslims and the Age of Exploration.* Herndon, VA: International Institute of Islamic Thought.

———, Ann El-Moslimany, and Sommieh Uddin. 2005. "Modeling Methods for Integrated Curriculum—Three Teaching Units," *ISNA Education Forum.*

———, and Munir Shaikh. 2004. "Defining Islamic Education: Differentiation and Applications," *Current Issues in Comparative Education* 7(1) December. www.tc.columbia.edu/cice/.

Durkheim, Emile. 1972. "The Development of Educational Systems." In *Emile Durkheim: Selected Writings*, edited by Anthony Giddens. Cambridge: Cambridge University Press.

Dushkin, Alexander. 1948 (November). "The Role of the Day School in American Jewish Education" *Jewish Education* 20(1): 13.

———, and Uriah Engelman. 1959. "Jewish Education in the United States." New York: Commission for the Study of Jewish Education in the United States.

Dwyer, James G. 1998. *Religious Schools v. Children's Rights.* Ithaca, NY: Cornell University Press.

Easton, David. 1957. "Function of Formal Education in a Political System." *The School Review*, 65, 304–316.

Eberle, Christopher. 2002. *Religious Conviction in Liberal Politics.* Cambridge: Cambridge University Press.

Eck, Diana. 2001 (June 6–13). "Muslim in America." *The Christian Century*, 20–25.

Educational Policies Commission. 1937. *The Unique Function of Education in American Democracy.* Washington, DC: National Education Association.

———. 1940. *Learning the Ways of Democracy: A Casebook in Civic Education.* Washington, DC: National Education Association.

———. 1951. *Moral and Spiritual Values in Public Schools.* Washington, DC: National Education Association.

———. 1955. *Publication Education and the Future of America.* Washington, DC: National Education Association.

———. 1961. *The Central Purpose of American Education.* Washington, DC: National Education Association.

Edwards, Anne Michaels. 1996. *Educational Theory As Political Theory.* Brookfield, CT: Avebury.

Elias, John L. 1976. *Conscientization and Deschooling: Friere's and Illich's Proposals for Reshaping Society.* Philadelphia, PA: Westminster Press.

Eliot, Thomas H. 1959. "Toward an Understanding of Public School Politics." *American Political Science Review*, LIII, 1032ff.

Etzioni, Amitai. 1996. *The New Golden Rule: Community and Morality in a Democratic Society.* New York: Basic Books.

Everhart, Robert B. 1977. "From Universalism to Usurpation: An Essay on the Antecedents to Compulsory School Attendance Legislation." *Review of Educational Research* 47: 499–530.

Farris, Michael P. 1995. "Abolish the Department of Education? Why Should Home Schoolers Care?" *Home School Court Report* 11 (1): 28.

———. 1995. "More than the Department—It's Time to Abolish the Federal Role in Education." *Home School Court Report* 11 (1): 1ff.

———. 1995. "The Parental Rights Act: Establishing a Standard of Liberty." *Home School Court Report* 11 (2): 1ff.

Farris, Michael P., and Scott Woodruff. 2000. "The Future of Home Schooling." *Peabody Journal of Education* 75 (1 and 2): 233ff.

Fried, Jacob. 1953. "Public School or Jewish Day School." *Congress Weekly*, May 25, 11ff.

Friedman, Lee M. 1942. *Jewish Pioneers and Patriots*. Philadelphia, PA: Jewish Publication Society of America.

Fromm, Erich. 1970. Introduction to *Celebration of Awareness: A Call for Institutional Revolution*, edited by Ivan Illich. Garden City, NY: Doubleday and Company.

Gallup, Alec M. 1986 (September). "The 18th Annual Gallup Poll of the Public's Attitudes toward the Public Schools." *Phi Delta Kappan* 68: 43ff.

Galston, William. 2001. "Political Knowledge, Political Engagement, and Civic Education." *Annual Review of Political Science* 4: 217–234.

Gartner, Lloyd P. 1969. *Jewish Education in the United States: A Documentary History*. New York, NY: Teachers College Press, Columbia University.

———. 1974. "Jewish Education in the United States." In *The Jewish Community in America*, edited by Marshall Sklare. New York, NY: Behrman House.

———. 1976. "Temples of Liberty Unpolluted: American Jews and Public Schools, 1840–1875." In *A Bicentenniel Festschrift for Jacob Rader Marcus*, edited by Bertram Wallace. Waltham, MA: American Jewish Historical Society.

Gelbart, Gershon I. 1963. *Jewish Education in America: A Manual for Parents and School Board Members*. New York: Jewish Education Committee of New York.

Gellner, Ernest. 1983. *Nations and Nationalism*. New York: Cornell University Press.

Gershuny, Jonathan. 1978. *After Industrial Society: The Emerging Self-Service Economy*. Atlantic Highlands, NJ: Humanities Press.

Gibbons, Cardinal. 1889. "Should Americans Educate Their Children in Denominational Schools." In *Denominational Schools*. New York: Kansas Publishing House.

Glazer, Nathan. 1972. *American Judaism*. Chicago, IL: University of Chicago Press.

Glenn, Charles. 1988. *The Myth of the Common School*. Amherst, MA: University of Massachusetts Press.

———. 1995. *Educational Freedom in Eastern Europe*. Washington, DC: Cato Institute

———. 2003. "Protecting and Limiting School Distinctiveness: How Much of Each?" In *School Choice: The Moral Debate*, edited by Alan Wolfe. Princeton, NJ: Princeton University Press.

Golden, Harry, and Martin Rywell. 1950. *Jews in American History: Their Contribution to the United States of America*. Charlotte, NC: H.A. Stalls Printing.

Goldman, Nahum. 1963. "Jewish Education and the Future of Jewish Life in the Diaspora." *Jewish Education* 33 (Winter): 2ff.

Goodside, Samuel. 1951. "A Social Studies Syllabus for Secular Teachers in Jewish All-Day Schools: A Companion Bulletin to the Social Studies Curriculum Bulletins of the Board of Education of the City of New York." PhD dissertation, New York University.

Green, Andy. 1990. *Education and State Formation: The Rise of Education Systems in England, France, and the USA*. New York: St. Martins.

Grinstein, Hyman B. 1945. *The Rise of the Jewish Community of New York, 1654–1860*. Philadelphia, PA: Jewish Publication Society of America.

———. 1969. "In the Course of the Nineteenth Century." In *A History of Jewish Education*, edited by Judah Pilch. New York: American Association for Jewish Education.

Grossman, Mordecai. 1945. "Parochial Schools for Jewish Children: An Adverse View." *Jewish Education* 16 (May): 20–25.

Gutmann, Amy. "Challenges of Multiculturalism in Democratic Education." http://www.ed.uiuc.edu/eps/PES-Yearbook/95_docs/gutmann. html 1995.

———. 1987. *Democratic Education.* Princeton, NJ: Princeton University Press.

Haddad, Yvonne. 1991. "The Challenge of Muslim Minorityness: The American Experience." In *The Integration of Islam and Hinduism in Western Europe,* edited by W.A.R. Shadid and P.S. van Koningsveld. Kampen: Kok Pharos Publishing House.

———, and Adair T. Lummis. 1987. *Islamic Values in the United States: A Comparative Study.* New York: Oxford University Press.

Harris, Greg. 1988. *The Christian Home School.* Brentwood, CA: Wolgemuth and Hyatt.

Hasan, Asma. 2002. *American Muslims: The New Generation.* New York: Continuum.

Hashim, Rosnani. 1999. "Islamization of the Curriculum," *American Journal of Islamic Social Sciences* 16(2): 27–43.

Hawley, W.D. 1995. "The False Premises and False Promises of the Movement to Privatize Public Education." *Teachers College Record* 96: 735ff.

Henig, Jeffrey. 2005. "Understanding the Political Conflict over School Choice." In *Getting Choice Right: Ensuring Equity and Efficiency in Education Policy,* edited by Julian R. Betts and Tom Loveless. Washington, DC: Brookings Institution Press.

Herberg, Will. 1955. *Protestant Catholic Jew: An Essay in American Religious Sociology.* Garden City, NY: Doubleday and Company.

Himmelfarb, Milton. 1960 (July). "Reflections on the Jewish Day School." *Commentary* 30, 29.

Hirschman, Albert. 1970. *Exit, Voice, and Loyalty.* Cambridge, MA: Harvard University Press.

Hofmann, Murad Wilfried. 1997. "Muslims as Co-Citizens in the West—Rights, Duties, Limits and Prospects." *The American Journal of Islamic Social Sciences* 14(4) (Winter): 87–95.

Holmes, Arthur. 1977. *All Truth is God's Truth.* Grand Rapids, MI: Eerdmans.

———. 1983. *Contours of a World View.* Grand Rapids, MI: Eerdmans.

Honor, Leo. 1955. "The Impact of the American Environment and American Ideas on Jewish Elementary Education in the United States." *Jewish Quarterly Review* xlv.

Hughes, John. 1841. "A Review and Refutation of the Remonstrance of the Public School Society and the Argument of Hiram Ketchum." *New York Freeman's Journal* (Special Report).

Hunter, James D. 1991. *Culture Wars: The Struggle to Define America.* New York: Basic Books.

Husain, Syed Saijad, and Syed Ali Ashraf. 1979. *The Crisis in Muslim Education.* Jeddah, Saudi Arabia: Hodder and Stoughton.

Institute for Advanced Studies in Culture. 1996. "The State of Disunion, Vol. II. *Survey on American Political Culture.* Ivy: In Medias Res Educational Foundation.

———. 2000. "The Politics of Character." *Survey of American Public Culture,* Vol. III. Charlottesville, VA: Institute for Advanced Studies in Culture, University of Virginia 2000.

Iverson, Robert. 1959. *The Communists and the Schools.* New York: Harcourt Brace.

Jakobovits, Immanuel. 1961 (February). "The Strengths of the Yeshiva Movement." *The Jewish Parent*, 5ff.

Jay, Honorable John. 1889. "Public and Parochial Schools." In *Denominational Schools*. New York: Kansas Publishing House.

Johnson, George. 1929 (August). "Contribution of Catholic Education to American Life." *National Catholic Welfare Council Bulletin*: 7ff.

Jorgenson, Lloyd. 1968. "The Oregon School Law of 1922: Passage and Sequel." *Catholic Historical Review* 54: 455ff.

———. 1987. *The State and the Non-Public School: 1825–1925*. Columbia, MO: University of Missouri Press.

Kaminetsky, Joseph. 1957. "Evaluating the Program and Effectiveness of the All-Day Jewish School." *Jewish Education* 27 (Winter): 39–49.

———. 1970. *Hebrew Day School Education: An Overview*. New York: Torah Umesorah.

Kapel, David. 1972. "Parental Views of a Jewish Day School" *Jewish Education* 41 (Spring): 28–38.

Katz, Michael. 1976. *A History of Compulsory Education Laws*. Bloomington, IN: Phi Delta Kappa Educational Foundation.

Keane, John J. 1889. "Should Americans Educate Their Children in Denominational Schools." In *Denominational Schools*. New York: Kansas Publishing House.

Keesee, Timothy. 1993. *American Government for Christian Schools*. Greenville, SC: Bob Jones University Press, 21.

Kelley, Dean. 1962. *Why Conservative Churches Are Growing*. New York: Harper and Row.

Kett, Joseph. 1973. "Juveniles and Progressive Children." *History of Education Quarterly* 13, (Summer): 191ff.

Key, V.O. 1961. *Public Opinion and American Democracy*. New York: Alfred A Knopf.

Keyworth, Karen. *Support Networks for Islamic Schools and Data Based Profiles*. http://www.4islamicschools.org/student_papers.html.

Khan, Muqtedar. 1999. "Collective Identity and Collective Action: The Case of Muslim Politics in America." *Muslims and Islamization in North America: Problems and Prospects*, edited by Amber Haque. Beltsville, MD: Amana Publications.

———. 2002. *American Muslims: Bridging Faith and Freedom*. Beltsville, MD: Amana Publications.

Khan, Shujaat A. 1999. "A Critical Review of Islamization of Knowledge in the American Perspective." *Muslims and Islamization in North America: Problems and Prospects*, edited by Amber Haque. Beltsville, MD: Amana Publications.

Klicka, Christopher J. 1995. *The Right Choice: Home Schooling*. Gresham, OR: Noble Publishing Associates.

———. 1998. *The Right to Home School: A Guide to the Law on Parents' Rights in Education*. Durham, NC: Carolina Academic Press.

———. 1999. "The UN Convention on the Rights of the Child: The Most Dangerous Attack on Parents' Rights in the History of the United States." http://www.hslda.org.

———. 2000. "Religious Freedom is Endangered But States are Fighting Back." http://www.hslda.org.

———. 2002 (January/February). "Charter Schools." *Home School Court Report*, 1–9.

Knowles, Gary, Stacey Marlow, and James Muchmore. 1992. "From Pedagogy to Ideology: Origins and Phases of Home Education in the United States, 1970-1990." *American Journal of Education* 100: 195–235.

Kosmin, Barry, Egon Mayer, and Ariela Keysar, 2001. "American Religious Identification Survey." http://www.gc.cuny.edu/faculty/research_briefs/aris/aris_index.htm.

Kramer, Doniel Zvi. 1976. "The History and Impact of Torah Umesorah and Hebrew Day Schools in America." PhD dissertation. New York, NY: Yeshiva University.

Kraushaar, Otto. 1972. *American Non-Public Schools: Patterns of Diversity.* Baltimore, MD: John Hopkins University Press.

Kumar, Krishan. 1997. "Home: The Promise and Predicament of Private Life at the End of the Twentieth Century." *Perspectives on the Grand Dichotomy: Public and Private in Thought and Practice,* edited by Krishan Kumar and Jeff Weintraub. Chicago, IL: University of Chicago Press.

Lannie, Vincent P. 1968. *Public Money and Parochial Education: Bishop Hughes, Governor Seward, and the New York School Controversy.* Cleveland, OH: The Press of Case Western Reserve University.

Leonard, Karen. 2003. *Muslims in the United States: The State of Research.* New York: Russell Sage Foundation.

Levinger, Lee. 1944. *A History of the Jews in the United States.* Cincinnati, OH: Union of American Hebrew Congregations.

Levinson, Meira, and Samford Levinson. 2003. "Getting Religion: Religion, Diversity, and Community in Public and Private Schools." *School Choice: The Moral Debate.* Princeton, NJ: Princeton University Press.

Lines, Patricia. 1991. "Estimating the Home School Population." Washington, DC: U. S. Department of Education Office of Educational Research and Improvement.

———. 1998. "Homeschoolers: Estimating Numbers and Growth." Washington, DC: U. S. Department of Education Office of Educational Research and Improvement.

Lischka, C.N. 1921 (June). "State Laws Affecting Parochial Schools." *National Catholic Welfare Council Bulletin.* 3: 21ff.

Lookstein, Joseph. 1960. "The Goals of Jewish Education." *Tradition: A Journal of Orthodox Jewish Thought* 3(1) (Fall), 34–43.

Lubienski, Chris. 2000. "Whither the Common Good: A Critique of Home Schooling." *Peabody Journal of Education* 75 (1 and 2): 207ff.

Machen, J. Gresham. 1995. *Education, Christianity, and the State.* Hobbs, NM: The Trinity Foundation.

Mack, Dana. 1997. *The Assault on Parenthood: How Our Culture Undermines the Family.* New York: Simon and Schuster.

Mahroof, M.M.M. 2002. "Toward the Islamization of History: A Historical Survey." *American Journal of Islamic Social Science* 17(1): 65–83.

Mann, Horace. 1957. "Ninth Annual Report." *The Republic and the School: The Education of Free Men,* edited by Lawrence Cremin. New York: Teachers College Press, Columbia University.

Martin, David. 1999. "The Evangelical Upsurge and its Political Implications." In *The Desecularization of the World: Resurgent Religion and World Politics,* edited by Peter Berger. Grand Rapids, MI: Eerdmans Publishing.

Mayberry, Maralee, J.G. Knowles, Brian Ray, and Stacy Marlow. 1995. *Home Schooling: Parents as Educators.* Thousand Oaks, CA: Corwin Press.

McCarthy, Charles. 1919. *History of the United States for Catholic Schools*. New York: American Book Publishing Company.

McKeown, Elizabeth. 1988. *War and Welfare: American Catholics and World War I*. New York: Garland Publishing.

Mead, Edwin. 1889. "Has the Parochial School Proper Place In America." *Denominational Schools*. New York: Kansas Publishing House.

Meyer, John W., and Richard Rubinson. 1975. "Education and Political Development." *Review of Research in Education*, edited by Fred Kerlinger. Itasca, IL: F.E. Peacock.

Mill, John Stuart. 1978. *On Liberty*. Indianapolis, IN: Hacket Publishing Company, 105.

Moes, Matthew. "Creating Islamic Culture in Muslim Schools." http://www.4islamicschools.org/student_papers. html.

———. "Islamic Schools as Change Agents." http://www.4islamicschools. org.

Monohan, A.C. 1921. *Correspondence*. NCWC Archives, Box 542, Washington, DC.

———. 1921 (June). "Work of the N.C.W.C. Bureau of Education." *National Catholic Welfare Council Bulletin* 3: 14ff.

Moreau, Joseph. 2003. *School Book Nation: Conflicts Over American History Textbooks from the Civil War to the Present*. Ann Arbor, MI: University of Michigan Press.

Morse, Samuel. 1835a. *Imminent Dangers to the Free Institutions of the United States Through Foreign Immigration*. New York: E. B. Clayton.

Muhammad, Amir Nashid Ali. 1998. *Muslims in America: Seven Centuries of History (1312-1998)*. Beltsville, MD: Amana Publications.

Muslim Americans: Middle Class and Mostly Mainstream, 2007, is available online from the Pew Research Center at http://pewresearch.org/.

Nash, Gary, Charlotte Crabtree, and Ross E. Dunn. 1997. *History on Trial*. New York: Alfred A. Knopff.

National Center for Education Statistics. 2001. *Digest of Educational Statistics*. Washington, DC: NCES.

———. 2001. *Private School Universe Survey, 1999–2000*. Washington, DC: NCES.

———. 2002. *Private Schools: A Brief Portrait*. Washington, DC: NCES.

National Council for Jewish Education. 1961. "Resolution on Community Support for Day School Education." *Jewish Education* 32 (Winter): 123.

NCWC. 1921 (February). "Opening of N.C.W.C. Bureau of Education." *National Catholic Welfare Council Bulletin* 2: 9ff.

———. 1921 (November). "Agreement of American Ideals and Catholic Teaching." *National Catholic Welfare Council Bulletin* 2: 13ff.

———. 1922 (October). "Bishop Gallagher's Able Defense of Catholic Schools." *National Catholic Welfare Council Bulletin* 3: 15ff.

———. 1923 (February). "Administrative Bishops of N.C.W.C. Hold Important Meeting." *National Catholic Welfare Council Bulletin* 3: 5ff.

———. 1924 (June). "Eminent Catholic Lawyers Successfully Defend Rights of Private School." *National Catholic Welfare Conference Bulletin* 4.

———. 1932. *Directory of Catholic Colleges and Schools*. Washington, DC: Department of Education.

Nimer, Mohamed. 2002. "Muslims in American Public Life." *Muslims in the West: From Sojourners to Citizens*, edited by Yvonne Yasbeck Haddad. New York: Oxford University Press.

Noll, Mark. 1999 (May/June). "Some Recent Battles." *Books and Culture.* 5, 3,: 30–34.
———, George Marsden, and Nathan Hatch. 1989. *The Search for Christian America.* Colorado Springs, CO: Helmers and Howard.
Organization of American Historians. 2004. "The Debate over History's Role in Teaching Citizenship and Patriotism." http://www.oah.org/reports/tradhist.html.
Pastoral Letter. 1829. "Provincial Councils of Baltimore." In *Catholic Education in America: A Documentary History,* edited by Neil G. McCluskey. New York: Teachers College.
Paterson, Frances R.A. 2003. *Democracy and Intolerance: Christian School Curricula, School Choice, and Public Policy.* Bloomington, IN: Phi Kappa Delta Educational Foundation.
People for the American Way. 2004. "Dereliction of Duty." http://www.pfaw.org.
Peshkin, Alan. 1986. *God's Choice: The Total World of a Fundamentalist Christian School.* Chicago, IL: University of Chicago Press.
Pew Research Center. 2007. *Muslim Americans: Middle Class and Mostly Mainstream.* Washington, DC.
Pierce v. Society of Sisters. 1926 United States Reports Vol. 268, Government Printing Office, Washington, DC.
Pipes, Daniel. 2005 (March 29). "What Are Islamic Schools Teaching?" *New York Sun.*
Quick, Abdullah. 1998. *Deeper Roots: Muslims in the Americas and the Caribbean from Before Columbus to the Present.* London: Ta-Ha Publishers Ltd.
Rahman, Mawdudar. 1994. "A Holistic and Institutional Analysis of Islamic Education." *The American Journal of Islamic Social Sciences* 11(4): Spring, 520–531.
Rashid, Hakim M. and Zakiyyah Muhammad. 1992. "The Sister Clara Muhammad Schools: Pioneers in the Development of Islamic Education in America." *The Journal of Negro Education* 61(2): Spring, 178–185.
Rauch, Eduardo. 1978. "Jewish Education in the United States, 1840-1920." *School of Education.* Cambridge, MA: Harvard.
Ravitch, Diane. 1974. *The Great School Wars.* New York: Basic Books.
———. 1978. *The Revisionists Revised.* New York: Basic Books.
———. 2003. *The Language Police.* New York: Alfred A. Knopf.
Ray, Brian D. 1999. "Home-Schooling on the Threshold: A Survey of Research at the Dawn of the New Millennium." Salem, OR: National Home Education Research Institute.
———. 2005. "A Home School Research Story." In *Home Schooling in Full View,* edited by Bruce Cooper. Greenwich: Information Age Publishing.
———, and Nick Weller. 2003 (May, 22–26). "Homeschooling: An Overview and Financial Implications for Public Schools," *School Business Affairs.*
Reese, William J. 1985. "Soldiers for Christ in the Army of God: The Christian School Movement in America." *Educational Theory* 35(2) Spring, 175–194.
Reich, Rob. 2002. "Testing the Boundaries of Parental Control in Education: The Case of Homeschooling." In *Moral and Political Education,* edited by Stephen Macedo and Yael Tamir. New York: New York University Press.
———. 2005. "Why Home Schooling Should be Regulated." In *Home Schooling in Full View: A Reader,* edited by Bruce Cooper. Greenwich: Information Age Publishing.

Rose, Lowell and Alec Gallup. 2000. "The 32nd Annual Phi Delta Kappa/Gallup Poll of the Public's Attitudes toward the Public Schools." *Phi Delta Kappan*: September, 41ff.

Rose, Susan D. 1988. *Keeping Them Out of the Hands of Satan: Evangelical Schooling in America*. New York: Routledge.

Rosenstock, Elliot D. 1969. "The Case for/against a Reform Jewish Day School." *Dimensions*. (Summer): 36ff.

Rubin, Philip. 1958 (September 8). "Why Jewish Day Schools." *Congress Weekly*: 12ff.

Rush, Benjamin. 1786. "Thoughts upon the Mode of Education Proper in a Republic." In *Essays on Education in the Early Republic*, edited by Frederick Rudolph. Cambridge, MA: Harvard University Press.

Ryan, James. 1922. *Catechism of Catholic Education*. Washington, DC: Bureau of Education, National Catholic Welfare Council.

———. Correspondence from January 23, 1924. In NCWC Archives, Box 122, File 159D. Washington, DC: Catholic University.

Sadlier, Agnes. 1894. *Sadlier's History of the United States*. New York: William Sadlier.

Schiff, Alvin Irwin. 1966. *The Jewish Day School in America*. New York: Jewish Education Committee.

Schlesinger, Arthur Jr. 1998. *The Disuniting of America: Reflections on a Multicultural Society*. New York: W.W. Norton.

Schumer, Charles. 2003 (May 10). "Saudis Playing Role in Spreading Main Terror Influence in United States." Senator's Press Release.

Schwartz, Stephen. 2002. *The Two Faces of Islam: The House of Sa'ud from Tradition to Terror*. New York, NY: Doubleday.

Segal, Samuel. 1955. "Evaluation of the Jewish Day School." *Jewish Education* 25 (Winter): 46–62.

Shelley, Thomas. 1989. "The Oregon School Case and the National Catholic Welfare Conference." *Catholic Historical Review* 75 (3): 439ff.

Sikkink, David. 1999. "The Social Sources of Alienation from Public Schools." *Social Forces* 78(1): September, 51–86.

Smith, Christian. 1998. *American Evangelicals: Embattled and Thriving*. Chicago, IL: University of Chicago Press.

——— and Sikkink, David. 1999 (April). "Is Private Schooling Privatizing." *First Things*: 16–20.

Smith, J. Michael. 2001 (July). "Encouraging the New Pioneers." *Home School Court Report* XVII.

Smith, Jane. 1999. *Islam in America*. New York, NY: Columbia University Press.

Smith, Tom W. 2002. "The Muslim Population of the United States: The Methodology of Estimates." *Public Opinion Quarterly* 66: 404–417.

"Speaker for School Bill: Ray McDougall of Salt Lake Defends Measure to Be Voted on Tuesday." 1922 (November 3). *Oregon Statesman*.

Spiegel, Irving. 1963 (November 17). "2 Reform Rabbis Back Day Schools," *New York Times*.

Stark, Rodney. 2003. *For the Glory of God: How Monotheism Led to Reformations, Science, Witch-Hunts, and the End of Slavery*. Princeton, NJ: Princeton University Press.

———. 2005. *The Victory of Reason: How Christianity Led to Freedom, Capitalism, and Western Success*. New York: Random House.

Steinberg, Bernard. 1979. "Jewish Education in the United States: A Study in Religio-Ethnic Response." *Jewish Journal of Sociology* 21 (1): 5ff.

Stevens, Mitchell. 2001. *A Kingdom of Children*. Princeton, NJ: Princeton University Press.

Strauss, Valerie, and Emily Wax. 2002 (February 25). "Where Two Worlds Collide: Muslim Schools Face Tension of Islamic, U.S. Views." *The Washington Post*, A1.

Sweeney, Elizabeth. 1928 (June 28). "Discharging the Duties of Citizenship." *National Catholic Welfare Conference Bulletin*.

Syme, Daniel. 1983. "Reform Judaism and Day Schools: The Great Historical Dilemma." *Religious Education* 78: 153–181.

Tauhidi, Dawud. 2007. "The Tarbiyah Project: A Holistic Vision of Islamic Education." Tarbiyah Institute. www.Tarbiyah.org.

Taylor, John Wesley. 1986. "Self-Concept in Home-Schooling Children." *Home School Researcher* 2 (2): 1–3.

Theissen, Elmer J. 2001. *In Defence of Religious Schools and Colleges*. Montreal: McGill-Queens University Press.

Thomas, Cal. "Where Are the Sleeper Cells?" March 7, 2002. http://www.jewishworldreview.com/cols/thomas1.asp

Tocqueville, Alexis de. 1945. *Democracy in America: Volume I*. New York, NY: Vintage Books.

Tyack, David B. 1966. "Forming the National Character: Paradox in the Educational Thought of the Revolutionary Generation." *Harvard Educational Review* 36 (1): 29–41.

———. 1968 (October). "The Perils of Pluralism: The Background of the Pierce Case." *American Historical Review*. 74ff.

———. 1976. "Ways of Seeing: An Essay on the History of Compulsory Schooling." *Harvard Educational Review* 46: 355ff.

Van Galen, Jane A. 1991. "Ideologues and Pedagogues: Parents Who Teach Their Children at Home." In *Home Schooling: Political, Historical, and Pedagogical Perspectives*, edited by Jane A. Van Galen and Mary Ann Pitman. Norwood, OH: Ablex Publishing.

Vitz, Paul C. 1986. *Censorship: Evidence of Bias in Our Children's Textbooks*. Ann Arbor, MI: Servant.

Walch, Timothy. 1978. "Catholic School Books and American Values: The Nineteenth Century Experience." *Religious Education* 73: 582–591.

Webster, Noah. 1790. "On the Education of Youth in America." In *Essays on Education in the Early Republic*, edited by Frederick Rudolph. Cambridge, MA: Harvard University Press.

———. 1800. *An American Selection of Lessons in Reading and Speaking: Calculated to Improve the Minds and Refine the Taste of Youth, and Also to Instruct Them in the Geography, History, and Politics of the United States*. 12th Edition. Boston, MA: Thomas and Andrews.

Weiss, Philip. 1995 (May 8). "Outcasts Digging in for the Apocalypse." *Time* 145: 48–49.

Welner, Kariane Mari. 2002 (March). "Exploring the Democratic Tensions Within Parents' Decisions to Homeschool." ERIC, document ED480141, http://www.eric.ed.gov.

Wenders, John T., and Andrea D. Clements. "Homeschooling in Nevada: The Budgetary Impact." http://www.education-consumers.com.

Wertheimer, Jack. 1999. "Jewish Education in the United States." In *American Jewish Year Book, 1999.* New York, NY: American Jewish Committee.

Whitehead, John, and Alexis Crow. 1993. *Home Education: Rights and Reasons.* Wheaton, IL: Crossway Books.

Wirt, Frederick M., and Michael W. Kirst. 1982. *The Politics of Education: Schools in Conflict.* Berkeley, CA: McCutchan Publishing Corporation.

Yacoob, Fawad. 2006. "Strengthening the Islamic Identity through the History/Social Studies Curriculum." Islamic Society of North America Educational Forum.

Yang, Philip and Nihan Kayaardi. 2004 (September). "Who Chooses Non-Public Schools for Their Children?" *Educational Studies* 30(3): 231–249.

Zimmerman, Jonathan. 2002. *Whose America? Culture Wars in the Public Schools.* Cambridge, MA: Harvard University Press.

Zine, Jasmine. 2007. "Safe Havens or Religious Ghettos? Narratives of Islamic Schooling in Canada." *Race, Ethnicity, and Education* 10(1): March, 71–92.

Index

About the Author

STEVEN L. JONES is Associate Professor of Sociology at Grove City College. He is co-editor of *Church-State Issues in America Today* (Praeger, 2007).